Industrial development and migrant labour
in Latin America

THE TEXAS
PAN AMERICAN SERIES

To Annick

JULIAN LAITE

Industrial development and migrant labour in Latin America

UNIVERSITY OF TEXAS PRESS
AUSTIN

International Standard Book Number 0-292-73826-9

Library of Congress Catalog Card Number 81-50281

The Texas Pan American Series is published
with the assistance of a revolving publication fund
established by the Pan American Sulphur Company

Printed in the United States of America

Contents

Tables

Illustrations

Acknowledgements

The field work for this study was carried out while I was a postgraduate student at the University of Manchester, and was financed by a British Social Science Research Council award. The writing and the broadening of the issues have been done during my time as a lecturer at Manchester University.

I am indebted to several people who helped me during the research and writing. Firstly, to the workers of La Oroya who received me warmly into their homes and with discretion into their political affairs: during 1971 some miners were shot and several Oroya workers whom I knew were fired, detained in jungle prison camps and had their union hall closed. Secondly, to the villagers of Ataura and Matahuasi who welcomed my wife, daughter and myself, and among whom we made many friends.

I owe both intellectual and personal debts to Norman Long and Bryan Roberts, who guided me in the field and who have commented almost continually on my work, through many long discussions. For their very useful comments and criticisms at various stages, I would also like to thank Adrian DeWind, Ronnie Frankenberg, John Goldthorpe, Gavin Smith, Denis Sulmont, Peter Worsley and several colleagues at Manchester.

In the collection of material I was assisted greatly by the management of Cerro de Pasco Corporation and by students from the Central University in Huancayo. Giovanni Mitrovic and Sally Grubb helped with coding some data, whilst Steve Pursehouse and Margaret Irvine wrote or expanded special computer programmes for me. The typing was done by Jean Ashton.

Last, but not least, is my debt to my wife. In the villages she brought up our daughter, emotionally supported me, and herself gained access to women's activities and gossip which probably would have remained closed to me. In England her recall of people and events has been crucial as has been her support during the writing of this book.

J.L.

1

Industrialisation, proletarianisation and migration

To a great extent, industrial production is now organised internationally. The degree of industrial development differs from country to country, but the technology is often similar and markets are world-wide. Multinational corporations accumulate and invest capital on a global scale, whilst domestic industrialists form part of an international pattern of supply and demand.[1]

Yet particular contexts vary. Industrialisation in the developed capitalist nations transformed labour-forces that were mainly agrarian into primarily industrial ones. In the Third World contemporary industrial development is frequently limited and dependent on the industrialised nations.[2] Industry coexists and articulates with substantial agrarian and commercial sectors. Much of the population continues to work on the land, and there are large numbers of entrepreneurs and migrant workers but only small groups of artisans and industrial workers. International economic factors and relations between sectors of the local economy together influence the formation of social groups. Industrial organisation generates similar pressures wherever it occurs, but the responses vary. The social structures that have emerged in the Third World are the result of these pressures and responses.

Understanding such group formation requires investigation of two important questions. The first concerns the extent to which industrial workers become proletarianised, a process which includes the transition from peasant to industrial proletarian and the development of a working-class culture and consciousness. The second concerns the extent to which contemporary industrial development requires proletarianisation, particularly in underdeveloped countries.

Proletarianisation[3] is the creation of 'free' labour. 'Free' labourers neither form part of, nor own, the means of production with which they work. They must sell their labour in order to subsist. If people are to be able to own and sell their labour, there must be the institution of private property. For the sale of labour to be necessary, the means of production must be controlled by one group in society. Money must circulate so that labour can be bought and sold, whilst the separation of the labourer from his product and from control of his work-task needs to be extensive. The worker must become a dependent wage-labourer.

Historically, proletarianisation involved the freeing of agrarian labour through the liquidation of common lands and the extension of commercial farms. Often the State directed this process, acting in the interests of industrial and commercial classes. Those who left the land were encapsulated by the urban–industrial sector in which they were housed and fed. The proletariat worked to a discipline set by industrial capitalists and their machines, different from the task-oriented duties and rhythms of agrarian life. Having become a commodity that could be bought and sold, labour had to be cajoled and motivated to meet the demands of profit and loss. 'Life' and 'work' were separated, and family structures adapted to meet industrial demands. Clubs and trade unions arose, expressing common proletarian interests, and a distinct working-class culture and consciousness emerged.

Proletarianisation occurs within a political and economic framework which does not determine group formation but sets limits on social change. To investigate areas of similarity and difference in this process political economy analysis must be complemented by an examination of the way groups and individuals actively respond. Actors affected by political and economic pressures orient to changes in the social structure and establish institutions and strategies to cope with them.[4]

The main elements of the political and economic framework[5] analysed in this study are as follows. The extent of industrial development sets limits on the number of workers and affects relations between the industrial and non-industrial sectors. Employment is also affected by the type of technology. The way in which the agricultural sector is organised influences the supply of labour and resources to industry as well as relations between the sectors. The State may foster industrial development and control the supply and organisation of labour. Examining these factors facilitates discussion of the links between the local, national and international levels. Their identification also permits distinctions to be drawn between capitalist industrialisation and that of Russia, or possibly China. However, this study is concerned only with the former.

Workers' responses to industrial development involve institutions such as the family and the trade union. Networks of kin, friends and workmates are established, to help people confronted by problems of survival and change. Group formation is affected by political parties and leadership. Attitudes to work influence involvement in the industrial sector and trade unionism. It is the variations in these elements which contribute to variations in industrialisation. In this study the focus is on migration from agriculture to industry, and it is the dimensions of a worker-peasant existence that are explored.

Migrant labour was part of the international trading economy before the industrial era, as settlers colonised the expanding European empires.[6] With the onset of European industrialisation, rural migrants were transformed into industrial proletarians, although the transformation was often difficult, since migrants tended to maintain themselves as worker-peasants. Today, mature industrial economies import cheap labour, while in the Third World labour migrates to local industrial centres. Migrant labour was thus an important factor in the development of the international economy. In trying to assess whether contemporary migrant labour is a transitional feature of that economy it is useful to distinguish between historical and contemporary processes.

Historical industrialisation

The growth of industry in capitalist Europe during the eighteenth and nineteenth centuries gave rise to an industrial proletariat. However, the nature and rate of working-class formation differed as between England, France, Germany and Spain. In England[7] during the sixteenth and seventeenth centuries the structure of the rural economy was systematically altered by a powerful landed and commercial bourgeoisie. The expansion of commercial farming and the enclosures deprived large numbers of people of their means of subsistence. The surplus population of 'free' labourers, having no rights to land, had little alternative but to migrate to the towns and larger villages where industrial employment was expanding. The new machines required a steady supply of unskilled labourers, as did mining, which at its peak employed several million people.

In the mines and factories the migrants were transformed into a working class. Mechanisation brought together large groups of workers who shared common tasks and living conditions. The similarity of their experiences and interests found expression in a common culture as the working class began to organise collectively. Drawing both on pre-industrial customs and their current circumstances, workers founded co-operatives and trade unions. Political and religious ideologies arose, voiced by leaders who advocated class struggle and alternative social systems. In the face of political opposition these men helped establish class consciousness among workers. Collectivism and solidarity became organising principles of working-class life. Within the three-generation extended family, dependent members were supported, and experience and occupations were passed on. Contacts made at work were reinforced in leisure clubs, while the street was an arena for the socialisation of the young. Working-class culture was reproduced in residentially stable communities.

This English experience is often cited in development studies as a general model of industrialisation and class formation. However, the English working-class emerged as the largest group in society whilst in underdeveloped countries today proletarians are often found in a few sectors and in limited numbers. Moreover there is increasing evidence that certain features of the industrial revolution in England were historically specific. Significantly, there were 'free' labourers before industrial change began, and so their transitional status was relatively short-lived.

Nevertheless, migrant labourers from Ireland fuelled the first industrial revolution for some time. The Irish came from small peasant farms and during the early nineteenth century worked temporarily at the harvest or in the building trade. They went back home to acquire land and marry. Then the famine both increased Irish emigration and made it permanent. No longer able to subsist in their own country, they went to industrialising Europe and to frontier America. Yet the old ties were kept up. One-third of the migrants returned to buy homesteads near their family lands.[8] While they were away their remittances provided vital support, and they expected to be included in the family inheritance. After 1852 there was little further subdivision of land in Ireland, while population growth continued. The Irish became part of the industrial working class and their peasant communities decayed.[9]

Generally, the organisation of agriculture differentiated England, with its 'free' labour, from Europe,[10] where there was a substantial stratum of peasants. In France, the revolution had destroyed the feudal system and freed the serfs, yet at the same time it had created a block of poor and middle peasants. Few groups of enterprising commercial farmers or 'free' labourers emerged. In England the pool of surplus employable labour was one in six of the total population; in France only one in twenty. During the first half of the nineteenth century agricultural prosperity reduced migration to the towns, slowing French industrialisation and hampering the growth of the working class. By mid-century the workers were struggling to maintain industrialisation against a conservative regime supported by a conservative peasantry.

In Germany, agricultural change was closer to the English pattern. In 1807 serfdom was abolished in Prussia, feudal landowners became capitalist farmers, and by 1849 there were 2 million rural labourers. The commercialisation of agriculture led to increased productivity, the expropriation of peasants' lands and migration to the towns. Not all migrants were 'free' labourers, however. Until 1914 Upper Silesian miners were worker-peasants, recruited from smallholdings within twenty miles of the mines. Only a third of their plots were economically viable and the owners eked out a living through temporary work in the mines. Expanding mining output after 1780 drew its labour from an increasing agricultural population, so that it was not necessary to alter the land-holding structure in order to provide manpower. Mine owners were content that their worker-peasants were able to feed themselves. Wives worked the land whilst their husbands were away. In 1890 one-fifth of all mineworkers were engaged in arable farming. A stable industrial proletariat emerged later, during the early twentieth century.

In Spain, only the northern regions of Catalonia and the Basque provinces industrialised during the nineteenth century. Not until mid-twentieth century were most provinces fully absorbed into the industrial economy. In 1971 one-third of the national labour force was still engaged in agriculture, and half of all agricultural land was farmed by peasants. This agricultural sector currently provides migrant labourers to the urban industrial centres of Spain and Europe.

Thus the pace of working-class formation varied across Europe, and differences in agricultural sectors were a contributing factor. In America[11] there was no surplus agricultural population to provide workers, and labour supply was a crucial problem. The solution was massive migration from Europe and the American south, and the large-scale use of capital. Immigrants were proletarianised, but they adopted racial and ethnic ideologies and identities rather than class-based ones. The new technology led to innovation and industrial expansion. Rising employment and wages in the automobile industry contrasted with the aging machinery and declining living standards of the British textile industry at the end of the nineteenth century.

Generally, technology[12] influenced working-class formation in a number of ways. Labour-intensive technology, as in cotton textiles, extended proletarianisation. Capital-intensive technology, as applied to mining, displaced workers. However, it also proletarianised them, either replacing petty-commodity producers by machine-operators, as in mining, or expanding an industrial sector such as the automobile industry.

State policies on industrial development also differed between European countries. In England the Enclosure Acts helped alienate agricultural smallholders whilst the Combination Act hindered proletarian political organisation. The Prussian State established a customs union, controlled the textile industry, regulated the sale of goods produced by artisans and intervened in the mining industry. Its support for industrialisation was in contrast to French policies in the middle of the century which favoured agriculture.

Finally, there were differences in the ways workers organised among themselves.[13] Denied access to the rural sector, English 'free' labour had to defend itself within the industrial milieu. Strong trade unions emerged in response to government oppression which in the early nineteenth century were radical and lent support to Chartism. Later, radicalism declined as labour found a role in institutionalised politics. In Germany workers and middle class were more divided, and this gulf, together with the influence of left-wing ideologies, helped to sustain radicalism. In France it was a particular radical political tradition that helped establish the Paris commune. American miners' leaders, espousing workingclass ideologies, fought bitterly with the leaders of urban industrial workers, who advocated nationalism. The latter won, circumscribing the development of working-class consciousness.

Historically, then, even though in the long run industrialisation had similar elements and consequences, there were important variations in the process. Today, it is the relationships between the extent of industrial development, the nature of the technology, agricultural structures, State policies and workers' organisation which affect the extent of working-class formation.

Contemporary industrial development

The developed and the underdeveloped nations now form part of an international industrial economy. Capitalist industrialisation generates free labour which in both types of society is transformed into a working class. At the same time, migrant labour has emerged. In Europe and America migrants from underdeveloped countries complement industrial workers. In the Third World peasants migrate to areas of industrial activity.

Industrial economies

Europe and America import cheap migrant labour which is employed alongside the working class. Capitalist penetration of underdeveloped societies created poor peasants unable to subsist on the land.[14] The surplus rural populations migrate both to their national work centres and to those of the industrialised countries. Companies can raise profits by paying low wages to these workers and maintain production by neutralising their political activities.[15]

In north-west Europe[16] there are 11 million migrant labourers, one-seventh of the industrial labour force. Their numbers fluctuate with economic cycles and State policies as they are first required and then dispensed with. One-tenth of the French labour force, two million workers, are migrants from Algeria, Spain and Portugal. The Algerians are mainly young bachelors from poor rural regions. They leave temporarily to earn money to support families or to learn a trade. Originally firms contracted whole villages, establishing in French cities concentrations of Algerians from a single locality. They are poorly housed and have low-status manual jobs. French workers think they undercut wages, and relations between them are poor. Receiving little support from French trade unions, they founded their own union in the 1960s. However long they work in France, ultimately they return to their families and villages.

West German industrialisation before 1914 was manned by Dutch and southern European migrants. During the second world war the State directed foreign labourers and after the war East European refugees helped in the reconstruction. Later Germany recruited labour direct from Mediterranean countries and by 1972 employed 2·3 million migrant workers. They are on temporary contracts and firms can keep wages low through labour turnover. Living in barracks, where wives are rarely allowed, different national groups have little contact with one another. At work they encounter resentment and they are reluctant to join trade unions for fear of reprisals from the employing agency. The German unions have made little effort to recruit them.

Few migrants settle in either France or Germany. Usually, they want to earn enough to buy a shop, or a house, or a taxi back home. Anyway, governments discourage settling. Some men realise their goals but most accrue a little savings, return to still overpopulated and economically stagnant villages, and find they must re-migrate. The barracks mostly contain men, there is little family life, and so they contrast with working-class communities.

The British experience differs owing to different State policies and labour catchment areas. Although the government recruited direct among second world war refugees, after 1951 migrants came from the Commonwealth. The voucher scheme of 1962 limited their numbers but allowed in dependants, probably transforming them into permanent immigrants with families. There has been no policy of periodic repatriation and despite problems of race relations, and an initial reluctance by trade unions to recruit migrants, they are now being assimilated into the class structure.

America[17] has both foreign and native migrants. Internally, labourers from the south and south-west move to California, the central wheat states and the north-east, harvesting vegetables and fruit. Contract workers living in camps, they have little formal or trade union organisation. Externally, labour is recruited from Mexico and the Caribbean. Labour shortages during the first world war led to a sharp increase in the flow of temporary Mexican field workers into south-west America. Between the wars the entry of these *braceros* was restricted. In the early 1940s both governments agreed on the direct recruitment of Mexicans to work on American farms. The Mexican government organised recruitment and transport, the American government, employment. From 1942 to 1964 4 million *braceros* were legally employed, not counting many 'wetbacks' or illegal entrants. The Mexicans hear of jobs through village contacts, remit money to their villages and return to them. They do not integrate with American farmworkers. Mechanisation has reduced agricultural employment and they are now seen as undercutting jobs and wages. It was always difficult to unionise the farmworkers but with the *braceros* it has proved almost impossible. They fear the employment agency and want mainly cash.

Thus in both Europe and America migrant workers on the one hand form part of the labouring proletariat, but on the other differ from the indigenous working class whom they complement. Cheap labour is required in sectors which are either unattractive to local workers or which have unstable markets characterised by short-lived booms. Overall, such labour helps maintain profit rates.Consisting often of young men, only sporadically involved in industrial work, its long-term interests lie outside the industrial economy and it does not readily assimilate into the working class. The social structures of the barracks and the home villages are not those of working-class communities. Such men are difficult to unionise and their residence is dependent on State policies. Clearly, different types of workers are identifiable within the industrialised economies.

Underdeveloped economies

In both industrialised and underdeveloped societies, migrant labourers and industrial workers complement one another, but in the latter the industrial proletariat is in a minority. In many Third World countries industrial development has been limited, dependent, unstable and capital-intensive.[18] Consequently, although there is a numerous working class spread throughout the Third World, in few countries is it large-scale.

The limited and dependent nature of this sort of industrialisation is shown by the fact that only 13 per cent of the labour force in underdeveloped countries work in industry, and their output is only one-tenth of the world's total. Much production is controlled by multinational corporations which invest mainly in the industrial sectors. In 1969 American direct investment in the Third World was $20 billion, three-quarters of it in industry.

Such foreign investment occurs because raw materials are found abroad and the labour there is cheap. Local wages must be high enough to attract men from other sectors. Agriculture is an important source of labour, and so industrial wages need only compete with low or non-existent rural wages. They do not have to guarantee worker subsistence. Products provided by workers' families in the villages supplement their wages. It is outside the industrial sector that families are maintained and the labour force reproduces itself. In addition, foreign labour is likely to be poorly organised and more susceptible to control than the trade unions of the industrial nations.

Instability is due to key Third World products, such as metals, being sold on fluctuating international commodity markets. As prices fall, multinational managements curtail production and employment at the periphery. Indeed, the corporations' involvement in underdeveloped countries' industry, where they specialise in particular products, may be more short-term than in the metropolitan economies, where they may be more diversified. At the centre, corporate management decides where it should invest around the globe.

The technology exported by the multinationals is capital-intensive, and their control of technological advance is such that even local producers must often purchase similar equipment. In Latin America and Africa, despite considerable investment during the 1960s, employment in manufacturing grew less rapidly than population increase, failed to rise as a percentage of total employment, and in some cases even declined in absolute terms. Moreover, such investment may displace already employed skilled labour as unskilled machine operators replace artisans.

There are several reasons for the exported technology being capital-intensive. Governments and aid agencies have been more concerned with output than with employment. Contemporary industrial technology is of this nature, in contrast to the labour-intensive machinery of the first industrial revolution. Capital equipment, deployed at home or abroad, is geared to meeting common international patterns of consumer demand. Labour costs are reduced. This is important even in countries where labour is cheap, for such costs include not only wages but also the overheads of transporting, housing and feeding the workers.[19] Managements try to opt either for developing a skilled, committed labour force by meeting these costs, or for operating with migrant workers who subsidise themselves through maintained rural links. Finally, a smaller labour force may be more manageable; strikes and shut-downs are a serious matter for companies operating with continuous process technology.

Such considerations lead directly to the question of the extent to which industrial development requires proletarianisation. Clearly, in some circumstances, thoroughgoing proletarianisation is efficient for, and may be necessary for, capitalist industrial expansion. In other cases, however, worker-peasants may be an efficient form of labour, since proletarianisation would raise labour costs. Such a situation approximates to the one discussed in this study, although the pressures from the State and in the agricultural sector for increasing proletarianisation are also recognised.

Besides the extent and nature of industrial development affecting class formation, the organisation of industry and agriculture is also important. Industrial production may be organised formally, with clear divisions between management and men, stipulated work-tasks and inflexible routines. The operations of multinationals are usually of this type. Local production may be informal,[20] household-based, using family labour or with co-operating artisans. Workers move between these forms of production or operate simultaneously in both. Similarly, in agriculture there are different forms of production with different types of labour. Generally, three types may be identified: common ownership of land worked by members of the community, small privately owned plots worked by peasants, and large commercial farms employing wage-labourers. Landless labourers migrating into formal industrial work may be more susceptible to the pressures for proletarianisation than peasants working in the informal sector but keeping their links with the land.

Governments attempting to industrialise can raise investment funds internally, by taxing agriculture and commerce, or externally through foreign loans. The former strategy alienates powerful interest groups, and producers avoid being taxed. Foreign loans[21] can open up dilemmas. The demands of outside investors may clash with national political aspirations, jeopardising the development programme and leading to instability. It is in such circumstances that military regimes emerge, trying to stabilise the situation. Some governments act in concert with foreign capital, while others favour domestic producers, but even these latter are under constant pressure from foreign investors.

State policies also affect labour organisation. Occasionally governments control workers direct, defining their status and limiting where they may work and reside.[22] In other cases the State provides a political framework for proletarian organisation. Trade unions help workers to develop a sense of common identity and establish their interests in opposition to others. Leaders advocate the claims of labour not only through the trade union movement but also in the national political arena.

Obviously, the range of factors affecting industrial development and class formation makes detailed comparisons difficult. Studies must attend to particular elements in particular situations. In the present case the analysis focuses on the proletarianisation of the worker-peasants making up the labour force of a multinational mining company. The process differs from historical widespread industrialisation in small-scale manufacturing. Yet it is similar to enclave development in other Third World countries. That is to say, it is important to identify the various elements and then relate the different forms of industrial development and labour organisation to one another. To this end, analyses of Africa and Latin America are relevant.[23]

In Africa[24] the most industrialised economies are those of the south. Industrialisation began with mining and the shipping of metals through the ports. Labour for industrial work was recruited both from local tribes and from those of central and east Africa, thousands of miles away. There had long been large-scale migrations in the north and west of the continent but this move to the south marked the increasing integration of Africans into the international industrial economy.

During the first decades of the nineteenth century, Europeans introduced commercial relations into south Africa. Previously the tribal economies had been self-sufficient. In Botswana economic production among the Bantu was household-based, with limited specialisation and some bartering. There was no regular production for a market. The Europeans traded for local ivory and at first such contacts neither imbalanced the native economy nor ended its self-sufficiency. Some households moved into commercial farming and between 1830 and 1870 several tribal economies were 'peasantised' as Africans began to sell agricultural products.

The situation changed during the second half of the century. Diamonds were discovered, but by the 1870s the full exploitation of the mines was being hindered by the reluctance of Africans to work there. They preferred to produce and sell crops to the Europeans and miners. This increased market led to the further commercialisation of agriculture and the emergence of a successful peasantry. The Europeans tried to solve the mine labour shortage in a variety of ways, with mine managers usually acting in concert with the colonial administration. Native commissioners directly pressed and obligated Africans to work, whilst the Native Labour Boards used the *chibaro* system of contracting labour to work temporarily. In the mines barrack compounds were built, to which entry and exit were strictly controlled. During the diamond boom they served both to detain Africans in the work-place and to regulate the smuggling of diamonds out of the mines. The boom ended in the 1880s and workers returned to the tribal lands. Imbalance was created in the rural economy and there was involution on the land as ex-migrants took up subsistence agriculture and markets closed. Falling agricultural production and overcrowding were exacerbated by European expropriation of land. Africans remained on the land as squatter peasants but their tenure was insecure.

The discovery of gold in South Africa accentuated imbalance in the rural economy. Difficult to mine and present in low-grade ores, its extraction required many workers. To ensure labour supply, mine management and colonial administrators again devised a number of solutions. Rural taxes were introduced. In Botswana the new tax on huts in 1899 meant that Africans needed cash to pay the tax. Some revenue came from selling goods to the miners, for with the re-expansion of markets peasants again produced cash crops. However, they found it difficult to compete with subsidised European farmers. At the same time, African insecurity of tenure increased the possibility of eviction. So limited agricultural income and evictions led to migration to the mines to raise cash to pay the taxes. In Zimbabwe the compound system was transplanted from the diamond mines and its functions expanded beyond the prevention of gold smuggling and the restriction of labour mobility. The colonial administration and mine management regulated the supply of provisions, established credit systems, arranged recreation and subverted political organisation in the compounds. To some extent, the supply of labour to the mines was stabilised.

Migrants came from within South Africa and farther afield. The opportunity to earn wages plus the drives of the Native Recruiting Corporation and the Witwatersrand Native Labour Association generated both short and long-distance migration. The agencies advanced money to the migrants, who used it to pay taxes and then worked off the debt in the mines. By the end of the century three-fifths of the workers in the Witwatersrand were from Mozambique, whilst Lesotho supplied 30,000 men to the mines and railways of South Africa.

Imbalance was systematically created in the previously self-sufficient tribal economies, resulting in migration in order to meet subsistence and cash needs. Tribal economies were not eliminated; rather, a migrant labour system emerged during the first half of the nineteenth century, which was circulatory. Africans migrated long distances to the industrial sector, worked there temporarily and then returned to their homelands, only to re-migrate after a short period. As well as the State policies, there were other pressures at work. Generally, population growth and low incomes in the rural areas were powerful influences. Particularly, different tribal structures exerted different pressures. In Tanzania men migrated in search of bridewealth in the form of cash to buy cattle. In east Africa the chieftain system among the Alur led to the chiefs accumulating wealth and an exodus of men trying to acquire savings outside the tribal system.

One example of the integration of tribal economies into the system of circulating migrant labour is that of the Tonga, living by Lake Nyasa, some 1,500 miles from the mines of Zimbabwe and South Africa. Tongan women became agricultural producers as the men migrated to the South African mines. At any one time two-thirds of the men were absent. Despite the distance, village contacts were maintained, for they knew they would return. Money was remitted to kin who upheld the migrant's status in the village by safeguarding his rights to land and helping his wife and children. Whilst away, some men even competed for village political offices. The village provided social security, and migrants supported this 'traditional' social structure even though working in a 'modern' sector.

Preserving 'traditional' tribal structures and continuing the migrant labour system was also the policy of colonial administrators. In Botswana the chiefs were allowed to administer tribal justice, hearing and judging requests and complaints. Chiefly jurisdiction extended into the mines, providing several advantages for the administration and managers. The system hindered commercialisation of the tribal economies and thus the growth of wages which would compete with mine wages. Chiefs were contracted as labour recruiters and in the mines they helped govern the compounds. At work the State maintained the men's migrant status. Labour was employed mainly on short-term contracts and housing was only for those with jobs. Pass laws were introduced: workers migrating into southern Africa needed permission and when it expired they had to leave. Internal migrants also needed permits, for freedom of movement was restricted to the tribal homelands. Misdemeanours committed at work usually meant deportation to the homeland.

At the same time there emerged in the industrial sector institutions and practices oriented to both rural and urban interests. Required to bury their own dead in accordance with custom, tribal groups established burial societies which brought members of the same tribe together. Savings clubs were set up and 'social societies' were formed. On occasion the object of the latter was the maintenance of rural religious beliefs in the town. An 'urban tribalism' emerged as a means of classifying a heterogeneous urban population, and tribal categories became a badge of identity and a guide to interaction. Young men of the same age-group and tribe helped one another by sharing lodgings and passing on information about jobs. Companions were sought within the ethnic group, as were wives, who preferably were found within the village. On occasion, tribal associations were mobilised for political ends.

However, complementing the workers' migrant status was their status as wage-labourers, with shared industrial experiences and confronted by a white management. Consequently there was a move from tribal-based to class-based social action. In Zambia industrial production was concentrated in the towns of the Copperbelt and the miners came from the Bemba and Ngoni tribes. Most conflict in the mines appeared to be between these tribes and was regulated by chiefs. In fact, they had entered different sections of the labour-force and the tensions were between different industrial interest groups. During the 1930s and 1940s strikes occurred which the chiefs could not control, and their authority was undermined. Immediately after the second world war mining unions were established which became the most powerful in Zambia, copper being the country's largest export-earner.

In South Africa the State has rigorously controlled labour, yet determined efforts have been made to instigate working-class politics. The first responses of workers to compound life were absenteeism, desertion, destruction of property and migration to less arduous work centres. In the 1920s the Industrial and Commercial Workers' Union tried to organise among the miners but magistrates deported those participating in union meetings; in 1929 it was disbanded. Some small African unions continued up to the 1950s but the Suppression of Communism Act virtually eliminated them too. Until very recently African trade unions and strikes have been illegal.

This situation has led to African workers adopting other means to express grievances. One alternative is direct action such as occurred in the docks and industrial estates of Durban in the late 1960s and early 1970s. Then, the government negotiated, but in other instances such as Sharpeville and Witwatersrand the response was repression and internment. A second alternative is the formation of an African shadow organisation paralleling a white or coloured trade union, one example being the National Union of Clothing Workers, which operates alongside the legal clothing unions, using their resources.

The expansion of the South African industrial economy has supported this transition from tribal to class-based social relations. Economically, South Africa almost ranks with the industrialised nations, and this has profoundly altered the migrant labour system.

Previously, subsistence agriculture was maintained within a capitalist framework such that it bore the costs of reproducing the migrant labour force. Migrants fed themselves and their families on products from the rural sector. Industrial wages were low, since they did not need to cover subsistence. However, since the end of the second world war subsistence production has declined. Household productive units have disintegrated and many landless labourers have emerged. Some have found work and two-thirds of the labour force are wage-labourers. However, unemployment is now 1·5 million out of a total of 9 million. The government does not allow this reserve army of labour to live in towns, but garrisons it on Bantustans. A pass system controls work in the towns. Thus the workers who now migrate are proletarians, quartered in rural areas. The contemporary migrant labourers in South Africa come from outside the country.

The extent of industrial development and State policies is transforming South African workers into proletarians, but in other African countries the situation is different. In Kenya, for example, wage-earners form only one-fifth of the work-force and only half of these are in the formal sector: construction, public works and some manufacturing. On the one hand, industrial employment is limited and most workers in the formal sector are migrants with maintained rural links. On the other, both colonial and independence governments have fostered the trade unions in that sector, from which political leaders have emerged. However, the independence governments have not been able to incorporate the unions into a national development strategy and the unions continue to engage in political struggle. It may be that this will lead to the crystallisation of class identity among unionised workers.

Another area of the Third World in which proletarian and migrant labour coexist is Latin America.[25] Again there are differences in the potential for working-class development and the transformation of migrant labour, both between Latin America and Africa and across Latin America itself. Urbanisation is greater in Latin America and generally there is a sharper break between town and countryside. It came under European control earlier than many parts of Africa, resulting in longer periods of commercial penetration of rural areas. In some countries immigrants from Europe and African slaves rivalled the indigenous population in numbers. Yet despite these differences, similar processes are at work in both regions. Rapid population growth and the use of machinery in the countryside produces urban migration.

Industrialisation in the cities leads to the emergence of dependent wage-labour.

The extent of industrial development in Mexico, Brazil and Argentina is greater than in most of Latin America. In Mexico, mining was important during the colonial period and continues to be so. Agriculture was commercialised early through *haciendas*, and northern beef and southern sugar were sold in America and Europe. To transport these products the British and French invested in railways. Later American investments in metal and oils added to this industrial infrastructure. There was colonial mining in Brazil too but the main industrial impetus came from the investment of returns from coffee, dairy products and cotton. The development of Sao Paulo, the leading industrial state, stemmed from the investment of coffee profits in railways and manufacturing. Today Brazil continues to divert agricultural resources and revenues into industrial expansion. Similarly, in Argentina, revenue from the sale of beef, cereals and dairy produce was invested in industry after the second world war, when agricultural commodity prices were high.

In all three countries a strong central government[26] has pursued industrialisation. In Mexico during the 1940s the State devalued agriculture in favour of industry, giving tax concessions and encouraging urban investment. Currently, Mexico plans to use its oil wealth to further industrial expansion. The New State in Brazil during the 1930s set up State institutions to help industry and built up domestic industries behind tariff barriers. Since the mid-1960s industrialisation has been the goal of the Brazilian military governments. In Argentina it was Peron who after the second world war used agricultural revenues to finance industry, even though the policy created rural distress and urban migration. Strong governments in all three countries have attempted to substitute domestic production for imports. This industrialisation has led to the formation of an urban working class.[27] The State has fostered its growth by adopting industrial policies and incorporating workers into government institutions. Governments have tried to regulate industrial conflict by recognising and controlling the unions.

However, industrial development is not only of this State-supported, urban-based kind. There are also enclave[28] sectors: foreign-controlled primary production for export, usually mines and plantations. Foreign management controls both investment in the enclave, including the type of technology employed, and the profits it generates. Enclaves are an extension of the industrialised economies and arise because foreign capital either displaces local exporters or instigates export production. In both cases enclave development follows the rhythms of the international, not the domestic, economy. Indeed, domestic cycles come to reflect those in the export sector.

Mining enclaves in Latin America are seen as having only a limited effect on employment and income distribution in the national economy. Between this export and other sectors there are deemed to be steep technological, financial and organisational gradients. The most important links are seen to be political, as foreign management manoeuvres within the underdeveloped society. In this study of Peruvian mining the limits to employment and development are very important. Yet the national and local links between mining and the Peruvian economy have been considerable. There is feedback into associated industries, and into agriculture and commerce near the mines. There is no sharp break between proletariat and peasantry, for many industrial workers are migrants who maintain contact with the rural areas.

Miners in Latin America have been seen as in the vanguard of working-class formation and likened to the industrial workers of nineteenth-century Britain and Europe.[29] Enclave investment gives rise to concentrated masses of workers, geographically and socio-economically isolated, who solidaristically band together. Similar groups[30] are Bolivian tin miners, Peruvian miners and sugar workers, Chilean miners and Venezuelan petrol workers. On occasion these workers are politically important. Peru, Chile and Bolivia depend on metal exports and the well organised mining unions are strategically placed to exert critical pressure on the balance of payments. The miners are radical, the bastions of nationalist sentiments *vis-à-vis* their foreign employers, espousing class rhetoric and ideologies. In Chile they supported the Socialist and Communist parties. In Peru they struggled for nationalisation of the mines. In Bolivia in 1952 they seized control of their camps and the near-by cities and with armed units secured the National Revolution in La Paz.

However, enclave industrial development also limits working-class formation. Export profits have flowed abroad and have not provided a basis for extensive industrialisation, a factor which has had two important consequences. Firstly, enclave workers find few other groups with whom they may readily identify. Concerted political action by this splintered proletariat is infrequent and short-lived. Isolated yet important, their participation in politics renders them vulnerable to retaliation. In Peru, Bolivia and Chile the political rights of miners have frequently been curtailed. Their politics is that of confrontation, in contrast to the incorporation of industrial unions in Mexico, Brazil and Argentina. Secondly, limited industrial development occurs alongside agriculture and commerce. This coexistence occurs also in the more industrialised Latin American economies. Throughout Latin America labour in the industrial sector is supplied by agriculture.[31] The industrial proletariats do not adequately reproduce themselves such that labour comes wholly from the urban industrial sector. As we have seen, the origins of the labour supply affect the extent of working-class formation.

Industrial labour has been supplied by immigration[32] or internal migration. In Brazil and Argentina an industrial proletariat has been formed by immigrants from Europe and the Orient, and by landless labourers from the large sheep, cattle, sugar and cotton *haciendas*. In Peru, Ecuador, Bolivia, Chile and to some extent Mexico, however, migrants also come from smallholding or communal peasantries and maintain their links with the land.[33] The transformation of these workers into an industrial proletariat is unlikely to be straightforward.

As in Africa, the causes of migration are population growth, declining opportunities in agriculture and the attractions of city life. Similarly, the nature of that migration varies.[34] Mechanisation forces landless *hacienda* workers to migrate permanently, but peasants may move only temporarily to supplement family income. Young men may like city life or may try to further their education, whilst their elders move to supervise children's education or re-establish family groups. Women go into domestic work, men into industry and commerce.

As in Africa, the consequence of migration[35] in the countryside is demographic imbalance as villages consist only of the women, the very young and the very old, with able-bodied men in the distant work centres. In the towns, migrants are supported by kin and establish informal social networks and formal organisations. Kin provide lodgings, while friends tell of jobs and wages. People from the same region – *paisanos* – form clubs to aid new migrants and organise leisure. As well as helping with urban life, these networks and clubs are a means of contact with the village. Kinsfolk bring food from the village to the migrants and safeguard their rural interests by working their land for them or maintaining their presence in village affairs. Migrants' clubs are places to discuss rural news and supply funds and services to the villages in the form of school books or a church roof.

Thus the town is not always the terminus of migration.[36] Often, migration does end there as people proceed in stages from the countryside, through provincial towns to the capital. Yet some return periodically to the rural areas because there is no work in the city, or on a death in the family, or because their savings target has been achieved. The potential for return migration from enclaves, which recruit direct from agriculture, is probably greater than from cities, but urban migrants also sojourn to and fro.[37] There are systems of circulatory migration in Latin America, just as there are in Africa.

Proletarian and migrant labour

Today as in the past, capitalist industrial development generates both proletarian and migrant labour. Often migrants are transformed into a working class, but any such change depends upon a range of factors and can be a lengthy process. Proletarianisation is affected by local factors in both industry and agriculture, and by international pressures. Focusing only on local industrial factors such as trade unions, strikes or political parties does not adequately encompass the process. Moreover, the political economy of industrial development must be complemented by analysis of the ways in which actors and groups respond to change and establish social structures. Only by attending to these features can different types of labour and labour processes be related to modes of economic development.

In underdeveloped societies urban working classes and migrant labourers work alongside one another. Contemporary industrial development recruits labour from peasantries whose decline is still uncertain. The context of proletarianisation is that of the articulation[38] of industry and agriculture, local and national structures, and different economic and social forms. In order to analyse the emergence of social groups in a situation of limited industrial development, workers in the Peruvian mining sector were studied. The major concerns of the study are the extent of industrial development and its technology, the organisation of agriculture and its links with industry, State policies with regard to development and labour, workers' organisation, including trade unions, families and social networks, and workers' attitudes. The focus is on the migration of worker-peasants. Thus the study is illustrative of the type of situation in which multinational corporations draw on peasant labour to be found throughout the Third World.

Notes

[1] Important analyses of global economic development have been offered by Frank, A. G., 1969; Wallerstein, I., 1974(a), 1974(b); Amin, S., 1975; Fröbel, F., *et al.*, 1977. However, analyses of the world economy overemphasise both the similarities between different types of capitalist and State-directed production and the extent to which socio-economic organisation at the national and local levels is determined by global factors.

[2] Dos Santos, T., 1969.

[3] Marx, K., 1957; Thompson, E. P., 1967.

[4] Weber, M., 1968.

[5] These elements are suggested by Hobsbawm, E., 1975.

[6] Portes, A., 1977.

[7] Marx, K., 1957; Thompson, E., 1965; Hobsbawm, E., 1968; Anderson, M., 1971; Foster, J., 1974; Hoggart, R. 1957.

[8] Hobsbawm, E., 1975.

[9] Arensberg, C., and Kimball, S., 1965; Brody, H., 1973.

[10] Hobsbawm, E., 1975; Marx, K., 1962; Price, R., 1972; Schofer, L., 1975.

[11] Hobsbawm, E., 1975; Thomas, W., and Znaniecki, F., 1958.

[12] Habakkuk, H., 1967.

[13] Foster, J., 1974; Thompson, E., 1965; Jensen, V. H., 1950; Hobsbawm, E., 1975.

[14] Berger, J., and Mohr, J., 1975.

[15] Castells, M., 1975.

[16] Castles, S., and Kosack, G., 1973; Trebous, M., 1976.

[17] Craig, R., 1971; Friedland, W., and Nelkin, D., 1971; Portes, A., 1977.

[18] Cardoso, F., and Faletto, E., 1970; UNIDO, 1973; Barnet, R., and Muller, R., 1974; Morawetz, D., 1974; United Nations, 1966; World Bank, 1976. Of course, the proportion of industrial workers in the total labour force varies throughout underdeveloped countries. In Africa in 1960 it was only 6·7 per cent, whilst in the Middle East it was 20·6 per cent. In 1966 in Latin America, it was 14 per cent.

[19] Wolpe, H., 1972.

[20] Hart, K., 1973.

[21] Kalecki, M., 1972; Alavi, H., 1972.

[22] Wolpe, H., 1972.

[23] The case of India is also of interest but the discussion of proletarianisation in the industrial sector is not, as yet, as fully extended as in the African and Latin American cases. However, see Lambert, R., 1963; Morriss, M., 1965; Sheth, N., 1968.

[24] Wolpe, H., 1972; Schapera, I., 1947; Bundy, C., 1972; Van Olsenen, C., 1976; Arrighi, G., 1973; Mitchell, J., 1956; Van Velsen, J., 1966; Epstein, A., 1968; Banton, M., 1969; Epstein, A., 1967; Gluckman, M., 1960; Mayer, P., 1971; Sandbrook, R., and Cohen, R., 1975; Bates, R., 1971; Sandbrook, R., 1975.

[25] Furtado, C., 1970; Glade, W., and Anderson, C., 1963; Lopez, E., *et al.*, 1967; Frank, A., 1969; Furtado, C., 1963; Baer, W., 1965; Diaz, Alejandro, 1970; Rock, D., 1975; Scobie, J., 1964.

[26] Cardoso, F. H., and Falletto, E., 1970, distinguish between the liberal, national populist and developmentalist States of Argentina, Brazil and Mexico. These important characterisations enable distinctions to be made not only between nations but also between State policies within countries at different times.

[27] Alba, V., 1968; Alexander, R., 1965.

[28] Cardoso, F., and Faletto, E., 1970.

[29] Di Tella, T., *et al.*, 1967; Bourricaud, F., 1970; Petras, J., and Zeitlin, M., 1968.

[30] Petras, J., and Morley, M., 1974; Lora, G., 1977; Nash, J., 1979.

[31] Chaplin, D., 1971; Sanchez Albornoz, N., 1974.

[32] Poppino, R., 1968; Scobie, J., 1964; Brant, V. C., 1977.

[33] Dandler, J., 1969; Lomnitz, L., 1977; Long, N., and Roberts, B., 1978.

[34] Cornelius, W., 1971; Herrick, B., 1965; Skeldon, R., 1977.

[35] Laite, A., 1974; Long, N., 1973; Mangin, W., 1970; Roberts, B., 1973.

[36] Skeldon, R., 1977.

[37] Lomnitz, L., 1977.

[38] Cardoso, F., and Faletto, E., 1970; Frank, A., 1969; Laclau, E., 1971; Stavenhagen, R., 1975.

2

Industrial development and mining in Peru

Contemporary Peru is a country of contrasts. Geographically, there are three very different regions – the coastal strip, the high Andes and the low-lying jungle. Economically, there are a range of sectors, some of which are technologically more advanced than others, although all are contained within a capitalist framework and commercial relations have permeated most areas of activity. The most striking economic contrast is between the industrial and the agricultural sectors, between modern machinery and wooden implements pulled by animals. That difference is reflected in the contrast between countryside and town. In most of Peru there is a sharp break from paved urban streets to rural *adobe* villages. Also, there are a range of social groups in both town and countryside whose life-styles are markedly divergent. Peasants are still illiterate and barefoot, industrial workers learn to control complex machinery; the urban poor huddle in slums whilst the very rich live in resplendent villas.

Throughout Peru agriculture is the predominant activity. Three-quarters of the population live and work in the countryside. However, the organisation of agriculture in the three regions varies. On the coast the main products are sugar and cotton, but they are worked under different systems. Sugar production is organised into large *haciendas*, with wage-labourers working for the *hacienda* family. Cotton production by contrast is in the hands of small-scale tenant farmers. During the 1970s the military government tried to organise both *hacienda* workers and tenant-farmers into large agrarian co-operatives.

In the highland Andes there is the same distinction between small and large-scale production. Large cattle and sheep rearing *haciendas* existed, employing ranch-hands and shepherds, but again the government attempted to turn them into co-operatives. The bulk of the Andean population, however, are peasants, and agrarian reform has not altered their way of life. Most are subsistence peasants, owning small plots of land or belonging to *communidades*, who produce a certain number of commodities for the market. Beyond the Andes lies the Amazonian jungle, which contains some coffee plantations as well as Indian tribes practising slash-and-burn agriculture.

However, agricultural production is not the only activity in the rural areas.[1] There is considerable artisan production of boots, hats, pottery, furniture and so on. These commodities are sold both in the travelling fairs which pass from village to village and in the provincial towns. Indeed, this commercial activity is very important in Peru. The transportation of commodities is crucial and the transport sector presents opportunities for entrepreneurial activity. The sale of products in the towns offers further opportunities for entrepreneurs who may specialise by product or by outlet, controlling access to markets.

The most important market is of course that of Lima, where some 3·2 million people live – 20 per cent of Peru's population.[2] Most of these people are the 'marginal' masses,[3] working sporadically in the 'informal' sector of the urban economy, eking out a hand-to-mouth existence through temporary jobs and petty trading. Alongside these people marginal to the urban core economy are the limited number of industrial workers, the state functionaries and the wealthy. No other cities approach Lima in size and influence. They are often administrative and commercial centres but they contain few industrial workers.[4] Only in the ports of the coast or the mining towns of the highlands does industry dominate.

The State functionaries of Peru are a large and influential group. They comprise teachers, administrators in the nationalised sector such as bank clerks, civil servants in government departments, the police and the military. They are white-collar workers with relatively stable positions and pension arrangements. The wealthy are the ex-*hacienda* owners, merchants and the administrators of foreign capital. The industrial workers are employed in car assembly plants, breweries, cement works and textile mills in Lima, while on the coast and in the highlands they are engaged in fishing and mining. They are relatively few in number, for only 20 per cent of the labour force work in the industrial sector. Five per cent of the labour force work in factories, 9 per cent are artisans and 2 per cent are in mining. To understand why these industrial workers are so few in number is to understand the nature of limited dependent industrial development in Peru.[5]

Industrial development

The first impetus came with the guano boom, from 1840 to 1860. Off the coast of Peru lay several small islands rich in guano, or bird droppings. In 1842 the government collaborated with local entrepreneurs to exploit this natural fertiliser. Although the price of guano collapsed in the 1870s, during the boom years a small group of Peruvian entrepreneurs emerged who had large amounts of capital to invest. This capitalist group invested in cotton, sugar and mining, introducing technological innovations in those industries. This new national bourgeoisie also considered plans for developing a railway network.

The government used its income from guano to pay off foreign debts and underwrite railway construction. The collapse of the guano market caused it to default on its railway bonds. In 1890 the debt was bought by W.R. Grace, an American, in return for the rights to operate the railways and exploit coal, oil, guano and mineral deposits. His shareholders assumed the name of the Peruvian Corporation. So the rights to much of the country's industrial potential passed into foreign hands and the industrial development promised by the guano boom failed to materialise.

During the 1890s, however, there came a second impetus to industrial growth as foreign demand for cotton, sugar and silver increased. Since the production of these commodities was controlled by Peruvians, the increased profits passed into the Peruvian economy and industrial investment rose. The one cotton textile mill was expanded and new ones were established. The brewery expanded, flour mills were built, and by the late 1890s there was further investment in the manufacture of chocolate, ice-cream, furniture and cigarettes. In 1900 the factory labour force in Lima was 6,500, while the artisan sector employed 16,000. Concomitantly there was an expansion of banking and insurance services, a new stock exchange was built, and electric power was introduced. This industrial investment was import-substituting and controlled to some extent by Peruvians. Thus during the first decades of the twentieth century the economy was not totally dependent on foreign interests. Rather, it was the interplay between local and foreign interests that imposed limits on development.

The rapid expansion generated by the export boom was not sustained. Limits on domestic food production raised Peruvian prices whilst those of imports fell. Industry became uncompetitive. Foreign loans dried up and the only industrial investment that occurred was in the mining sector. There, an American consortium, the Cerro de Pasco Mining Company, began buying up mines in the central highlands in 1902. This shift away from industry was permitted for two reasons. Firstly, much industrial production was in the hands of small-scale immigrant entrepreneurs who had little political muscle. Secondly, the national bourgeoisie who controlled the rest of industry had other interests. They were also export producers, import merchants and bankers who could switch resources from one sector to another. So the boom in cotton and sugar exports during the second decade of the twentieth century attracted their funds, rather than the industrial sector.

During the 1920s the country's export performance declined whilst foreign investment rose. Sugar and cotton prices dropped, although copper exports expanded. However, the expansion of copper output was due to American investment, which produced a lower return of funds into the Peruvian economy than did domestic investment. This pattern became general as the share of foreign-controlled exports rose from one-sixth of total exports in 1920 to one-half in 1930. The government of President Leguia tried to compensate for this lack of export funds by public spending on construction works. To finance it, the government borrowed abroad, establishing a pattern of heavy external debt financing which has remained to the present day. The funds went to a small group of property speculators and the high profits in the construction industry diverted resources from industrial investment. During the 1920s there was a net decline in employment in the cotton industry.

For many Latin American countries the world depression of the 1930s meant a switch to import-substituting industrial production and interventionist governmental policies. In Peru, however, the economy was already depressed by 1930, the manufacturing sector was moribund and there was little enthusiasm for government intervention following the failures of the 1920s. So Peru focused on export production, a strategy which enabled her to recover quickly from the depression, but which led to further dependence on foreign capital.

By 1936 cotton exports had regained their 1929 level and mining output recovered from 1933 onwards. The recovery in metals was headed by lead, zinc and the precious metals. Whereas foreigners owned the copper mines, it was Peruvians who owned the lead and zinc deposits, and they invested in those metals. The government helped these local entrepreneurs by purchasing ore concentrators and opening a Mining Bank in 1941 which gave credit to small-scale Peruvian mines. The output of these mines outstripped that of the largest producers. In 1942 Cerro de Pasco's proportion of mine output was only one-quarter that of the national total. It seemed that a local bourgeoisie was establishing itself in the mining sector, but the rise of local interests in mining was limited. The revival of metals outside foreign control meant that there was no clash of interests between foreign and local capital. But the largest metal deposits still remained in foreign hands, as did the sources of machinery and technology.

In other industrial sectors there was also a limited revival of exports during the 1930s. Oil production increased, but limited supply cut short this boom. Peruvian sugar was squeezed out of world markets by foreign government preferences for Cuban and British Empire sugar. Cotton enjoyed a protected price during the 1930s, as America supported its own producers, but this led to overproduction and falling output during the second world war. High food prices after the war reinforced the move out of cotton and into using land for food cultivation. Throughout the 1930s President Benavides kept government spending at a low level, limiting state intervention in the economy.

Such restrictions on government spending led to dissatisfaction among Peru's emerging middle class, who began to support APRA, the centre nationalist political party. In order to weaken APRA's appeal, President Prado, elected in 1939, began a policy of fiscal expansion. From 1939 to 1948 government spending grew nearly fivefold. However, it followed no coherent policy and there were few mechanisms to channel investment into the industrial sector. In 1945 President Bustamante was elected with a mandate to continue government expansion, but again his attempts lacked consistency. The return to interventionism in the late 1940s seemed as big a failure as the experiment of the 1920s. Indeed, from 1930 to 1950 there was no systematic support programme for industrial development. Occasional measures had been taken. For example, tariffs had been introduced in 1934 to protect domestic textile production, while some support had been given to mining. Sporadic industrial development had occurred:

during the early 1940s manufacturing expanded at 10 per cent per year. But from the mid-1940s imports became competitive, domestic inflation continued and there were shortages of machinery. The industrial sector stagnated and no cohesive industrialist class emerged.

At the beginning of the 1950s the economy was open to foreign intrusion and had no strong domestic industrial interests. From 1950 onwards the country became increasingly integrated into the international industrial system. Exports were the key elements in the economy, government policies were *laissez faire* and foreign capital entered and left with little constraint. During the 1950s Peru attracted more foreign investment than most Latin American countries. The economy expanded and then boomed in the early 1960s. However, this growth did not lay the foundations for autonomous industrial development. Rather, investment was due to multinational corporations which produced consumer goods and imported advanced technology into a country which became increasingly dependent on foreign investment.

A large measure of external penetration came in the mining industry. As relative metal prices changed so the importance of local entrepreneurs declined whilst that of foreign producers rose. At first foreign dominance was re-established in copper production. Then, in the mid-1950s, the American corporation Marcona Mining bought large iron-ore deposits. Local entrepreneurs were not prepared to compete for these deposits, and the government offered local interests little support. The dynamism of the mining sector during the 1950s was based on foreign capital, and the returns on investment flowed abroad. The fall in lead and zinc prices in the 1950s weakened domestic mining interests. Thus when foreign mining companies reduced investment in the mid-1960s it meant an overall decline in mining investment.

This pattern of boom, decline and lack of investment was repeated by Peru's other exports, cotton and sugar. Irrigation projects begun by President Odria in the 1950s led to increases in the supply of both products. At first the market took up these increases. The price of cotton rose with the Korean War, but in the 1960s competition from synthetics led to over-supply and land was switched to food production. Peruvian sugar finally gained access to the American market, but no increases in production followed. Foreign banks were taking over the sugar *haciendas* and limiting the flow of funds into that sector. The investment in the sugar industry was not removing production bottlenecks.

Only in the fish-meal industry did domestic investment seem to produce sustained industrial growth. The fishing industry expanded during the 1950s, attracting local entrepreneurs. Despite the influx of foreign capital during the boom of the 1960s, local capital still dominated the industry. Fishing revenue remained in the domestic economy through wages and investments in boats and canneries. However, high profits led to over-fishing. By 1970 fish reserves were low and in 1972 the industry collapsed. As it collapsed, so did Peru's export structure. From 1950 to 1959 exports had doubled in volume, and from 1959 to 1962 they had risen again by two-thirds. From 1962 to 1968, however, they rose by only one-fifth, and in 1968–75 they fell by one-third.

The overall lack of domestic investment in industry and the weakness of the export structure led Peruvian governments back to intervention during the 1960s. Since the second world war population growth had been putting pressure on land-tenure systems, leading to rural unrest and migration to the towns. Urbanisation meant a growing demand for local manufactured products and was accompanied by the rise of a middle class. During the 1950s the middle class were denied access to power by President Odria, but in 1963 they secured the election of the Accion Popular party, led by President Belaunde. Belaunde adopted interventionist economic policies in both the industrial and the agricultural sectors.

Export promotion had had some spin-off into industrial development. There was a group of local entrepreneurs linked to export promotion, and foreign exporters in Peru began to diversify. The Grace company moved into chemicals, paper, biscuits and machinery, while Cerro de Pasco Corporation began producing explosives and furnace bricks. By 1960 one-third of manufacturing activity in Peru was export-linked, and local entrepreneurs allied with foreign interests in joint ventures. Such alliances led to an increasing concentration of economic control within the industrial sector.

These developments were reinforced by economic and political factors. A rise in domestic demand during the 1950s attracted investment into paper, cement, tyres, textiles and some consumer durables. An industrial promotion law in 1959 gave incentives to industrial investment, whilst devaluation in 1958 made local products competitive. Yet this support was not co-ordinated. All types of industrial investment were encouraged, and the result was a wave of foreign investment in Peruvian manufacturing. It trebled between 1960 and 1966, and in the latter year over half the total output of most manufactured goods was produced by foreigners. Whilst growth occurred in the food industries and in consumer durables, there was little expansion of the capital goods industry. Foreign domination of industrial development meant that imports in the industrial sector were high, whilst domestic returns were low. Although manufacturing increased its share of the national product from one-seventh to one-fifth between 1950 and 1968, the increase did not mark the rise of a strong national bourgeoisie. Rather, local entrepreneurs worked with foreign capital and rapidly switched funds out of industry when conditions were unfavourable.

At the same time as intervention increased in industry, there were also attempts at government reform of agriculture. The reforms were aimed at the large-scale commercial farmers on the coast. However, Belaunde's plans made Peruvian agro-commercial entrepreneurs reluctant to invest, and so during the 1960s agricultural exports hit production bottlenecks. A rise in domestic demand in the 1970s resulted in an increase in food imports.

This limited and unstable industrial development has led to the formation of a working class.[6] Two main proletarian groups have emerged. The first is the urban–industrial working class,[7] found mainly in Lima, employed in factories and in the port of Callao. The second group comprises the workers in the enclave sectors, mainly sugar, mining and petrol. Both groups have strong and well organised trade unions, leaderships which project class ideologies and a history of strikes and struggle against employers and the government. On occasion, these workers have combined in general strikes to influence national policies. However, these moments of cohesion are exceptional. The main characteristics of the working class are that it is small and splintered.[8]

Labour organisation emerged primarily in Lima at the end of the nineteenth century. Artisans, such as bakers, who were becoming proletarianised formed occupational associations. In Callao the longshoremen established a union, as did the textile workers in Lima. During the first decade of the twentieth century these groups engaged in direct action and strikes for better wages and working conditions. The ideology of the workers' organisations was mainly anarcho-syndicalist, but during the second decade of the twentieth century this orientation changed. Rifts developed between the artisans' guilds and the industrial workers' trade unions which were exposed during the struggle for the eight-hour day. The unions organised independently of the guilds and in 1919 called a general strike in support of the eight-hour day. Their success in this struggle, the growing interest of politicians in the labour movement, and the example of the Russian revolution opened new political directions among workers' organisations. A faction emerged supporting President Leguia, a Socialist group formed, and so on.

This build-up of the labour movement was checked in 1919 when President Leguia assumed office. Throughout the 1920s workers' organisations were repressed. Only towards the end of the decade did political organisation re-emerge as Mariategui formed the Socialist Party of Peru and Haya de la Torre introduced APRA. The fall of Leguia in 1930 permitted the emergence of a central workers' federation, the Confederacion General de Trabajadores del Peru. Affiliated to the CGTP were the mining unions and the coastal agricultural workers, among whom were socialist and communist elements. However, the anarchist bakery employees and the Aprista textile workers resisted domination by the CGTP. The divisions in the labour movement were already apparent. But these workers' organisations were permitted to function for only a short time, and for most of the 1930s the labour movement was again repressed. APRA continued to consolidate its position among the textile workers, but the communist and socialist groups were weak. To some extent, competition for workers' allegiance came from the state as President Benavides created workers' social security organisations and regulated industrial conflict.

It was during and after the second world war that the labour movement was able to expand and consolidate. The governments of Presidents Prado and Bustamante tolerated political parties and trade unions during the mid-1940s. The textile workers in Lima embarked on strikes which were taken up by bread workers and bus workers. In 1944 there was a general strike from which APRA emerged much stronger than before. Unions were founded in the mining sector and a new workers' Confederacion de Trabajadores del Peru was established. Once more, however, independent union organisation was short-lived. President Odria came to power in 1948 and he outlawed APRA while at the same time supporting anti-APRA unions. Until 1956 Odria incorporated these unions into his paternalist policies, aided by industrial expansion. Independent trade-unionism only reappeared after his demise. During the 1960s the unions again operated freely, engaging in strikes, forming central federations and influencing national politics.

Clearly, a working class has formed among the urban-industrial proletariat of Peru. In the textile factories and the ports, among bread workers and bus drivers, proletarianisation has established the basis for working-class organisation. These workers produce and reproduce within the urban-industrial sector. They have strong trade unions with a long history of struggle and articulate leaders who have political ideologies, contacts and influence. On several occasions these workers have acted in concert, engaging in general strikes which have had direct national consequences. At the same time, it is clear that the labour movement has been limited by sporadic industrial development and government intervention. It has also been politically divided as different industrial sectors have supported different political ideologies.

However, analyses of working-class development also embrace the enclave sectors, focusing on the similarities between enclave workers and urban-industrial workers in the cities. The mining sector in particular is seen as a milieu for working-class formation.[9] The miners are characterised as living in isolated communities which develop solidaristic social values and standards. In these communities there are identifiable common grievances and a recognisable economic opponent in the form of the industrial employer. Social mobility out of these communities is restricted, and so protests over wages and conditions take the form of direct conflict with the employer.[10] These characteristics are seen as common to other Latin American miners and similar to those of the traditional working class which emerged in Europe and England during the nineteenth century. This view of the miners as forming a homogeneous, solidaristic traditional working class is adopted not only by social scientists but also by political groups in Peru. Not least of these was the Military Junta which came to power in 1968 and embarked on a programme of industrial development. This government viewed the miners as a political element crucial to development plans.

By 1968 Peru was faced with increasing foreign domination, rising imports, limited growth of the industrial labour force, a weak export sector and a government which was borrowing heavily abroad. There was also growing nationalist sentiment in the country, but President Belaunde did not have the constitutional freedom to implement his reforms. Consequently the military, led by General Velasco, took control in 1968 and proclaimed the Peruvian revolution. The army had intervened in politics before, in 1930 and 1962, but only to form temporary administrations. Velasco's government was strongly nationalistic and had a long-term programme of economic reform.

The aim of the Military Junta was to stimulate key exports and feed back that stimulus into domestic demand and industrial development.[11] Industrial expansion was to increase employment, with one-quarter of the new jobs created between 1970 and 1975 in this sector. Output was to rise at 12 per cent per year. To implement its policies, the government nationalised key industries such as oil and fishing, and later mining. It took over the marketing of products first, and then their production. At the same time it assumed control of financial institutions, encouraging a flow of funds into the industrial sector.

However, in terms of industrial development the Junta's experience has been of only limited success. The military have been faced with the same dilemmas as previous governments. Investment for industrial growth may be generated internally by taxing the agricultural and commercial sectors, or it may be raised externally by foreign borrowing. The former creates the dilemma that higher taxes may lead to lower revenue as economic activities move outside or below the taxable domain. The latter brings in its train the problem of reconciling national and foreign economic interests. Despite their nationalist rhetoric, the military were constrained to opt for the second alternative, borrowing abroad.

In the early 1970s bottlenecks appeared in the export sectors of the economy. Oil supplies were running out, agricultural exports could not be expanded without large-scale irrigation, and fishing was reaching its ecological limits. The mining industry became the key to development plans. Mineral exports account for half Peru's export earnings, and these are used to pay off the interest on long-term development loans. In the 1970s huge sums were needed to exploit new copper deposits. Only multinational corporations could supply these funds. However, the mining sector is highly unionised and constitutes a bulwark of nationalist sentiment. The question for the Military Junta, as for other twentieth-century Peruvian governments, was how to reconcile the attitudes of foreign investors with the political sentiments of the strategically powerful miners. The Junta resolved its dilemma, as other governments had resolved theirs, by disciplining the miners.

The dilemmas[12] faced by the government stem from the instability of peripheral capitalist development. In political terms that instability results in limited industrial development, frustrated economic policies and frequent changes of government. Often, political take-overs are instituted by the military, who step in to establish law and order. In underdeveloped countries minority political groups compete for control of government, and on occasion the military assumes that it is the only agency which can enforce national unity.

In socio-economic terms the consequences of limited, unstable, dependent economic development in Peru have been twofold. Firstly, the social structure has not been transformed from an agrarian to an industrial one. The bulk of the population are still agriculturalists; the commercial sector is large, the industrial sector small. In 1970 45 per cent of the labour force were employed in agriculture.[13] Between 1950 and 1970 the commercial sector grew from 7 to 11 per cent of the labour force, and the service and government sector from 17 to 21 per cent, while the percentage of mineworkers declined. A large-scale working class has not emerged.

The second consequence of economic instability has been the persistence of migration between economic sectors. It is a stable feature of the social structure. Most migration is from the countryside to the towns. From the mid-1960s to the mid-1970s urbanisation increased from 50·2 per cent to 55·3 per cent, while Lima grew at the rate of 6 per cent per year.[14] Much migration is to Lima,[15] and in the metropolis the majority of migrants find work in the 'informal' sector of the economy, portering or shining shoes and cars. Some enter the more formal sectors such as the service industries or commerce, but only a few become part of the industrial labour force.

Whereas this one-way drift to Lima is perhaps the most important migratory flow, it is clear that there are also processes of circulatory migration between economic sectors and geographical regions. Although migrants move from agriculture to industry and from the country to the town, they maintain their interests within and between these sectors and locations. Rather than committing themselves to any single sector, they try to keep their options open across various sectors. The maintenance of this range of interests and alternatives means that migrants move back and forth between sectors as circumstances change. Circulatory migration is a response to economic instability.

One instance of maintained links between agriculture and industry illustrative of circulatory migration occurs in the highland mining region. Mining in the central highlands is an important industrial enclave. The industry's development has been unstable, with wide fluctuations in employment, and capital-intensive, leading to much larger increases in output than employment. Moreover, the mines have been owned by a foreign multinational corporation which has restricted the return of revenue into the domestic economy. People who migrate from the rural sector to the mines know that this type of employment is limited and unstable, so they keep up their interests in the rural sector. Their response to industrial development establishes an important difference between these workers and a traditional solidaristic working class. It is consequently a major focus of this study.

Contemporary mining in highland Peru

Peru is one of the world's great mineral producers,[16] providing 4 per cent of the West's mined copper. With Chile, Zambia and Zaire it controls the international consortium CIPEC. In 1970 copper contributed 38 per cent of the value of Peru's mineral output, with gold and silver providing 14 per cent, iron 13 per cent, zinc 8 per cent and lead 6 per cent. The mining sector employed some 80,000–90,000 people, or one-tenth of the industrial labour force. It is divided into three sub-sectors: small, medium and large. Small-scale mining includes lesser Peruvian companies and prospecting individuals. Medium-scale mining is carried out by Peruvian entrepreneurs who work in conjunction with large foreign companies and the state.

Large-scale mining dominates the sector. Until they were nationalised by the government in the mid-1970s it was carried on by large American concerns. Today the state collaborates with foreign investors over new mining projects. In the early 1970s three American companies were by far the most important: Cerro de Pasco Mining Corporation, Marcona Mining and Southern Peru Copper Corporation. Marcona became important after the second world war when direct American investment in Peruvian mining and smelting rose from $55 million in 1950 to $155 million in 1953, mainly on account of Marcona's investments in iron ore deposits. It is a subsidiary of Utah Construction Company. Southern Peru Copper Corporation produces copper from the large Toquepala mine near the southern coast of Peru, which opened in 1960. Southern was owned mainly by the American Smelting and Refining Company, with 61·5 per cent of the shares, while Dodge had 16 per cent and Cerro Corporation 22·3 per cent.

Cerro Corporation was the parent company of Cerro de Pasco Mining Corporation – CdeP – which it owned totally. Cerro was one of the seven multinational giants which controlled four-fifths of the West's supply of non-ferrous metals. All seven concerns have interlocking directorships. One of the key companies of the seven is American Metals-Climax, which is controlled by the Chase Manhattan Bank, in turn part of the Rockefeller empire. Not only was Peruvian copper controlled by foreign interests, it was also consumed by them. At the beginning of the 1970s, of just over 200,000 tons produced, slightly more than 3,000 tons remained in the country. The rest went in exports to the United States, which took 58 per cent, to Europe, 24 per cent, to Japan, 12 per cent, and 6 per cent to the rest of the world.

American domination of iron mining was total, for Marcona controlled 98 per cent of production and CdeP another 1 per cent. Non-ferrous metals accounted for 69 per cent of mining as a whole, and of that CdeP and Southern controlled 70 per cent of the capital investment, 71 per cent of sales and 82 per cent of copper production. Other foreign interests did exist, in the form of other American companies and Japanese, French and British mines, but their combined output was less than that of the large American companies. There were also Peruvian interests, mainly in medium-scale mining, but these were controlled by CdeP. Of the 220 mining companies in Peru, 100 were owned or controlled by CdeP, which had as members of its own board the managing directors of fourteen medium-sized companies. There was thus no strong indigenous capitalist interest in the mining sector. The national mining employers were in alliance with American capital.

Although CdeP had slightly less book-value capital invested in Peru than Southern, it was the most influential corporation. CdeP owned all three refineries in the country and two of the four smelters. It could press smaller companies to sell its ore at reduced rates, since they had no alternative refining outlet. As well as controlling many smaller companies it also owned or controlled nearly all the engineering industry, making ammunition, metal rods, steel castings and lead alloys. At the same time, Cerro owned wire and cable mills in Lima, as well as an oil company exploring in the jungle.

Multinational investment in Peru reaped high profits. Between 1950 and 1970 $790 million were repatriated to the United States from subsidiaries in Peru, $669 million of this during the years 1960–70. During the same twenty year period the American mining corporations invested only $284 million in the country, so that the outflow of funds was three times the inflow. The rate of profit on this capital is difficult to calculate owing to accounting procedures, but for Marcona it has been estimated to vary from 30 to 130 per cent, while for Cerro it has fluctuated around 30 per cent.

The mining investments of CdeP were mainly in the central highlands, where in the early 1970s the corporation operated seven major mines.[17] These employ about 6,000 workers. The largest is Morococha, with 1,500 workers, the smallest Cobriza, a recently opened mine with 600 workers. All are underground and some shafts, like those at Casapalca, are very deep. The technology is capital-intensive where the rock layers permit. The miners live in barracks built by the corporation round the pit-heads. The majority of them are young bachelors who work there for short periods. They live several to a room and eat communally. There is little provision for family life, and one school suffices for the children of migrants raised in the barracks. Although the mines are centres of wage-labour, they are work centres rather than urban centres.

In addition CdeP operated two major administrative and refining centres in the highlands, located in the towns of Cerro de Pasco and La Oroya. Cerro de Pasco is also a mining location, while Oroya is the administrative heart of highland mining operations, with the main refinery situated there. It is in these towns, rather than in the mines, that the pressures of proletarianisation are most felt. In Cerro de Pasco the corporation employed some 3,000 workers, in Oroya around 6,500. In both towns, workers have their families with them and so there are family dwellings, schools and colleges.

Oroya lies 4,000 metres above sea-level. It is the largest mining town in Peru as well as one of the most important railway centres. Through it passes the main road from the capital to the towns of the highlands. However, it is some five hours' journey to Lima, and several hours by road to the highland towns of Junin, Cerro de Pasco and Jauja. Consequently Oroya presents an isolated picture of a crowded jumble of shacks and huts huddled high in the Andes. The town straddles the Mantaro river, which cuts a deep gorge through the mountains. On one side is the municipal township of Old Oroya, a maze of slums and shacks which creep up the sides of the hills. On the other, on the only available flat land, are the long rows of barracks which house the labour force. The town is completely dominated by the vast CdeP refinery. Huge chimneys emit a poisonous smoke that has devastated the region

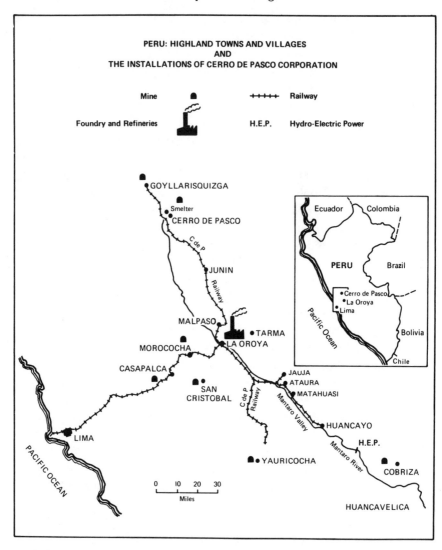

PERU: HIGHLAND TOWNS AND VILLAGES
AND
THE INSTALLATIONS OF CERRO DE PASCO CORPORATION

and given it the appearance of a lunar landscape. Refuse from the refinery pours into the river, which has become acidic, and is borne downstream.

Twenty-six thousand people live in Oroya. Most of the work-force are directly employed in the refinery, whilst the remainder are dependent upon that labour force for their own livelihood. There are six major social groups. The first are the refinery's blue-collar workers, or *obreros*, who number 5,300. The second are the refinery's white-collar workers, or *empleados*, who number around 1,200. Thirdly, there are the schoolteachers, bank clerks, railway officials and municipal administrators who are employed by the government. Then, there is the town's petty-bourgeoisie, which is divided into two groups. On the one hand are the native Oroyinos who own land and houses in Old Oroya and rent these out to the industrial workers and their families. On the other are the immigrant traders who operate restaurants, garages and bus services. Finally, there are the urban poor who are employed by the bourgeoisie of Old Oroya. They work in the informal sector as waiters, garage attendants or labourers and form a veritable 'reserve army' of labour, often living off kinsmen or friends until a vacancy appears in the industrial labour force. Living just outside Oroya are the refinery management. Engineers and accountants, these Americans and Europeans live a colonial life, with servants and golf.

The living and working conditions of *empleados* and *obreros* are quite distinct. *Empleados* are mainly office workers, many inhabiting a large administrative block away from the refinery itself. Even when employed in the refinery complex, *empleados* usually have small offices to themselves. They are employed for long periods and have acceptable redundancy arrangements. After twenty-five years' service they may retire on full pay. They are paid monthly, in *soles*, between $80 and $400 per month (in 1971). They also receive substantial fringe benefits in the form of subsidised food and schooling, and good medical care. The *empleados'* housing is located away from the refinery and the smoke, and consists of comfortable three or four-storey flats with two-to-three-bedroom apartments.

In contrast, the circumstances of the *obreros* are very poor. The *obreros* are employed on a daily basis and paid weekly in *soles* at a rate of between $2 and $4 per day (in 1971). They must work until they are sixty before they can retire on half-pay. If they leave before then, as most do, they receive a small severance sum. Their fringe benefits are much fewer than those of the *empleados* and they have no access to the houses of the *empleados*, owing to a weighted points system.

The *obrero* housing consists of rows of barrack-like huts in which each family is apportioned one room. Families of eight or nine persons live in this one room and sleep together on beds stacked up to the ceiling. The rooms are two metres square and may have a small kitchen annex, completely taken up by a stove. Washing and sanitary arrangements are communal. At one end of each row is a tap and some wash basins. At the other end is a privy from which excrement passes direct into the Mantaro river. Situated around the refinery, these *campamentos* receive the full force of the descending smoke. Those *obreros* who do not qualify on the corporation points system for a *campamento* seek accommodation in Old Oroya, where conditions are even worse. There, rooms are divided by cardboard and plastic sheets and often no washing and sanitary facilities are available. Central taps provide for the former and the open street for the latter.

The working conditions of the *obreros* are those set by an ageing refinery. The noise in the works is deafening and many *obreros* develop a basic hand language. It is often dark under the ovens and gantries and wet and uneven underfoot. It is very dangerous, the dangers lying not only in accidents but also in illness and disease. Mining has the second highest accident rate of all industries in Peru.[18] Deaths in pit disasters are regular occurrences, whilst fractures, crushings and bruisings are common. At the same time, Oroya workers are also subject to lead poisoning, which results in paralysis and death. In 1952 surveys[19] showed that lead in the air in Oroya departments was 125 times internationally agreed safety margins. Measures were brought in to alleviate the situation, and by 1965 there had been some improvement. However, the *obreros* know that refinery work is dangerous and damaging, and so aim to work there only for short periods.

Within the industrial sector itself, then, there are two major strata, clearly defined and distinguishable. It is in the early morning entry to work that the differences between the two groups seem most pronounced. At the refinery gates hundreds of *obreros* gather, hawking and spitting in the cold, thin air, rattling their billy-cans and slapping the side of the *empleados'* bus as it noses through the crowd. Yet, despite these work-place differences, both *obreros* and *empleados* often come from the same village, are members of the same family, or grew up together. They call upon these extra-industrial links to handle the problems of industrial life and so, outside the refinery gates, the divisions of the work-place are occasionally blurred.

The *obreros* are mainly young men, with an average age of thirty-five, while the *empleados* are older, their average age being thirty-nine. The different distribution of ages between the two groups is more marked, however. Over one-third of the *obreros* are under thirty, whilst nearly three-quarters of the *empleados* are between thirty and fifty. The bias towards the younger end of the *obrero* age range reflects the recruitment of young, unskilled *obreros*, while the sharp drop in the employment of *empleados* after fifty reflects the pension arrangements of these white-collar workers.

Table 1. *1971 CdeP Oroya work-force: age by occupational group*

	Empleados		Obreros	
Age in years	N	%	N	%
18–29	238	22	1,551	34
30–49	768	71	2,464	54
50+	76	7	548	12
	N = 1,082 = A		N = 4,563 = B	

[For A, B see appendix]

Since many *empleados* are promoted from the *obreros*, and since their working conditions are better, the *empleados* had on average worked longer with the corporation in Oroya than the *obreros*. The former had worked for fifteen years on average and the latter thirteen. Again, however, it was the distribution in years worked which revealed major differences. Over half the *obreros* have worked in Oroya for less than ten years, compared with only one-third of the *empleados*. In fact, one-third of the *obreros* have worked in Oroya for less than five years.

Table 2. *1971 CdeP Oroya work-force: numbers of years worked*
with CdeP in Oroya, by occupational group

	Empleados		Obreros	
Number of years worked	N	%	N	%
Less than ten years	411	38	2,373	52
Ten years or more	671	62	2,190	48
	N = 1,082 = A		N = 4,563 = B	

[For A, B see appendix]

Unlike the younger men working in the corporation's mines, the majority of the Oroya workers are married with families. Two-thirds of the labour force are married and around one-fifth of both *empleados* and *obreros* are bachelors. However, whereas one-fifth of the *obreros* admitted that they were cohabiting, none of the *empleados* did. Cohabitation is a normal feature of highland life, but the *empleados* may have felt constrained to emulate the public mores of the corporation's foreign staff.

That emulation may also have influenced family size, for, although both *obreros* and *empleados* had on average 3·2 children, the greater age of the *empleados* meant that they had had longer to procreate. Detailed statistical analysis of family sizes, in which age was controlled for, showed that *obreros* continued to have children after *empleados* had stopped. Along with emulation, the reasons were twofold. Firstly, the *empleados* were more educated and so presumably had better access to contraceptive advice. Secondly, they had the promise of a pension as security for their old age. The only provision *obreros* could make was to ensure there would be children to support them.

Obreros and *empleados* differ as regards the range of their occupations and salaries as well as in age, industrial experience and family size. *Empleados* are found in a much wider variety of occupations than *obreros*. They range from clerks and typists to accountants and engineers, whilst *obreros* are usually either unskilled men or skilled mechanics, electricians or carpenters. Thus the salary range for *empleados* is much greater than that for *obreros*, most of whom are concentrated on similar and close wage-points.

These differences between the two industrial strata are reflected in the fact that they have established different unions. The *obrero* trade union is the Sindicato de Trabajadores Metalurgicos de La Oroya – the STMO. It is the largest single union in Peru. All *obreros* become members of the STMO after three months unless they opt out; the union embraces 87 per cent of the *obreros*. Its structure and legal existence are similar to those of unions throughout the world. There is an elected president, with a yearly term of office, and an elected committee of some fifteen members, who are in turn chairmen of elected sub-committees. There are also a number of shop stewards, representing and elected by corporation work-groups, as well as a women's committee, which has advisory status. The meetings of the STMO are well attended, occasionally by up to 2,000 workers; its strike calls are solidly supported, and the rhetoric of its leaders is that of class struggle.

The *empleado* union, the Associacion de Empleados de Yauli – the AEY – is, on the other hand, a much less impressive affair. Although two-thirds of the *empleados* are unionised, the meetings of the AEY are not well attended, take place in a class-room and are mainly concerned with policy matters. The AEY rarely went on strike, and when it finally did so the rhetoric was of grievance and negotiation, not of class struggle and social revolution. The relations between the AEY and the STMO were characterised by uneasy politics rather than mutual trust.

Just as the refinery and its smokestacks dominate the barracks of New Oroya, so the large STMO hall dominates the slums and shacks of

Old Oroya. Without doubt, Oroya gives the impression of being an industrial town. Yet few of the industrial workers were born there. Rather, they came from the surrounding countryside, and their families remain there, for their dependants far outnumber the total population of the town. The industrial workers maintain and develop their links with the rural areas from which they came. Complementing Oroya's status as an 'industrial town' is also the fact that it is a 'migrant town'.

In 1961 two-thirds of all those working in the Peruvian mining sector were migrants.[20] Mining was the industry with the second largest proportion of migrants. In Oroya, only one-sixth of the *empleados* and one-tenth of the *obreros* were born there. The rest came from the near-by highland Departments of Junin, Pasco and Huancavelica, or from the city and Department of Lima. Over two-thirds of the *obreros* and just over half the *empleados* came from within fifty miles of Oroya. One reason for this large local recruitment of labour is straightforwardly ecological. Oroya lies at an altitude of 4,000 metres, and lowlanders do not find it easy to acclimatise. So over nine-tenths of the total labour force comes from the highlands.

Table 3.   *1971 CdeP Oroya work-force: place of origin by occupational group*

	Empleados		Obreros	
Place of origin	N	%	N	%
Oroya	173	16	456	10
Junin (minus Oroya)	530	49	2,920	64
Lima (city and department)	64	6	137	3
Cerro de Pasco	97	9	365	8
Huancavelica	32	3	411	9
% of total work type		83		94
Rural = 200–10,000	554	51	3,268	72
Urban = 10,001+	528	49	1,295	28
	N = 1,082 = B		N = 4,563 = A	

[For A, B see appendix]

The status of Oroya as a migrant town is reflected in many dimensions of the workers' lives. Three important aspects of the work situation are education, the distribution of migrants throughout the refinery complex, and labour turnover. Outside the work situation, migrant links influence kin and village networks, the establishment of regional clubs, and strategies with regard to industrial work, among other things.

Educational attainment is perhaps the single most direct influence stratifying the refinery labour force into *obreros* and *empleados*. In order to become an *empleado* some secondary schooling is required, and the higher positions demand university education. Two-fifths of the *empleados* have had secondary schooling, and a quarter of them are university-educated. In contrast, the great majority of *obreros* have only primary education, although a third of them have some secondary schooling.

Since the workers were not born in Oroya, and the corporation recruited only those of eighteen years old and over, it is clear that these educational differences are established in the workers' places of origin, not in the work location. Statistical analysis shows that it is the Peruvian Departments with the highest educational levels and facilities that send the best-qualified migrants. The prime example is Lima city, with its numerous colleges and universities, which provides a disproportionate number of *empleados*. On the other hand, the provinces of Junin, with the poorest educational facilities, provided the *obreros* with the lowest educational qualifications. Thus education, one of the main factors affecting occupational stratification in the industrial milieu, exerts that influence from the place of origin through the structure of the migratory stream.

The second influence of migration is seen in the distribution of workers throughout the corporation departments in Oroya. Recruitment to this large, formal organisation is purportedly based on the universalistic criteria of age, sex and education. Certainly, as has been shown, these three are very important. Alongside them, however, a set of informal recruitment criteria also help to structure the labour force: village and kinship links.

Migrants from different Peruvian Departments are distributed non-randomly throughout the corporation departments, as the distribution of *obreros* shows. There are two reasons. The first is 'formal' and operates at the Departmental level. Certain corporation departments require higher educational standards than others, for example Administration. Certain Peruvian Departments supply better-educated migrants, such as Lima. Thus there is a concentration of Limenos in Administration.

The second reason is 'informal' and operates at the village level, although its cumulative effect is demonstrated at the Departmental level. Certain villages 'capture' certain corporation positions and departments. A migrant who gains a position of some influence in a section will recruit his compatriots to that section. A village network is built up as these in turn recruit more people from the same village. Particular men – and often these are *empleados* – become known to other migrants as being well-placed. They are asked to provide news about jobs and even jobs themselves and so become gatekeepers of the industrial labour force.

Table 4 shows the effects of these influences on the distribution of the labour force. Huancavelicenos have grouped in the Foundry and other industrial departments, while migrants from Pasco have moved into Railways and non-industrial departments. Limeños and Huanuceños also have colonised Railways and non-industrial work. Further statistical analysis of the Railways department shows that certain villages from Cerro de Pasco are over-represented there. Table 4 does not include Junin, whose preponderance distorts statistical analysis, but the same patterns are found by village and province in Junin. Migrants from the thirty-one villages of Jauja province distributed throughout the twenty-two corporation departments are clustered in particular departments, revealing the extent to which rural migrants have captured industrial salients. But, although these informal contacts structure the *obrero* labour force, the same is not true of the *empleado* work force, where formal criteria predominate.

As well as influencing the structure of the labour force through education and distribution, migration also influences it through labour turnover. Very few people were taken on by the corporation at the beginning of the 1970s, and the characteristics of the men who left differed from those of the ones who stayed. Those who left were younger, better educated and had not worked for the corporation as long as those who had stayed. At the same time, those who left were not from the highlands, but from the cities. Thus the labour force increasingly contained workers from rural origins with maintained rural links.

Table 3 shows the extent to which the industrial labour force is rural in origin. Half the *empleados* and three-quarters of the *obreros* were born in the countryside. Overall, three-quarters of the Oroya workforce comes from villages, most of them from villages in the Department of Junin. Junin has five provinces, and three of these – Jauja, Concepcion and Huancayo – compromise the Mantaro Valley area. The Mantaro

Table 4. *Distribution of obreros from Peruvian Departments through CdeP departments*

| Peruvian Department | Specific CdeP departments | | | | | | | | | | Type of CdeP department | | | |
| | Foundry | | Electrical | | Engineering | | Admn. | | Railways | | Industrial [Foundry+Elect. +Engineering] | | Non-industrial [Admn.+other services] | |
	N	%	N	%	N	%	N	%	N	%	N	%	N	%
Ayacucho	42	71	2	3	6	10	8	14	1	2	50	81	9	17
Huancavelica	335	88	3	1	22	6	14	4	8	2	360	88	41	10
Huanuco	47	71	3	5	3	5	6	9	7	11	53	72	14	19
Lima	67	52	5	4	22	17	18	14	16	13	94	67	30	22
Cerro de Pasco	126	40	34	11	42	13	35	11	78	25	202	58	69	20

N = 950 = *obreros* from five Peruvian Departments   N = 922 = *obreros* from five Peruvian Depts.

$X^2 = 203$ = Highly significant $X^2 = 31$ = Highly significant

[For significance tests see appendix]

Valley supplies around one-fifth of the refinery labour force and has a long history of contact with the mining sector. In order to investigate the links between the industrial and rural sectors, the Mantaro Valley, and selected villages within the valley, were chosen for study.

The valley[21] lies at some 3,000 metres, fifty miles to the south-east of Oroya and around two hours' journey from the town. It is fifty miles long, two to three miles wide and contains numerous villages and *comunidades*. The dominant economic activity is agriculture, practised under a *minifundia*, or smallholding system, centred on household subsistence farming. In 1961 nine-tenths of the farm units in the valley were under five hectares, and the trend was toward increasing fragmentation of land ownership. There were some larger farms, up to 600 hectares, and there was some renting of large extensions, but it was the *minifundistas* who predominated.

Alongside agriculture, commercial activities are very important. Much of the commerce is centred on the two towns of Jauja and Huancayo, which, respectively, straddle the northern and southern ends of the valley. Much is also carried on in the villages themselves. Most villages have shops and market-places where agricultural produce is bought and sold as well as some industrial products. There is also a system of rotating fairs which move from village to village. The occupations embraced by this commercial activity are not only those of trader and shopkeeper, but also transporter and driver. The transportation of agricultural and artisanal goods to the mines and to Lima is an important commercial activity.

Household subsistence agriculture and a range of commercial activities are thus two elements in the socio-economic structure of the valley. The third is labour migration. The villages supply labour to the mines and to Lima. At the same time they are part of a larger migratory process which embraces the highlands, the mines and the capital. The process is not just a one-way flow of labour from the land. Rather, the migratory patterns are complex and partly circulatory. Migrants go off to the mines or Lima, and then return to their villages. While this rural–urban–rural migration is taking place, there is rural–rural migration as people move into villages where men are working away from home.

Seasonal migration from the poorer villages lying at the foot of the eastern valley side provides female agricultural labour to work in the fields of the more prosperous villages, as well as supplying temporary male labour to the mines of Huancavelica. The women from the poorer villages work either for large land-holders or for the families of migrants. Often the migrants remit cash to their families for the hiring of this temporary labour.

The migrants in the towns stay for varying lengths of time and then either return to their village or go on to Lima. Some sever their links with the land and are joined by their families. This process occurs in stages or steps as the migrants move from village to town to metropolis. With step migration, some contact is maintained with the rural areas in the form of visits and letters, but urban interests come to replace rural ones. Other migrants keep their links with the land and maintain their families in the village. This form of circulatory migration is characterised not by the replacement of interests but by efforts to maintain interests across different sectors.

Circulatory migration is a process which contains feedback. The migratory flows affect, and are affected by, the socio-economic structures in the villages and towns. In the highlands the elements in the migratory process are complex and are constituted in three major cycles. The first is that of industrial production, linked to the movements of the world's metal markets. As this cycle turns, so highland employment fluctuates. The second is that of peasant production. The peasant household is both a production and a consumption unit and its structure alters with births, marriages and deaths. As the household cycle turns, so migration is called for to supplement family income. The third is the individual life-cycle. As individuals age, so they meet the life-crises of marriage and provision for children and parents. Often such provision is made through the returns from migration.

Notes

[1] Long, N., and Roberts, B., 1978.

[2] United Nations, 1975.

[3] Quijano, A., 1968.

[4] Roberts, B., 1975.

[5] The following analysis draws to a large extent on Thorp, R., and Bertram, J., 1978.

[6] Sulmont, D., 1974, 1975.

[7] Blanchard, P., 1974.

[8] Larson, M., and Bergman, 1969; Payne, J., 1965.

[9] Bourricaud, F., 1970; Kruijt, D., and Vellinga, M., 1977; Quijano, A., 1968. However, Bonilla, H., 1974, and Chaplin, D., 1967, have drawn attention to the

important transitional and migratory status of the miners.

[10] These characteristics are outlined by Kerr, C., 1954.

[11] Instituto Nacional de Planificacion, 1970.

[12] Fitzgerald, E., 1976; Kalecki, M., 1972.

[13] Banco Central, 1961, quoted in Thorp, R., and Bertram, J., 1978.

[14] United Nations, 1975.

[15] Skeldon, R., 1977.

[16] Bollinger, W., 1972; Brundenius, C., 1972; De Wind, A., 1977; Purser, W., 1971; Thorp, R., and Bertram, J., 1978.

[17] CdeP documents.

[18] Accidentes de Trabajo, 1970.

[19] Del Carpio, G., 1967.

[20] Censo, 1961.

[21] Long, N., and Roberts, B., 1978.

3

The industrial development of highland mining

There have been four major periods in the history of mining in Peru.[1] The first is the pre-Incaic age, in which limited amounts of metal were mined with limited technology. The second is the Incaic period, in which the mining industry was an integrated part of an agricultural society. Again, capital and technology were limited during this period, but the organisation of labour was on a large scale. The third period was the colonial epoch, during which merchant capital provided funds for the working of the mines. However, this mining was based on the super-exploitation of labour which led to the virtual collapse of indigenous agricultural systems. The fourth period is the modern era, dating from the turn of the present century. In this period, mineworking has become capital-intensive rather than labour-intensive, as industrial capital has sought to exploit Peru's mineral wealth. Despite these changes, however, it is possible to discern continuities in processes and structures from one period to the next.

Mining in Peru up to 1900

Metalworking, mainly of gold and copper, has been practised in Peru for over 2,000 years. Tools and ornaments were fashioned of metal in both coastal and highland civilisations. However, it was with the establishment of the Inca state in the mid-fifteenth century that copper and bronze were produced on a larger scale. Metal implements began to be employed by the peasantry as they used bronze-tipped ploughs, whilst artisans used copper and bronze chisels. The use of gold and silver was restricted to the nobility, in the form of ornaments and sacred objects. The extraction of metals by the Incas was mainly from surface ore deposits or from shallow mines, mainly silver. The ores were mined with stone hammers and bars tipped with copper, and smelted in small ceramic furnaces. The mines were the property of the Incas, who organised local production.

Labour was recruited from the surrounding provinces. The indigenous population was required to render labour service to the Inca state under the *mita* system. Those living near-by worked in the mines during the four warm months of the year when they were operational. The miners came in groups of twenty to fifty, accompanied by their wives, and worked for one month at a time until they were replaced. The migrants then returned to their lands. Mining was secondary to agriculture, and the four warm months were the ones in which agricultural activity was at its lowest. The base metals that were mined and smelted were used by the peasantry and the army, while the precious metals were reserved for the state functionaries and the priests. Hence, the mines and the hills from which precious metals were extracted became sacred. Festivals were held around mining shrines, religiously reinforcing the authority of the Inca state at the point of production.

The challenge to the Incas came from Spanish imperialism, and it was the conquest of 1532 which brought Peru into the international economy. However, whereas Inca rule was overthrown by the Spaniards, the organisation of the state was maintained and put to colonial use. At first the *conquistadores* merely plundered existing stocks of gold and silver. When these were exhausted there arose the problem of mining and refining further quantities, and the organisation of the old Inca state was called on for this.

Most important for the Spaniards were the silver mines of Potosi and Huancavelica, and later those of Cerro de Pasco.[2] At first the mining technology was similar to that used by the Incas, but soon surface ores were depleted and deeper ones were being mined, which required refining. The skilled work of mining and refining was done by the Indians, but the Spaniards directed them into more and more hazardous conditions, particularly at Potosi, which was opened in 1545. The dangerous nature of the work began to pose problems for labour recruitment.

To mine and process the silver required large numbers of workers. Prior to 1572 this labour was recruited voluntarily and for wages.

Revenues to the Spanish Crown came from capitation taxes, and the Crown wished to safeguard the native population as a source of revenue. In the Caribbean forced labour had decimated the population and so, anxious to preserve the population in Peru, the Crown regulated minework. Thus in the mines, prior to 1572, were to be found *hatunrunas*, sent by *encomenderos* to earn money for their tribute; *tindarunas*, required to work for six-month periods in Potosi by the colonial administrators, and recruited on a payment basis; and *yanaconas*, who were free subjects but were probably in debt to the Spanish administrators. In Potosi the miners were required to live within the town walls, where they were prevented from escaping and checked for smuggling. They were sold consumption goods and were paid in silver.

By the late 1560s, however, it became increasingly necessary to deepen the mines and extend the processing system, and so new mining laws were passed in 1572. A million and a half Indians throughout Peru were relocated into *reducciones*, and each year one-seventh of this population had to pay its tax in labour to the Crown. In Potosi an Indian was expected to work every third week for four months. These *mitayos* worked alongside voluntary labour and usually did the unskilled and heavy work. Both forced and voluntary labour was paid, however, for both types of labourers had to purchase food. This was supplied by traders, and the wages were taxed by the Crown.

The forced labour *mita* of the Spaniards differed from the Inca *mita* in that, whereas the latter was a subsidiary part of an agricultural system, the former was a dominant part of a colonial system. Through poor conditions the Indians died in the Spanish colonial mines. At the same time conditions in the rural areas, from which they were drawn, deteriorated. Irrigation systems fell into disrepair, and disease and famine wasted the old Inca society. The result was the decimation of the Indian population.

During the late seventeenth and eighteenth centuries the mining industry expanded only slowly.[3] The mines went deeper and deeper, and it became more and more difficult to contract labour. Mines were leased out by the Crown, but owing to rising costs even this did not stimulate production. Local merchants moved into the vacuum, financing miners who would then turn all their production over to the merchants. This directed funds away from the Crown and led to the erratic exploitation of mines. Finally, the mines were thrown open and worked independently, but from 1812 they declined until, by the wars of independence, production had almost ceased.

The mines became flooded during the wars and, if they were to be worked again, needed to be drained. At this point the steam engine was introduced: its first application was in 1816, to pump out water. The steam-driven rotary drill and the locomotive meant that mechanised exploitation was now a possibility. In the 1820s funds were raised in London and Lima for the re-opening of the mines, but Peru lacked an infrastructure that could support mechanisation. There were no facilities for getting the machines in or the ores out. There were no manufacturers to supply spare parts, nor were there schools to provide a supply of engineers. Thus the British attempts to industrialise the mines were a failure.

The potential for the development of an economic infrastructure that would support the industrial exploitation of the mines came with the guano boom of 1860–80. Grace and the Peruvian Corporation took over the economic legacy of the boom and began to invest in industrial projects.[4] One of the most important was railway construction, which directly affected mining. In the central highlands lay the silver mines of Casapalca, Morococha and Cerro de Pasco. Ore from these mines was transported by llama and mule to the Central Railway, which extended from Lima a short distance into the highlands. The output from these mines was very limited, but the extension of the railway by the Peruvian Corporation altered this. As the line reached the Casapalca and Morococha mines, foreign and national investors were able to bring in the machinery to open new mines and install ore concentrators. The increased output was shipped out along the railway. Production at Cerro de Pasco was still limited, owing to the transport bottleneck, however, and to alleviate the situation, and to tap the agricultural resources of the region, the railway was pushed on to the village of La Oroya, arriving in.1893.[5]

Oroya was a highland *comunidad* containing some 150 adults and controlling 1,000 hectares of communal land. It lay in a valley, 4,000 metres up, and was situated by a bridge over the Mantaro river. Land around the village was used for raising some crops, whilst the valley slopes and the high land were used for grazing cattle and sheep. Most of the *comuneros* were solely peasants, and most of them were shepherds.[6] However, there was some socio-economic differentiation in that around a quarter of them were engaged in mining and trading, and some *comuneros* controlled more land and livestock than others. Most had rights to both riverside valley land and to upland, but some had rights to land close to the village itself which were to become valuable as the village expanded.[7]

The arrival of the railway was one event in a process of socio-economic change which had been affecting Oroya for some time. During the first half of the nineteenth century migrants came and settled there. They were drawn by the mines of near-by Yauli, as well as by the opportunities for raising sheep and cattle. During the 1850s the world prices of wool and meat had risen dramatically, and migrants had been attracted into farming. During the fifteen years up to 1850 there was a marked pattern of both short and long-distance immigration. Parish records show that migrants came from the Mantaro Valley, some fifty miles to the south, and that they were long and medium-term residents of Oroya. They came also from Tarma, and one of these took up the post of toll collector on the bridge of Oroya.[8] Shepherds driving sheep and cattle over it were required to pay the toll. Like other migrants this man began buying houses in the village and lands of the *comunidad*. This process of land alienation had been going on since at least 1880, as the *comunidad* records show.

Surrounding Oroya were two other *comunidades* and five *haciendas*, which had also been affected by these processes of change. The *comunidades* of Huaynacancha and Sacco were somewhat larger than Oroya, controlling 2,200 and 7,000 hectares respectively and comprising 200 to 300 adults each. As in Oroya, the main activity of the *comunidades* was the rearing of cattle and sheep, but again there was some economic differentiation.[9] In Sacco, half the *comuneros* were shepherds and a few were traders, but around one-third worked in the small silver mine operational there during the nineteenth century. In Huaynacancha there was evidence of land alienation similar to that which had been occurring in Oroya. In fact in all three *comunidades* the tendency towards the dispersal of communal land through inheritance was being reversed and rights to land were becoming concentrated in the hands of outsiders.

In the case of Sacco, this alienation had led to the formation of one of the five adjacent *haciendas*. This *hacienda* – Tallapuquio – had once been part of the communal land and was worked in usufruct by a *comunera*. On her death her communal rights passed to her two children. In 1870, however, two other *comuneros* from Sacco occupied the land, claiming that it was common land, and the case was taken to court. The children of the *comunera* won the case but lost the land, for it was promptly claimed by their lawyer in payment for his fees. In 1891 the lawyer died and the *hacienda* Tallapuquio passed to his daughter.

The remaining *haciendas* ranged from 1,500 to 6,000 hectares in size and were owned by families living in the region, by families from the near-by town of Tarma, and by a joint-stock company in Lima.[10] Their economic activities were predominantly pastoral, and so they consisted either of families or of managers with small shepherd labour forces which could control large numbers of sheep and cattle. The *haciendas* also used the practice of *huaccha*,[11] whereby shepherds from *comunidades* adjacent to *hacienda* boundaries would tend their own, as well as *hacienda*, sheep on *hacienda* land.

As with the *comunidades* during the nineteenth century, the *hacienda* lands were repeatedly bought and sold. One dominant family in *hacienda* purchases were the Santa Marias from Tarma. In 1861 the mother Santa Maria bought the *hacienda* adjacent to Oroya's communal land on the valley floor from a group of three widows and two spinsters.[12] In 1869 her son expanded the family interests along the river bank, and in 1874 he bought the neighbouring *hacienda* from its widowed owner. In 1890 this land was resold to the widow's daughter but changed hands again in 1895 when she was bought out by her sister. At the end of the century the fourth *hacienda* was also in the hands of a woman whose father had bought out the last remaining Spanish family in 1845. The fifth was owned by a joint-stock company in Lima which rented the land to a shepherding manager.

It was clear that the arrival of the railway in Oroya would transform the region and open up commercial opportunities. The Peruvian Corporation had contracted the building of the line to E. Thorndike and H. Meiggs. The latter always intended to continue it to Cerro de Pasco, where he had already purchased ore deposits. The former joined forces with members of the Santa Maria family to exploit the new trading opportunities.

The expansion of the mines of Casapalca and Morococha and the economic activity generated by the building of the railway persuaded the government to draw up plans for a new town in Oroya. The railway was being constructed by a large hired labour force, many of whom were Chinese, using materials shipped in from the United States. The mere presence of this workforce was stimulating economic activity, and the extension of the railway to Cerro de Pasco promised further possibilities. The opportunities were seized by those who could readily mobilise resources and take advantage of the situation.

One method of mobilising cash to exploit the new situation was to float a joint-stock company. In 1892 the Santa Maria family formed a limited company, La Compania Mercantil de la Oroya, which controlled a strategic forty hectares of the family's *hacienda* land. The capital of 100,000 *soles* was raised as shares, and the new company advertised its aims as being to rent land and construct hotels, offices and markets. The Mercantil had five directors, one of whom was Thorndike and another the younger son of the family. Together they encouraged household servants who had been granted land by the family during farming days to sell back their plots. In turn the Mercantil began to sell and rent land for development. Land was sold first to the railway company in 1892 and subsequently to individuals for the building of houses and shops. One of the purchasers was the family's elder son, who established a flourishing general store.

The arrival of the railway in La Oroya also stimulated mining activities in Cerro de Pasco once again. The transport bottleneck was eased slightly, as ores could at least be transported to the Oroya railhead. Between 1892 and 1893 production of copper at Cerro de Pasco jumped by two-thirds.[13] This increase in output was consolidated in 1897 when the government demonetised silver at the same time as copper prices began to rise. By 1898 production was three times its 1897 level, and Peruvian capital was being invested in the mines. Some of it came from wealthy local miners, but most was raised in Lima by Peruvian businessmen.

However, the boom in Cerro de Pasco was short-lived. The miners were quickly reaching the flood-line in the mines and so exhausting the accessible ores. The Peruvian Corporation had run into financial difficulties and was unable, or unwilling, to continue the line from Oroya to Cerro de Pasco.[14] This meant not only that the transportation of ore was expensive, but also that the cost of coal for smelting was almost prohibitive, for it came on llama-back from near-by coal deposits. It was, in fact, the transporters who were making money out of the copper mining rather than the miners. Thus the miners did not have the money to finance a railway extension and the transporters did not have the incentive.

Then in 1898 J. Backus and J.H. Johnston, two American engineers who had worked with Meiggs, approached the government with an offer to build the extension and drain the mines.[15] In return they claimed the mineral rights of the area they drained. The Peruvian mine owners opposed the scheme, for they did not want both mines and railway to come under foreign monopolistic control. Through their association, the Sociedad Nacional de Mineria, they offered to build a railway to the coal deposits and a road to Oroya, arguing that theirs was a non-monopolistic solution. The government, however, decided to split the two projects and tendered the railway and drainage options separately. The railway tender was taken up this time by Thorndike. The drainage contract was bid for by French, British and Peruvian interests, and finally went to the Peruvians in 1900. By this time, however, the water level had been reached in the mines, there was a sharp drop in the price of copper, and many miners began to sell out.

Despite the problems in Cerro de Pasco, by 1900 Oroya had been transformed from a small village into a bustling railhead. Not only was it a centre for the transportation of ores, much of the agricultural activity of the region also focused on it. Both sheep and cattle were herded to Oroya to be sent, either live or slaughtered, to Lima. However, important though these changes were, they were but the first phase of a process of industrial development that was to transform the town completely. The second phase was the monopolisation and exploitation of the mines by American interests.

Mining in the central region from 1900

Monopolisation and capitalisation

During 1901 and 1902 the mines in Cerro de Pasco were bought up by a small group of American financiers and engineers. In 1902 this group formed the Cerro de Pasco Mining Company and by the end of the year had purchased 730 mines and 108 coal mines in the region for a little over $2·65 million. It also purchased during that year the La Oroya–Cerro de Pasco railway concession from C. Thorndike.[16] In order to compete, the remaining Peruvian interests pushed on with the draining of the mines despite the company's efforts to stop them. In 1908 the company was forced to come to terms with the Peruvians and bought up the drainage rights. At the same time, in conjunction with Backus and Johnston, Cerro de Pasco Mining Company was eliminating local capitalists from Morococha. Only one Peruvian miner, L. Proano, held out, but eventually he too was bought up. In 1919 J. Backus and J.H. Johnston sold their interests to Cerro de Pasco Mining Company.

The company had acquired a monopoly of the major mining activities in the area, and had several major ore and coal deposits scattered throughout the central highland region. Consequently the main problem, the transport bottleneck, still needed to be solved. In 1904 the Cerro de Pasco Railway Company, a subsidiary of the mining company, completed the line from Oroya to Cerro de Pasco. This immediately reduced ore freight rates but CdeP still found it cheaper to import coal from Britain and New Zealand and transport it to Cerro de Pasco on the railway than bring it on llama-back from the deposits at Goyllarisquizga, only twenty miles away. In 1908 the railroad from Cerro de Pasco to Goyllarisquizga was completed, reducing coal freight costs from \$20 to \$4 per ton.[17]

At first, the extension of the railway network seemed to have solved the transport problem. However, monopolisation and easier transport led to an expansion of output. In Casapalca, for example, production rose from 1,000 tons per year in 1889 to 160,000 tons in 1916.[18] To cope with these increases CdeP installed ore concentrators at Casapalca and Cerro de Pasco, and built a smelter at Tinyahuarco, near by. But, it soon became clear to CdeP that moving large quantities of ore and coal around the highlands was an expensive business. The company decided to solve the problem through capitalisation, and embarked on the construction of a central refinery at Oroya.[19]

The refinery posed certain specific requirements. It had to be centrally located relative to ore and coal deposits in order to minimise transport costs. It needed a large area of flattish land, not easy to find in the Andes. It required plenty of water for in-process use, and thus had to be near a river. There had to be means of waste disposal, and again a river would serve the purpose. Finally, it required a large labour force and room to accommodate its workers. This meant the refinery had to be near a supply of labour and in a situation where housing could be erected.

All these considerations favoured Oroya as the new site, and the fluidity of the land negotiations there provided the opportunity to procure land. Under Peruvian law mining companies could lay claim to land by annexing it for mining purposes. Attention then had to be paid to the type of land claimed – urban, rural or communal – and the purpose for which it was required. In March 1918 CdeP laid claim to the land of the Mercantil, stating that it wished to build a refinery upon it. In response Thorndike offered to sell all the Mercantil to CdeP. Knowing that the Mercantil had not fulfilled its promises to the government as regards urbanisation plans for Oroya, the company extended its claim to all the Mercantil's lands, valuing it at a low agricultural rate. Amid protests, the Santa Marias sold out in 1919 and a director of CdeP became the Mercantil's president.[20]

Having acquired its prime site, CdeP began the construction of the refinery in 1919. Capital equipment and skilled labour on two-year contracts were shipped in from abroad, while unskilled labour was recruited from the neighbouring districts. Requiring space to store materials and house workers, CdeP expanded on to the *hacienda* Tallapuquio, which it had bought in 1912, to install a hydro-electric plant, and purchased the remaining 6,000 hectares of the Santa Maria *hacienda*.

Although CdeP was solving its transport and location problems, it was running into financial difficulties. In 1917, when the decision to construct the new refinery was taken, metal values were high – copper stood at $0·33 per pound, CdeP was paying dividends and the $6 million investment was considered worthwhile. But, these high copper prices were due to the United States' entry into the first world war. When the war ended, copper prices slumped, falling to $0·15 per pound in 1920. The completion of the new refinery would cut both freight and fuel costs by half and so CdeP pushed ahead with construction.[21] Until the new plant was in operation the older installations kept unit costs high and restricted large-scale exploitation of the rich ore-bodies at Cerro de Pasco and Casapalca. The cost of the refinery had risen to $15 million and the company was anxious to pay off the debt.

In order to procure labour for the building of the refinery CdeP relied heavily on the system of sub-contracting, or *enganche*.[22] The company contracted an *enganchador* to provide men to work the mines and refinery. The *enganchador* paid the men in advance and they then worked off the debt in the mines. This system was used also to provide labour to the jungle, and was seen as so pernicious that a law was passed in 1910 limiting its use. Disagreement over the law had split the Peruvian Senate, and in 1920 the system still flourished, since mining companies felt it was the only way to guarantee a labour supply. Nearly all the 2,000 labourers constructing the refinery were *enganche'd*, working off thirty to ninety day debts. In just two and a half years the refinery was completed and refining began in 1922.

CdeP was concerned only with the extraction of copper from the rich ores, containing 10–12 per cent metal, compared to Bolivian ores containing only 1 per cent. There was no attempt to filter the smoke from the refinery, and short flues were installed to recover metal particles from the smoke. Consequently 100–125 tons per day of lead, bismuth, sulphur dioxide and arsenic immediately began to be deposited on the surrounding countryside. The effect on the crops and livestock of the *haciendas* and *comunidades* was catastrophic. Owing to the different nature of their productive forms, the reactions of the *haciendas* and *comunidades* differed. From the *haciendas*, because the land was private property and control was in the hands of a few, the response was a concerted market calculation of costs and alternative investment. On the part of the *comunidades*, owing to the communal nature of ownership and the size of the collectivity, it was differentiation and a search for alternative means of subsistence.

To the south of Oroya six large *haciendas* had from 1904 to 1906 formed a joint-stock company, the Sociedad Ganadera de Junin. As soon as the refinery opened the Sociedad found that its sheep and cattle were dying of diarrhea, lack of edible vegetation and direct poisoning. The death rate among its cattle rose from 3 per cent to 18 per cent per year. The *hacendados* brought political pressure to bear on CdeP through government contacts and managed to get a smoke commission set up to assess the damage. This commission was established in 1923 and was to be the first of five.

As the commission deliberated, more and more claims for damage were lodged against CdeP, for the smoke affected an area fifty miles in diameter, whilst waste deposits were water borne even farther afield. In this situation CdeP embarked on two lines of action: it filtered the smoke and it bought up the *haciendas*. Smoke filtering was embarked upon for two reasons. The first was public opinion. The general outcry and accompanying political agitation were so strong that both CdeP and the government had to be seen to be doing something. The second reason was that by 1925 the metal content of CdeP's ores was declining. For example, the content of Cerro de Pasco ores had dropped to 5 per cent copper. Concentration processes were revealing traces of lead and zinc and the pyrite bodies at Cerro de Pasco promised huge quantities of zinc.[23] So the company installed filtering processes both to cut down pollution and reclaim metals. The filtered particles were 50 per cent lead in content, and one ton per day of bismuth was recovered, with a value of $1·5 million per year.

The immediate reason for the purchase of the *haciendas* was that it relieved CdeP of lawsuits and future indemnifications. The company knew that, faced with claims for damage from a large number of sources, it would have to fight each one lest a single test case should lead to indemnities for all the others.[24] CdeP also knew from experiments carried out with test animals that seemingly doomed animals could in fact recover, given proper care and attention. Thus, even though smoke output was being reduced, the expensive purchase of the *haciendas* could be made to yield financial pay-off in that the company would be able to feed its own mine and refinery labour force at cost price.

The acquisition of the *haciendas* began, and those with the most troublesome court cases were the first purchased. The Sociedad, with 14,000 cattle, 16,000 sheep and 1,000 horses, and extending over 115,000 hectares, was acquired in 1924 for $1,368,000. Next came Quiulla, and then Punabamba, Paria and Paucar. By 1930 CdeP had purchased 228,490 hectares for $1,851,000, plus another $180,000 to their owners for smoke damage. Thus, alongside the monopolisation of highland mining interests, there occurred the extensive take-over of large-scale highland agriculture. American-trained experts were hired to improve livestock and a new CdeP Farms Department was created. The *hacendados* took their money and invested it elsewhere, some in the commercial opportunities opening up in Oroya.

The response of the *comunidades* was less coherent. The effect of the smoke on their lower-lying lands had been disastrous. Almost overnight the sulphur dioxide had burned the barley of the Oroya *comuneros*. The high walls of the Mantaro river valley acted as a flue, conducting the smoke to the communal lands of Huaynacancha and destroying the barley there too. From 1922 to 1924 the *comunidad* of Oroya lost 278 cattle, 3,874 sheep and 200 mules and horses through smoke poisoning.[25] As for human beings, the ash, falling like rain, caused skin diseases and hair loss. It was clear that subsistence agriculture could not continue near the refinery, a conclusion borne out by the fact that today not a blade of grass grows for miles around.

However, under Peruvian law, while private land could be bought and sold, communal land could not, and so compensating the *comuneros* was not a straightforward matter. In contrast to the private piecemeal land sales of the nineteenth century, CdeP could not publicly alienate whole *comunidades*. Compensation for communal land expropriated or polluted would have to be by means of an agreed donation of land situated elsewhere. At the same time, there were conflicts of interest within the *comunidades* themselves. Some *comuneros* were subsistence peasants, interested in taking up land offers and continuing their agricultural life. Others, like the migrants who had come from outside, were more interested in cash compensation from CdeP, which they could use to invest in Oroya's commercial opportunities. Cash indemnification was forthcoming for affected livestock and private land; land indemnification for affected communal land.

CdeP's original mining claim on the property of the Mercantil included land belonging to Huaynacancha. In 1918 CdeP offered to compensate the *comuneros* partly with cash and partly with land in the Yauli region. It met with the response that Huaynacancha was not a *comunidad* and that anyway the Yauli *comunidades* were defunct. Instead the peasants of Huaynacancha claimed that they were private landholders and should be compensated more fully in cash. CdeP needed the land for the refinery buildings, and it was occupied by several peasant families, so the company agreed to a full cash indemnification and paid up.

The negotiations with the *comunidad* of Oroya were longer and more complex. The land of Oroya had been ruined for agricultural use, and besides CdeP wanted it for some more installations and a waste dump. So it valued the *comunidad* land. This valuation produced the first split in the *comunidad*. Private landholders came forward demanding a separate valuation, preferring an individual deal to being part of an overall settlement. Most of these were migrants and they were indemnified in cash.

In compensation for the communal Oroya land, CdeP purchased a *hacienda* near Tarma. This led to a second split in the *comunidad*, since only those who had rights pertaining to ruined communal land could claim an interest in the new land. The others received compensation in cash only for crops and stock lost. At the same time, the *comuneros* with rights to the new land were offered either part of the ex-*hacienda* or cash for their ruined land. This produced a third split in the *comunidad*. Half the affected *comuneros* opted to take the new land, and these were predominantly the older, larger landholders. The rest of the *comuneros* preferred to stay and take the cash. They were younger, and many were already employed by CdeP, or the railway, or in house-building.[26]

However, neither this solution to the compensation problem nor the divisions in the *comunidad* were clear and simple. The cash indemnity for crops and stock was only for the next twenty years and had to be renegotiated in 1943. Those *comuneros* who remained and raised livestock around Oroya would once again petition. Moreover, those who went to Tarma kept up familial links with those who remained. Often it was the parents who moved to Tarma and continued to farm, while the children worked in Oroya. As the area round Oroya became increasingly polluted, so more and more *comuneros* joined relatives near

Tarma.

In 1943 a new smoke commission began to re-evaluate damage and calculate indemnity. As with the *haciendas*, however, CdeP realised that the process could be unending, and prevaricated. In response, Oroya, Huaynacancha and Sacco formed a federation, and used their links with APRA to influence President Bustamante. Again CdeP came under pressure and again it offered to buy its way out of the problem. A second *hacienda* was acquired and offered to the *comuneros* in return for their communal land. In 1947 the exchange went through.

By this time the land in and around Oroya was worthless agriculturally but it had become valuable urban propery. The *comuneros* invested their compensation money in the construction of houses and shops in the town centre. At the same time many of them retained their rights to land within the old village. As migrants poured into the town to work in the refinery, so the *comuneros* rented out houses to them or catered to their consumption needs with restaurants, shops and garages. After 1925 the number of CdeP workers in Oroya rarely dropped below 2,000, fluctuating between 3,000 and 6,000. The original *comuneros* could work in the refinery *and* pursue commercial activities. Several fortunes were to be made in this way, particularly by leaders of the old *comunidad*.

Finally, CdeP was in similar conflict with the *comunidad* of Sacco. Like the other *comunidades* Sacco received compensation for stock and crops, although the soil was not polluted. What was at issue was the land of *hacienda* Tallapuquio, once *comunidad* property. During the 1930s CdeP rented it to an intermediary who in turn sublet to shepherds. The intermediary and Sacco were in continual conflict over grazing rights which came to a head in 1934. The *comunidad* threatened legal action but withdrew, only to renew its claim in 1954. Over the next ten years the land changed hands several times, until the matter was finally resolved by CdeP offering cash help to village schools and houses in return for rights to stretches of land.

Thus CdeP came to control a large area of the central highlands. More than this, it had 'smoked out' the highland peasantry, who had lost their means of subsistence and were forced to migrate to Oroya to find work. Whilst they were in the mines CdeP could exploit this wage-labour twice over by paying low wages and by selling them the output from its own *haciendas*. This is certainly the view of CdeP's tactics in the central highlands taken by some authors.[27]

Whether or not the company really intended to smoke out the

peasantry and create a labour force dependent on its products is, however, far from certain. Several other features of the situation cloud the issue. Firstly, there was already a supply of labour to the mines, and migration was a long-established process. Secondly, there was no immediate increase in the work force at Oroya and Morococha, the two installations nearest the affected villages. In the mid-1920s the total employed in these two centres did rise from around 4,000 to around 5,500, but it declined after that. Thirdly, while Oroya, Sacco and Huaynacancha suffered badly, other villages were less severely hit and the damage was often temporary. Those villages whose agricultural economy was destroyed by the pollution formed only a small part of the labour force. Moreover, workers from those villages took up nearer employment in the CdeP Farms Division as it expanded.

But, whereas CdeP may not have been faced with a problem over the number of labourers it needed, it was concerned with the quality of its labour. Mining certainly requires some skilled men, but the operation of a refinery requires many more. It demands mechanics, machine operators, drivers and many more whom CdeP had to train itself. The maintenance of a skilled labour force was a prime concern from 1924 to 1974. Despite several attempts, it was a problem CdeP was never able to solve. Even though the pressures of proletarianisation on these workers were very strong, yet still they maintained interests outside the industrial sector which enabled them to endure hard times and further their other interests.

Proletarianisation

Monopolisation and capitalisation had put the company in almost total control of some of the richest ore deposits in the world. Like the Incas and Spaniards before them, the Americans had to find some way of sustaining a large semi-skilled labour force to extract the ore for them. In order to solve this problem, the company organised the indigenous peasantry into the largest industrial labour force in Peru. To this end, it set about proletarianising them.

The main characteristics of the process of proletarianisation have been outlined in Chapter 1. Here, the major initial pressure came from the efforts of the management to treat labour as a homogeneous commodity. In the Peruvian highlands that treatment embraced wage-payment, dwelling patterns and employment decisions. Most workers were crowded on to a single wage-point, and previous variations in income resulting from self-employment or contract work were eliminated. Regular payment in wages or company tokens began, much of which was spent on standard goods in the company store. The workers were herded together into similar urban dwelling areas, and their common problems became visible not only in the work-place but in every sphere of life.

Perhaps most important, however, proletarianisation rendered the workers similar with respect to decisions orientated to market contingencies. Decisions about the size of the labour force, the direction of new investment, the ratio of labour to capital and the negotiated price of labour were now made by a foreign management operating with a finely calculated profit and cost rationale, full knowledge of the market, and the ability to introduce modern, capital-intensive technology. The result of these market-oriented decisions was the massive cycling of labour back and forth between the highland industrial areas and the rural sectors as world demand for metals fluctuated.

The first dimension of proletarianisation was the payment system CdeP introduced.[28] At the turn of the century, before the company arrived on the scene, the wages of non-contract miners in the highlands ranged from $0·30 per day for a labourer to $0·70 per day for a 'pick-man'. On *enganche* contract work, miners received $7·50 for one metre of advance at the ore-face, achieving $1·50 per day under good conditions. Labouring night and day, they could work thirty-six hours on and twelve hours off, during the three to four month stretches which they worked. They could thus earn nine days' wages per week, payable either to themselves or to the *enganchador*.

With the arrival of CdeP, the payment system altered. At first the labouring day-rate was raised to $1·25 to attract men back to the flooded and abandoned mines, but once the company's presence had been established, new payment policies were adopted. The drive to mechanise operations in order to overcome flooding and increase output meant an increase in the variety of skilled occupations. Skilled men were paid above the prevailing rate, at $2–$2·50 per day. At the same time the wages for labourers were reduced, until by 1912 they were only earning $0·50 per day. In addition, owing to mechanisation, the company could, in some instances, lay men off while paying those remaining slightly more. In the boilerhouse at Cerro de Pasco sixteen men tended the coal furnaces, earning $1·15 per day, but with the introduction of petrol only two men were kept on, earning $1·75 per day.

As well as rationalising the pay structure, the company also introduced payment by 'scrip'.[29] Ready-money wages were paid on the 10th of each month, but at the end of each day the labourer received a metal disc which could be exchanged the next morning for a cardboard one. Several cardboard discs could be handed in at the cashier's for a bond which enabled the worker to purchase articles at the company store. The bond issued one week was not valid for the next, and so the store was ensured a steady turnover. Such 'scrip' money had been declared illegal in 1879 and again in 1903, but it took action in the Peruvian Senate in 1909 and 1911 to finally put an end to it. Only eight years later, however, the company adopted yet another means of paying its workers – in pure gold and silver. The rise in value of the Peruvian pound made it more economical for a mining company to pay in gold, rather than trade that gold for dollars and then back into pounds at an inflated rate.

Monopolisation and proletarianisation were occurring not only in the mines but also on the *haciendas* purchased by the company. During the nineteenth century full-time shepherds had received $2 per 100 head of cattle, while a cowherd was paid $35 per year. The company paid *hacienda* labourers $0·40 per day and gave them the right to graze their own stock and cultivate plots of land. The highest wages of $0·55 per day went to herdsmen caring for cows in calf, while some small remuneration was paid to families who delivered milk to the company's milk plants.[30] For many agricultural workers these were the first wages they had ever received for agricultural work.

From the miners' wages there were various deductions. $0·05 per day went to pay for the provision of hospitals at Cerro de Pasco and Goyllarisquizga. This was a high exaction, since the former had only three beds and the latter served to register miners for compensation rather than to treat the sick. There was also a deduction of $0·05 per day for the oil burnt in miners' lamps, an injustice that was to lead to one of the first strikes.

Deductions from wages were also made to finance the second dimension in which proletarianisation was occurring – that of urbanisation. Those who took up company housing were allowed it free at first, but then had to pay $1 per month for a somewhat dubious privilege:

. . . the houses for work-men were very poor, much below the type installed in Chile which were also considered as inadequate at the time . . . The workmen's houses seen in Morococha were really disgraceful, they could hardly even be classified as hovels.[31]

The building of the refinery attracted a steady flow of migrants to Oroya. As well as the 2,000-strong indigenous labour force, CdeP contracted the skilled erection work to the American Bridge Company, and gangs of American steel erectors were shipped to Peru. Initially the company provided lodgings only for the skilled white labour force, so the indigenous workers sought accommodation in Oroya, or in small stone dwellings called *chosas*. While construction was in progress:

... the American Bridge crew erecting all steel work were men of great courage and efficiency but wilder than beasts. Liquor was a perpetual necessity and with so large a wild gang the Town of Oroya also became wild and Old Oroya converted itself into a sort of vice town.[32]

It was only after the refinery had been completed, and CdeP was seeking to establish a skilled, stable labour force to run it, that the workers' barracks were constructed.

The third proletarianisation pressure on the workers was management's treatment of them as a homogeneous commodity when taking market-oriented decisions. The expansion of the mines led to a large increase in the number of workers employed, but a marked feature of that employment was its variability. In the fifty years since the industrial development of the mining sector, employment and prosperity in the highlands have fluctuated with the fortunes of the industrialised world, as shown by figs 2–4.[33]

The completion of the refinery and the commencement of production had a twofold effect on labour migration. The new refinery was much more efficient than the smaller ones at Cerro de Pasco and Casapalca, and so could handle vast increases in output while employing only a few men. Hence, the first effect was a massive flow of migrants back to their native villages, produced by the release of construction labour and the reduced demand for refining operatives. So great was this returning volume of labour that special trains were put on to take them back to the Mantaro valley. The second was a flow of labour into Oroya, due partly to the effects of pollution and partly to the industrial and commercial opportunities opening up there.

From 1920 to 1925 corporation[34] employment fluctuated between 7,000 and 8,500, increasing with the rise in copper production in 1923 following the price rise that year, and then slumping in 1924 as falling copper output reflected the decline in the price. During the two years after 1924, however, as the corporation began production of lead and zinc due to filtering, both employment and output rose steadily. Yet by

1926 metal prices were falling again and 1,000 men were laid off in the Morococha mine. The building of the Yauricocha railroad and rising metal prices at the end of the decade pushed up employment once more and migrants again flocked in:

> ... guards were placed on all boundaries and at all entrances and roads, and even arms, when necessary were used with government permission. But in one case all precautions failed due to the building of the Yauricocha railroad; men, families, horses, burros, cattle, sheep, dogs, etc. trafficked day and night over the *haciendas*.[35]

By 1929 there were over 13,000 workers on the payroll, an increase of two-thirds since the opening of the refinery.

In 1930 the first shock of the depression hit the region as copper prices tumbled from $0·18 per pound in 1929 to $0·08 in 1931, with similar falls in lead and zinc. In Oroya a mineworkers' conference was being held and, after clashes with the police, the conference leaders were gaoled. Sympathy strikes and the imposition of martial law gave the corporation a warrant for draconian measures to alleviate its economic difficulties. The strikes were turned into a lock-out. Seven thousand men were fired, the Yauricocha mine was closed and the total labour force was halved. All told, by 1932 9,000 men had been laid off and employment was only one-third of its 1929 level.

Now the migratory flows were reversed as migrants flooded back to their villages and lands in special trains or on foot. In Oroya only one furnace remained in operation, workers' wages were cut twice, CdeP's shares fell from $120 to $5 and production was so low that the corporation paid no taxes, bringing threats of nationalisation from Lima. In 1933 the French-owned Huaron mine closed and its workers also returned to their villages seeking sustenance. Many of them were *enganchados* unable to afford transport, and a long column of workers and their families filed through the Andes on their way back to the Mantaro valley. It was a four-day walk, but many took longer, having to work in the fields by the wayside to earn sustenance for the next day's march.

Gradually the industrialised world pulled out of the depression and from 1934 metal prices began to rise steadily. Corporation output – particularly of lead, which by 1940 was half the total – rose accordingly, and employment began to expand again. But with the onset of the second world war stagnation returned to the mining sector. Throughout the war metal prices were pegged and although demand increased it was met by parent American producers finally utilising

CORPORATION OUTPUT OF REFINED COPPER, LEAD AND ZINC
DURING THE 20TH CENTURY

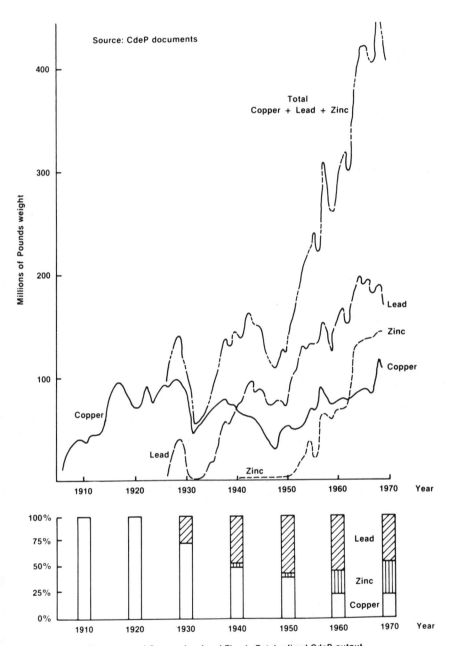

Percentage of Copper, Lead and Zinc in Total refined CdeP output.

METAL PRICES DURING THE 20TH CENTURY

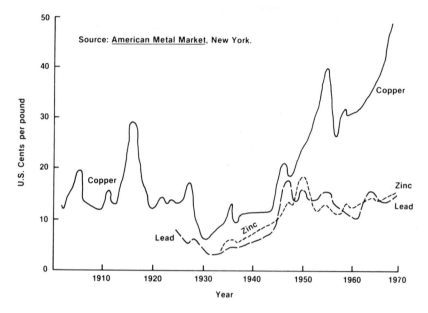

CORPORATION EMPLOYMENT DURING THE 20TH CENTURY

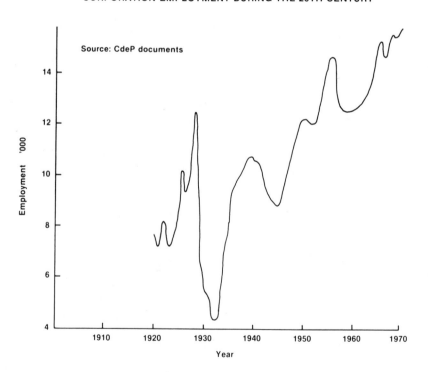

their installed U.S. capacity to the full. Thus, although CdeP's Peruvian output did rise slightly, owing to increased lead production, both copper production and total employment declined markedly.

Only since the end of the war has output risen significantly and employment passed the level of the late 1920s. From 1945 to 1951 the prices of lead and zinc increased seven times, quadrupling CdeP's lead production. The equally dramatic decline in prices at the end of the Korean war led to a reduction in the corporation's copper production and a check in its output of lead. There was thus a slight decline in employment in the early 1950s, but by the mid-1950s output and employment had risen once again. The slump in metal prices at the end of the 1950s, their revival in the early 1960s and decline in the mid-1960s are again reflected in CdeP output and employment. The record figures of the late 1960s and early 1970s were a consequence of the high prices ruling at the end of the decade.

These three proletarianising influences, then, have led to the formation of the industrial labour force whose contemporary characteristics were outlined in the previous chapter. Undoubtedly, the migrating peasantry of the central highlands have been rendered industrially homogeneous in that their conditions of work, payment and residence are very similar. Owing to these pressures, the fortunes of these highland industrial wage-labourers have depended to a large extent on the price and production cycles of the world metal industry.

With the arrival of CdeP and the subsequent processes of monopolisation, capitalisation and proletarianisation, the mining industry underwent a post-colonial transformation as dramatic as the colonial post-Incaic transformation. The Peruvian mining industry became capital-intensive where before it had been labour-intensive. Since 1920, although output has increased seventeenfold, the labour force has only doubled. This change in labour–output ratio is due partly to the productivity of the Peruvian metalworker,[36] but mainly to decisions by corporation management to introduce capital-intensive technology to their Peruvian operations. The low labour–output ratio plus the low wage rates meant that *obrero* labour costs were always around only one-tenth of total costs.

However, two points must be borne in mind with respect to this transformation of the mining industry. The first is that several of the features of the new industrial situation were present in former times. Large-scale migration was one of them, socio-economic differentiation in the highlands was another, while the export of ores to foreign markets was also long established. Moreover, the industrial development of the region began not with the capitalisation of the mines but with the extension of the railway, and it is important to distinguish the different impact of these two phases. The second point is that, although workers were much influenced by the pressures towards proletarianisation, they did not become a passive adjunct of a technological system. Rather, migrants developed their own strategies to cope with industrial work which often drew on non-industrial resources. Perhaps the main device evolved in response to industrial life was the trade union.

Notes

[1] De Wind, A., 1970.
[2] Boggio, M., 1972.
[3] Fisher, J., 1975.
[4] Miller, R., 1975.
[5] Stewart, N., 1946.
[6] CdeP documents.
[7] Laite, A., 1978.
[8] Wilson, F., Sussex University.
[9] CdeP documents.
[10] *Ibid.*
[11] Martinez Alier, J., 1972.
[12] CdeP documents.
[13] Bollinger, W., 1972.
[14] Miller, R., 1975.
[15] Bollinger, W., 1972.
[16] *Ibid.*; McLaughlin, D., 1945.
[17] Bollinger, W., 1972.
[18] *El Comercio*, 30 November 1919, Lima.
[19] Jachanowitz, A.
[20] CdeP documents.
[21] Colley, B., 1969.
[22] De Negri, M., 1911; Mostajo, F., 1913; Noriega, A.
[23] De Wind, A., 1977.
[24] CdeP documents.
[25] *Ibid.*
[26] *Ibid.*
[27] CIDA, 1966; Malpica, C., 1970.
[28] Mayer von Zulen, D., 1919.
[29] Colley, B., 1969.
[30] *Ibid.*, 1969.
[31] *Ibid.*, 1969.

[32] *Ibid.*, 1969.

[33] CdeP documents.

[34] In 1915 Cerro de Pasco Mining Company became Cerro de Pasco Copper Corporation and is henceforth referred to as 'the corporation'.

[35] Colley, B., 1969.

[36] De Wind, A., 1977.

4

The political organisation
of the mineworkers

Capitalisation, monopolisation and proletarianisation all militated towards the formation of a stable labour force in the mining sector. To these factors operating in the industrial sector the response from within that sector has been unionisation. The mining unions have become the largest and most powerful in Peru. Not only are they solidaristic and tenacious, they are also in a strategic economic position, controlling the supply of metals and thus the country's export earnings. Their organisation is formal and bureaucratic, the rhetoric of the leaders that of class and social revolution; support for the unions is widespread and dependable.

The growth of formal labour organisations in the mining sector has been seen as a modernising and moderating influence on the miners.[1] It has been argued that they are prone to violence and that early union leaders were militant revolutionaries. Formal unionism has led to the emergence of moderate leaders who control the potential violence of their members and through negotiation integrate the labour force into the political processes of the state. From an initial period of spontaneous political unrest during the first phase of industrial development the miners have passed into an era of modern political negotiation through formal organisation.

An historical analysis of the growth of unionisation in the mining industry does not reveal a unilinear passage from expressive violence to negotiated moderation, however.[2] Rather, there have been swings to and from violence and moderation, and formal and informal political organisation. What historical analysis does underline is the importance of relations between the unions and the state. Political organisation in the mining sector is not a function only of factors internal to that sector, such as arduous work, wage-levels or aggressive management. Rather, it depends also on external factors, such as relations with the state, discussed here, and support from the rural sector, discussed later.

The variations in modes of political organisation and activity in the mining sector are related to the dilemmas of the state over development policy. The government's problem has been to ensure a flow of external funds for industrial investment whilst at the same time placating the political feelings of the miners, who have always been the guardians of anti-imperialist sentiment. Throughout the twentieth century the answer has been found in the repression of the miners by the state, with important consequences for union organisation.

Labour organisation prior to 1944

Although labour unrest in the form of wage haggling, downing tools and brawling was probably recurrent in the 19th century, it was the monopoly control of the mines by CdeP that led to organised confrontation between management and men. Monopolisation resulted in a similar management for the men, who all worked under similar conditions with a common knowledge of one another, stemming not only from the work-place but also from their places of origin. *Enganchadores* would contract gangs of men for particular mines from particular villages. So men with a common bond began to negotiate with a common employer.

The conditions in the mines were arduous in the extreme. The men worked twelve-hour shifts and, often through sheer fatigue, accidents were frequent. One winch operator was not relieved for thirty-six hours and finally fell asleep over the winch handle, resulting in five men plunging to their deaths.[3] One newspaper[4] estimated that from 1902 to 1911 over 1,000 men had perished in the mine of Cerro de Pasco alone. The wrong sort of dynamite was used, one mine was full of gas, and pneumonia was common as men emerged to a freezing 5,000 metres above sea-level after working in suffocating heat. Boys sometimes died on their first day as, frightened to go down the mine, they drank large quantities of beer on the surface, with fatal effects during a rapid descent or ascent. The attitude of the management was another source of accidents, as safety rules were neglected and the men bullied. In one instance two drunken Americans killed a Peruvian, and, even though a court established homicide, corporation pressure ensured that no action was taken.[5] Fines were common, and if a sub-contracted labourer fled and was caught he was fined 70 per cent of his outstanding debt to the contractor.

Under these conditions discontent was endemic. In 1908 an explosion at Cerro de Pasco led to miners there downing tools and returning to their village of Chongos in the Mantaro valley. In 1909 the railway firemen struck, demanding more money and a nine-hour day, as a result of which five of them were deported. Later in the same year there were strikes over pay cuts.

The high point of labour unrest in the first decades of the twentieth century, however, was over the struggle for the eight-hour day in 1919.[6] In January that year the miners of Morococha and Casapalca struck over the 'scrip' system and in support of a national strike demanding the eight-hour day. Confrontation with the army ensued, since no police force existed. The soldiers fired on the workers, who responded by wrecking mine installations, which in turn led to the closure of the corporation store. While these miners returned to their villages the men of Cerro de Pasco put in a demand for an eight-hour day through their organisers, the Workers' Humanitarian Committee. The committee cautioned against a strike in view of the lack of funds, but in fact it proved unnecessary, since the next day, following the government's acceptance of the general strikers' demands, the corporation instituted the new hours.

The demand for an eight-hour day originated with national political groups, and strikes in support were linked to national strikes. Out of its success emerged a series of formal workers' organisations in the shape of friendly societies and working men's clubs. Entitled 'Sixteen Friends', 'Billinghurst Workers' Society',[7] and so on, these clubs met in 1919 to choose 'a candidate representative of the working class' for the forthcoming elections.[8] They federated to form a General Workers' Union, describing itself as part of the Workers' Syndicalist Movement. The union certainly had popular support, for 300 workers were present at the election of its committee and for a short while it represented workers' interests to the corporation.

However, after the elections in 1919 President Leguia seized power, and during his eleven-year term of office he increasingly repressed organised workers' movements. During his dictatorship political affiliation meant alienation from the central bargaining structure of Peruvian society. In the mines the decade of the 1920s was a period of underground organisation as Mariategui circulated his periodical *Labor* and organised a cultural circle in Morococha. The major event of the period for labour activity was the building of the refinery at Oroya.

Municipal Oroya simply could not cope with the sudden influx of workers and life there became violent. There was only a small police force, and justice was often rough. One well documented incident[9] occurred when, after a night of violence between Peruvians, police and Americans, several Peruvians were arrested. The next day the refinery workers went on strike, marched to the jail, and released them. The police captain, who tried to restrain them, was seized and killed. The police fired on the crowd, killing several people, and they retreated to the old town. The incident subsided and work continued on the refinery.[10]

It was not until 1929 that more formal efforts at worker organisation were instigated in the central mining region. Opposition to President Leguia was mounting towards the end of the period, particularly among persecuted workers, and in 1929 the underground Peruvian Communist Party formed the Confederacion General de Trabajadores del Peru, the CGTP.[11] In the same year the miners of Morococha founded their union during a successful strike. In 1930 Leguia was replaced by Sanchez Cerro, and at first it was thought that the new President would be more liberal. The initiative taken by Morococha was followed by corporation workers in other mines, and in Oroya, where the Metalworkers' Union, the STMO was founded.

The corporation, however, resisted these moves toward unionisation, refused to recognise the workers' committees, and set up its own. These in turn were rejected by the workers, who marched through Oroya until they were fired on by police and six were killed. The situation remained tense, then deteriorated rapidly. The CGTP was trying to organise a National Federation of Mining Workers and called a Mining Congress which opened in Oroya in November, shortly after the police attack. Sixty-one mining delegates were present, representing some 20,000 workers. It was attended by political and university representatives. Alarmed by the possibility of a national mining organisation, the corporation contacted the government and '... between the Government and the Corporation it was decided to deport the agitators ...'[12] In the early hours of the morning forty-six delegates were picked up by the police and taken to Lima. In Oroya the workers marched on the police station and demanded the return of their leaders. They were fired on, and retreated to corporation installations, taking with them two American employees as hostages.

Negotiations began between government, corporation and the newly formed STMO. The STMO threatened to strike and the CGTP threatened a general strike. The government agreed to release the leaders in return for the hostages. The men were exchanged and a reception was organised in Oroya for the released leaders, to which the near-by corporation workers of Malpaso were invited. As they marched to Oroya they were fired upon by police, and twenty-three were killed. The incensed marchers ran back to Malpaso, killed three foreign managers and destroyed property there. When the news reached Lima the CGTP again called a general strike, while the government's response was to draft more troops into Oroya and declare martial law. The general strike went ahead, but although it paralysed transport, textiles and municipal services it did not continue for long and soon only the miners were still on strike. Peace returned to the mining centres as the government, the corporation and the unions sought agreement.

The government was by then faced with a dilemma. The world mining situation had changed drastically during 1930. The prices of copper and lead had tumbled, the world was in the grip of the depression and CdeP had no intention of starting up production again at the record level of 1928 and 1929. The corporation turned the strike into a lock-out and the miners received no support from the government. Indeed, the government itself was embarking on restrictive economic programmes as it halved public spending between 1928 and 1931. It had no wish to alienate either potential investors or potential markets in a difficult situation, and so the miners paid the cost. When workers were finally taken on, some months later, 9,000 men had lost their jobs and the labour force had been cut by two-thirds.

Peru was racked by a political and economic crisis during the early 1930s. President Sanchez Cerro was replaced, only to return a year later, and neither he nor the other temporary Presidents were favourably disposed towards the labour unions. In the mining sector political activity resumed the clandestine form it had taken during the 1920s and remained that way. Shortly after becoming President in 1933 Benavides outlawed political parties. In Oroya and the mines underground political meetings were held and forbidden journals secretly read. In each section of the corporation there was a delegate, selected by the men, who would negotiate for his work group with the management over work conditions and bonuses. But there was no question of the corporation recognising workers' representatives on general issues.

Thus, prior to 1944, trade unions in the mining sector had for most of the time been both illegal and actively suppressed. The form of political organisation had swung from legal to illegal, and as it did so the form changed from formal to informal. At the same time the mode of political activity oscillated from confrontation to caution. Indeed, the periods of formal union organisation in mining are marked by the violent termination of their legality. Unionisation led to confrontation, not integration. Yet, even when unions were banned, industrial relations were carried on by other means. The geographical closeness of Oroya workers meant that they could engage in collective action without formal organisation like that of the early 1920s. The proximity of workers and management meant that informal bargaining was a routine feature of industrial work. After the second world war the trade unions were to play a more prominent role.

Labour organisation, 1944–72[13]

President Prado had replaced Benavides in 1939 and in 1944 he sought the support of APRA, the Peruvian nationalist party.[14] In return for APRA's support of Bustamante, a centre candidate, Prado lightened the repression against APRA. Immediately APRA and the Communists founded the Confederacion de Trabajadores Peruanos (the CTP) in Lima, and this came to be dominated by Apristas. In Oroya the Yauli workers' defence took on an Aprista lawyer.

At the same time, encouraged by the end of repression and alarmed at the rapid price rises occurring in Peru, a small group of about ten men began to meet in Oroya to discuss a possible wage claim. Most of them were section delegates and most were Apristas and Communists. Finally three volunteers took the claim to the corporation, which promptly threw it out. However, CdeP was faced with a labour shortage and knew that the men wanted higher wages and union recognition. So it countered by proposing workers' committees to discuss wages and salaries. The men responded by holding a general assembly of workers which decided to form a union and delegated the Aprista lawyer to draw up a constitution. The corporation backed its own proposals and a workers' commission travelled to Lima to put their case before President Prado.

After some prevarication the government gave the workers a 15 per cent pay increase and ordered that the union be recognised. So, in the first few months of Bustamante's presidency in 1945 the STMO secured recognition, as did the re-formed CGTP and the railway workers' union in Cerro de Pasco. In the following year the mining unions of Casapalca, Cerro de Pasco and Morococha were recognised; all told, between 1945 and 1947 thirty-eight unions were recognised in the mining sector.

After one year in existence the STMO put in its first wage claim, which was turned down. Under pressure to establish its own position and alleviate the severe inflation continuing to affect its members, the STMO declared a strike. The strike lasted twenty-two days, and the union was able to pay strike money from its accumulated funds as well as send a fleet of lorries to the Mantaro valley in search of maize and potatoes. Shopkeepers in Huancayo, Jauja and Oroya gave extended credit to the strikers and the unions of Morococha and Cerro de Pasco contributed to the strike fund. Finally the dispute was settled by Ministerial intervention and wages were raised to $1 a day, having doubled in the two years since 1945.

Also in 1947 the Central Mineworkers' Federation was formed and affiliated to the APRA CTP. This body began to advise the STMO, and together they drew up a range of negotiating points relating to medical assistance, working conditions and so on, which they determined to put to the corporation as a collective agreement alongside direct wage demands.

In Cerro de Pasco, however, Federation intervention had led to the deportation of their lawyer, and in the riot to release him the regional prefect had been killed. Martial law was declared, and the situation turned against the miners as Odria took over the presidency. The CTP was dissolved, APRA persecuted and the STMO threatened. The union was defended, however, by CdeP. Mining had just moved out of its period of labour shortage, and the corporation did not want labour troubles to jeopardise the boom promised by a sharp rise in prices. In 1949 the workers were given another 50 per cent pay rise.

However, once again the culmination of formal union organisation had been the development of links with national political groups and then the estrangement of the mining unions from the state. During Odria's seven-year presidency, from 1950 to 1956, the latter were closely controlled. Only leaders acceptable to the corporation and the government were allowed to take office. There were no major pay rises during this period and no strikes.

In 1956 Odria was replaced by President Prado, who again had received APRA support. Once more Apristas could organise among the mining unions, where they vied with the Communists for control of both individual unions and mining federations. It was during this period that union leaders sought to establish close relations between the mining unions and the state, and tried to moderate violence on the part of the workers. But the period was to be short-lived, lasting only five years.

The strikes that occurred shortly after President Odria's downfall were accompanied by violence. In 1957 and 1958 the men walked out, and in the latter year there was considerable violence in Cerro de Pasco.[15] Workers attacked foreign staff, corporation installations and staff housing in an explosive riot. Engaged in wage negotiations at the time, union leaders called for moderation so that the talks would not be jeopardised. Compared to the 1930s, when union leaders were rallying miners against imperialism, it seemed that their modern counterparts were concerned with negotiation and moderation.[16]

However, the violence in Cerro de Pasco was not a spontaneous upsurge. The workers were engaging in direct action just as they had done throughout the twentieth century. A colleague had been detained and then dismissed, and the direct action in support of him had escalated into confrontation with the police. Much of the violence that ensued from that confrontation was then turned against the management, with whom the men had long-standing grievances. However, the calls for moderation by the union leaders cast them in the role of conciliators. The outcome of the pay negotiations was a rise of 22 per cent for the miners.

After the strikes in Cerro de Pasco the union leaders continued their policy of orderly negotiations with the state. They also continued to struggle among themselves as Apristas and Communists fought for control of the national mining federations and thus the means of access to the state. The demand for the pay rise had been put by the Central Federation of Mining and Metal Workers, an organisation controlled by APRA. After the award the Central Federation negotiated mutual aid agreements with other mining unions to form the National Federation of Mining and Metal Workers. The Communists took over the National Federation while APRA retained control of the Central Federation. During the late 1950s and early 1960s the two groups fought for control of the two federations. But, while these two parties were vying for control at the national level a new political force was gaining momentum locally.

To maintain the credibility of the claim that they represent the miners, mining federations must include the STMO under their umbrella. Not only is the STMO the largest union, it is also the most strategically placed, being at the heart of the highland mining system, and it is the most influential, providing national union leaders. Gaining control of the STMO and splitting it away from national policies was a tactic employed several times by competing political groups. Before 1962 those groups were the Apristas and the Muscovite Communists. From the beginning of the 1960s, however, they were challenged by a new alliance of the Maoist and Trotskyist left.

During 1961 the STMO had managed to win several demands on account of the links between its new president and the Accion Popular party, which presented the demands to President Prado. Anxious not to provoke unrest in an election period, Prado had acceded. It seemed that the period of negotiated relations with the wider political scene was to continue. However, early in 1962, elections in the STMO brought in a new leadership, described by CdeP Security as 'extremists of various kinds'.[17] These leaders immediately lodged a 35 per cent wage claim with the corporation. Meanwhile, in July, the military, led by Perez, had effected a coup in Lima, alarmed at the possibility that Odria might return to power supported by APRA.

In Oroya CdeP prevaricated over the wage claim and finally rejected it. The mineworkers called for a strike in December. Fearing trouble, the corporation requested extra police, and as the night shift came off work pickets and police took up positions. The pickets tried to enter the refinery to persuade the day workers to leave, and were fired on by the police. At this, some 1,000 workers stormed the refinery, setting fire to the plant, cutting telephone wires and blocking the central highway. The refinery went up in flames, managers were taken hostage and Oroya was cut off for a day until troops arrived and put down the riot. This was not spontaneous violence but an organised political demonstration. Similar political unrest was occurring amongst other groups of Peruvian workers.

Since the late 1950s guerilla activity had been increasing in the country as a whole.[18] Encouraged by the Cuban revolution, Hugo Blanco was organising armed resistance among the peasants in La Convencion valley in the southern highlands. De la Puente had formed APRA-Rebelde in 1959, a militant splinter group from APRA, and in

1962 this changed its name to the Movement of the Revolutionary Left, MIR. MIR was to embark on guerilla action in the central highlands in 1964. The corporation and the government believed that the miners' and peasants' political unrest were connected:

... it was the influence of the Communists ... they are having much trouble in Ica and Cuzco ... Outside agitators were seen in Oroya, especially Cubans or men trained in Cuba.[19]

To break the threat of insurgency, the government rounded up and imprisoned some 2,000 people, including several dozen from Oroya.

The initial attempts at political action by left-wing elements were not crowned with success. After the Oroya incident the conservative elements in the military toppled Perez and left-wingers were persecuted. Once again a period of formal, legal unionism had led to the development of ties with national political groups, action by the STMO in the political arena, confrontation with the state and estrangement from the negotiated political process. Among the mining union leadership the left was in disarray, and for five years control passed back into the hands of the moderates. From 1962 to 1967 there were no major mining disputes.

The events of 1962 had, however, foreshadowed a new pattern of political activity in the mining sector. Towards the end of the five-year lull, activity among the miners once more became geared to events at the national level. As this activity escalated it became clear that the struggle in the mining unions was now between the Communists and the left,[20] rather than between APRA and the Communists. As union tactics again turned to confrontation this split in the unions was to prove a decisively debilitating factor.

During 1967 and early 1968 the mining unions moved out of their passive phase. Strikes by CdeP unions not only gained them pay increases but also tested a mutual aid pact which had recently been signed. At the national level APRA reorganised the National Miners' Federation, while the Communists set up a Trade Union Committee, out of which was to come a second Communist CGTP. Unions in small-scale mining were also becoming active, and some had marched to Lima to plead their case and win pay rises.

Then, in October 1968, the military seized power from President Belaunde and proclaimed the Peruvian revolution. The sympathetic treatment by the new military junta, led by Velasco, of a southern mining union wage claim convinced a group of workers in the STMO that there had been a basic change of line in Lima. Waving Peruvian flags and singing the national anthem, they ousted the old union leaders and installed themselves in their place. A new phase of union activity had opened up.

The new STMO leaders immediately disaffiliated from the APRA CTP and wrecked the Communist CGTP Regional Federation of mining unions. Instead they formed an alliance of the fourteen CdeP unions and lodged a wage claim with the corporation. After some months of bargaining, twelve of the unions accepted a CdeP offer, but Oroya and the mine of Cobriza remained obdurate. These two unions struck for twenty-three days, and then decided on a March of Sacrifice to the capital. In October 1969 several hundred men and women undertook the march. Despite repeated attacks by the police they arrived on the outskirts of Lima, where a settlement was negotiated with the government. The success of this settlement, and the example of the younger militant Oroya and Cobriza leaders, led to the election in other mining camps of a more aggressive leadership.

With the coming of the Peruvian revolution and the election of militant mining leaders, new political milieux had formed at the national and local levels. However, at the national level the same development policy dilemmas were to confront the military, who were to resolve them by adopting authoritarian measures at the local level as previous governments had done. At the local level the dilemma for the miners' leaders was whether to confront or compromise with the military regime. The Communists were to adopt a compromise strategy, but it was the left who were to embark on confrontation and their own eventual isolation. Thus, within the mining sector, union activity swung between the confrontation tactics of the left and the compromise politics of the Communists.

In 1970 the left formed a federation of the fourteen CdeP unions from members of the previous alliance, leaving the Communists with only one lever of influence in the central mining region – the president of the STMO. Apristas controlled a commission set up by the corporation unions to discuss their new eighteen-month work contract with CdeP. These discussions became bogged down, and when the CGTP threatened to take them over the commission broke up in disarray and advised the unions to strike.

This was the first opportunity presented to the new left-dominated corporation federation, and it immediately called a strike. The CGTP, always fearful that social disorder would provide a warrant for a right-wing coup, tried to resolve the situation. A second march to Lima was organised, the CGTP presented the miners' claims to the government, and the government acceded. In return the CGTP pledged Velasco the miners' support and claimed a success for compromise.

Work contracts, however, do not cover wage agreements, and the response to compromise from the federation was a claim for a 70 per cent increase. The corporation rejected this, and again the federation called a strike. At the same time the southern mining unions of Marcona and Toquepala also struck for more pay, while in the central highlands *empleados* and railway unions came out in sympathy with the CdeP *obreros*. This time the left had confronted the government with near-total paralysis of the mining sector.

The Communists could do little in the central region, but they did control the southern unions, and after a week the CGTP negotiated an offer acceptable to Marcona and Toquepala. As well as splitting south from centre, the offer also divided the central unions. One by one they returned to work, leaving only Cobriza and Oroya still out, until after thirty-one days they too capitulated. Encouraged by its success in the south, the CGTP tried to commit all mining unions to a pledge of support for the military junta, but the CdeP federation would have none of it, and broke off all links with the CGTP.

The adoption of a strategy of confrontation by the left led, during 1970, to seventy-one strikes in mining.[21] These accounted for one-third of all strikes in the country as a whole and two-thirds of national man-hours lost. Four-fifths of the mining man-hours lost were in strikes against the corporation. The most important reasons behind them were economic, in that the demands were for more pay or better bonuses. Since the corporation prevaricated at each new demand, the negotiations broke down and the strikes dragged on. It was the aim of the left-wing leaders to raise miners' political consciousness by matching these economic demands with political ones. The ultimate aim was to heighten workers' consciousness to such an extent that they would support demands for the nationalisation of the mines. So the left-wing federation searched for issues upon which to build economic and political confrontation.

Early in 1971 working and living conditions became the issues of confrontation. The federation demanded that the corporation should provide cost-price meat and milk for its workers, and pay a rent subsidy. In support of its claim the federation called a strike, but when asked by the CGTP to declare sympathy with the southern unions, again on strike over wage negotiations, refused to do so. After ten days the STMO men returned to work, following appeals from their Communist president. Some miners stayed out longer, but, lacking STMO support and harassed by the police, they went back some weeks later.

The question of meat, milk and rent had not been resolved, however, and again the left urged the STMO to strike action. This time the appeals of their president went unheeded, and the STMO struck. The government's reaction was drastic. The same night, leaders from the CdeP unions were arrested, including the president of the STMO. The CGTP threatened a general strike in sympathy with the union leaders and called on the STMO to support it. At an electric meeting a young folk hero of the left pleaded with the STMO workers not to back a general strike. The time and the issues were not right, he argued, and the CGTP officials would be secure in Lima while miners would be killed by military action. His appeal succeeded, but his dramatic vision was later to come true.

While the union leaders were under detention the government made clear the dilemmas it was facing at the national level.[22] Between 1970 and 1971 there had been a sharp fall in the price of copper which seriously damaged the country's balance of payments. From $0·80 per pound in March 1970, the price slumped to $0·50 per pound in March 1971, and as the year turned Peru's $300 million reserves were dropping at the rate of $25 million per month. During 1970 the trade balance had showed a surplus of $440 million, but the money was used to pay off invisible deficits, so that when it fell to only $140 million in 1971 the balance of payments was under considerable strain. The future of metals too was gloomy, for the forecasts were that world production was rising at twice the rate of consumption. This deteriorating market situation was exacerbated by the decline in production. In the first quarter of 1971 the government estimated that output had fallen by $20 million, resulting in a loss of tax revenue to the exchequer.

The government had always made it clear that it would seek external aid to finance its industrial development programme.[23] However, outside interests were still nervous about investing in Peru. Despite the fact that the economy had grown 7·5 per cent during 1970 the balance of payments was in difficulty and the country's internal policies were not encouraging. The government had nationalised an American oil company in 1968 and had joined the Andean Pact.[24] In March 1971 the five Andean Pact countries had ratified a new agreement concerning foreign investments. In future the governments concerned would work 'in harmony' with them. This statement had produced a swift negative reaction from the American Council, a body representing some 230 U.S. companies controlling four-fifths of U.S. investment in Latin America. Its negative view was shared by the Congress of Latin American Industrialists, who denounced the Pact statutes as 'dangerous for the future of foreign capital'.

Such caution on the part of foreign investors was worrying for the Peruvian government, which early in 1971 had started to negotiate a $780 million loan from the World Bank as well as a $20 million new American mining investment. During 1970 and early 1971 the state had taken over unworked ore deposits in Peru and established control over the marketing of metals through the new state company Minero Peru. But new mining investment would require foreign loans.

Peru intended to work 'in harmony' with foreign capital through the establishment of labour communities. The labour community, (also called the industrial community, the mining community and so on) would replace the limited company, and all members of the old limited companies would become shareholders in the new communities. All members would have voting rights and all would participate in electing the board of directors.

The change-over from limited company to community was to be a gradual one, with workers slowly building up to 51 per cent of the shares. The labour community purported to solve dilemmas for the government. The acquisition of shares by workers was to be so gradual that foreign investors would not be frightened off. The CdeP federation of unions calculated that it would take the corporation workers 129 years to own 51 per cent of its shares. Moreover, since workers were members of the community, there would be no need for a trade union, which again was attractive to foreign investors. At the same time workers' political aspirations would be assuaged, since they were purchasing foreign capital and would have representatives on the board. In this way the government hoped to encourage foreign interests to begin investing the $1,000 million necessary to exploit Peru's five largest ore deposits, without unduly antagonising industrial labour.

Whilst the government was explaining its case to the detained union leaders, the Communists and the left publicly made clear their attitudes to labour communities, the military regime and each other. The communist CGTP accused the left of supporting the multinational corporations in their plot to undermine the Peruvian revolution by reducing output. The CGTP threw its weight behind the military government and the labour communities. The left accused the CGTP and the military of being anti-syndicalist. The labour communities, claimed the left, would result in the abolition of the trade unions; and anyway, the mining communities were a poor substitute for the nationalisation of the mines. The battle lines between the three groups were drawn, and finally the left began its push for the nationalisation of the big mining companies.

The mining union leaders were released from detention and formed a commission of the CdeP federation, delegated to draw up a new work contract. While the commission deliberated, the federation continued its policy of confrontation. Workers from the small mine of Vinchos, in Cerro de Pasco, had marched to Oroya to ask the STMO for its help in a wage claim. The STMO organised soup kitchens and the federation threatened to strike in support of the Vinchos miners. However, the STMO president undertook to represent them. With the help of the CGTP he won a small increase. This infuriated the left but was accepted by Vinchos, and another strike threat was averted.

Then the commission presented the new work contract to the corporation. It called for a six-hour day, two months' annual holiday, a twenty-fivefold increase in bonuses, 1,000 high-school scholarships and pay increases that would give the lowest-paid worker the same hourly rate as he then got per day. The milk and meat issues were also reintroduced. The corporation pointed out that owing to falling prices and strikes it had actually made a loss in 1970, and in the first month of 1971 production was down by $72 million. It asked the government to shelve the new work contract for a year, and the STMO came out on strike.

During the strike two informers paid by the corporation were discovered and publicly interrogated in the STMO hall. Police action to rescue them was labelled as repression by the left, and the CdeP federation felt it now had the right issue at the right time to broaden the strike call. It called a general mining strike in opposition to the mining community, and demanding the nationalisation of the mines. The CGTP denounced the strike and sent two delegates, along with two government representatives, to Oroya to resolve it. Their combined pressure persuaded the STMO workers to go back to work.

The cloak of moderation thus fell upon the shoulders of the CGTP, which was declared by the government to be the means through which mining workers could be defended from extremists. The conciliatory approach of the CGTP was held up as an example to striking agriculture and fishery workers, and the CGTP consolidated its position as the institution that dealt direct with, and was respected by, the government. Unions affiliated to it once more pledged their support for Velasco. This time, in the mining sector, the left had lost ground and the political advantage lay with the Communists.

On the external front too there were changes. In trading terms things were still going badly for Peru. On 1 May the Bolivian government had nationalised the American-owned Matilde mine, one of the 3 largest sources of zinc in the world, and Chile continued to threaten nationalisation of her mines. In response, the U.S. Congress Agricultural Committee imposed a tax of $20 per ton on sugar imported from countries which had nationalised U.S. investments. The tax did not come into effect immediately, but it posed a threat to Peru, which had nationalised the U.S. oil company. Moreover, the continuing low demand for copper which had taken the price below Zambia's cost of production had prompted a meeting of the CIPEC producers – Chile, Peru, Zaire and Zambia. Two of these countries were adopting nationalisation as the solution to their problems, and the dilemma for Peru was that while she wanted co-operation on some trading and pricing matters she did not, in her search for foreign finance, want to be associated too closely with the nationalisers.

In that search, however, she was making some headway. On 1 May delegates from the Peruvian Central Reserve Bank met representatives of the Inter-American Bank. After the meeting the latter declared the country to be a satisfactory home for external finance and some weeks later announced that it would unfreeze the $11 million which Peru had been promised several years earlier. External reaction to the Andean Pact foreign capital regulations had been cooled by the Economic Minister's insistence before the U.S. Chamber of Commerce for Peru that the emphasis would be on profit-sharing rather than capital take-over and that he could guarantee 'the maximum security to foreign investors'. The next day the Minister was in Paris, meeting Peru's established creditors and representatives of the World Bank and preparing the ground for a massive loan.

Peru's foreign debt stood at $1 billion, and she was attempting to repay interest on it from her trade surpluses. Her dilemma was that she could not hope to stimulate investment while paying off the debt, yet would never get further foreign finance if she reneged on the payments.

The Paris group offered the Minister two alternatives: either they would help refinance the foreign debt, or Peru would keep up the repayments while opening her doors to foreign investment provided by the Paris Group. The Minister took the second option, affirmed that the regime would pursue '. . . a policy of stability, both on the external and internal fronts . . . to create a generally favourable situation for the participation of foreign private capital . . .'[25] and in July returned to Lima saying that 'the doors were now open'.

Hence by July 1971 external events were moving in the country's favour. Southern Peru announced that it would invest $20 million in the mine at Cuajone – the largest private investment ever undertaken in Peru. Minero Peru announced sales of metals to China and Spain. U.S. oil companies declared their interest in searching for oil in the Peruvian jungle and the threat of a sugar quota embargo was lifted by the United States.

However, the mining sector still held the key to the confidence of external finance on account of its importance to the balance of payments. In 1971 this importance was heightened when the output of the fishing industry, traditionally earning a quarter of Peru's foreign exchange, slumped by one-third because of over-fishing. The effect of this, plus the fall in metal prices and the loss of mining production, meant that in the fourth quarter of 1971 the balance of payments was in deficit by $65 million. The government could do nothing about the fish, nor could it influence metal prices. So the mining strikes emerged as the only short-run factor upon which it could hope to have any effect.

In the mining sector the left was pushing for nationalisation of CdeP and had ousted the Communist president of the STMO. The CGTP, on the other hand, had resolved the strikes in the southern mining region with personal Ministerial help. While the CdeP federation denounced the corporation's prevarication over the new work contract, the CGTP, on behalf of the industry as a whole, offered two days' free work to support Minero Peru. The isolation of the left was underway.

Negotiations with the corporation over the work contract dragged on for several months, until, to resolve the issue, individual corporation unions threatened strike action. The southern mining companies had not given their unions the promised wage increase, and several smaller mines in the central region had been on strike for some time. A strike over the work contract by the CdeP federation would thus result in a general mining strike, but before playing this card the left tried to negotiate direct with President Velasco.

The corporation federation asked him to nationalise CdeP. Velasco, however, was being made aware of the consequences of expropriation. The sugar quota embargo had worried him, and in Bolivia a right-wing coup had taken place under the leadership of H. Banzer and with U.S. assistance. With the nationalisation of her copper mines Chile's isolation was beginning. Hence, Velasco publicly cited the Bolivian example and turned down the miners' request. The CdeP federation responded by calling a general mining strike in support of the work contract and nationalisation.

This time the government was faced with total paralysis of the mining sector. The left had chosen its ground carefully. The strike was over both economic and political issues. The men solidly supported the economic issues, and so the CGTP could denounce the political measures but could not resolve the basic economic differences. The result appeared to be deadlock. Two government Ministers were dispatched to Oroya, where they met a hostile reaction from federation delegates. The latter pointed out that the $7 per day increase they demanded was merely symbolic and that $0·80 would be acceptable. But they insisted on policy statements regarding nationalisation which the Ministers could not give them. The deadlock was broken by force.

In the Cobriza mine a row about moving machinery during the strike had escalated into violence.[26] The miners had retreated to the union building, taking two hostages. Despite radio pleas by federation union leaders the hostages were not released, and troops were sent in to rescue them. Civil liberties were suspended in the central region, the union halls in Oroya, Cerro de Pasco and Cobriza were seized, and in Cobriza five miners were killed. Union leaders in all the mining camps were detained and taken to jungle prison camps.

The government offered the miners a $0·40 increase and gave them seventy-two hours to return to work. With their unions closed down, their leaders detained, and facing redundancy threats, the men returned to work. The ex-president of the STMO negotiated in Lima for the release of the detainees and the CGTP posed as the workers' champion. The Oroya workers were unconvinced, however; they broke into the ex-president's house and attacked the man who three years earlier had taken the platform by storm.

Thus the government had kept its pledge to 'open its doors' and maintain internal stability. There were several consequences of the way it had resolved the dilemma. Externally the Japanese and Poles announced a strong interest in Peruvian mining and metal refining, while the U.S. Commercial Mission to Latin America urged its members to invest in the country. Early in 1972 the World Bank finally agreed to lend Peru $780 million over three years, $220 million being earmarked for mining. Internally the mining unions were weakened. In Oroya few people turned up at union meetings and the leaders were concerned mainly to recuperate their forfeited jobs. The government went ahead with establishing the mining communities and elections were held for the worker representatives on the Cerro de Pasco board.

Government policies with respect to the corporation did not stop with community elections, however, for in January 1974 CdeP was nationalised. In fact the corporation had offered its Peruvian assets for sale some time in 1970–1, but the government had demurred for a variety of reasons. It wanted to negotiate over the price, and delayed in order to bring it down and to inspect its own reserves to see whether the requisite foreign exchange was available. It seems probable that some of the money from the World Bank was used to purchase the corporation.

The other reasons centred on new investments and political manoeuvring. The corporation maintained that its Peruvian subsidiary was losing money because of strikes, and new investment could not be considered as long as the unions threatened to interrupt production. On its part, the government did not want to appear to accede to left-wing union demands for nationalisation. Further, nationalising the mines with the unions intact would lead to major difficulties for the new mining communities, which would somehow have to dislodge the strongest unions in the land. By breaking the mining unions the government resolved the corporation's fears about new investment and cleared the ground for the mining community. The direct action by the government in Cobriza and Oroya seemed at one stroke to solve a whole series of dilemmas.

The industrial development of the highland mining sector has led to the growth of unionisation there. Processes of monopolisation, capitalisation and proletarianisation have been accompanied by the organisation of the industrial labour force into trade unions. The unions are probably the largest, best organised, most influential and most politicised in Peru. They defend the market interests of the mineworkers with great tenacity.

However, internal factors alone to not explain the growth of unionisation. Nor has the relationship with the main external agency of the state been one of progressive integration. There has been no move from spontaneous violence to formal negotiations, as has been suggested by some authors.[27] It is true that before the second world war the concentration of workers meant that, without a union, they were able to engage in direct action, while since the war the trade unions have negotiated on their behalf. But unionism does not necessarily entail the demise of direct action. The miners have continued to engage in both, according to whichever promises greater efficacy at the time. Nor has the union leadership been hegemonic, increasingly advocating moderation. Rather, it has been split over which course of action to pursue at particular times.

The efficacy of union actions has been affected by relations between the mining unions and the state. The relationship has swung from integration to confrontation, and as it has done so the mode of political organisation has moved from formal to informal and from acquiescence to violence. The miners have not been incorporated into the political apparatus of the state. Even with nationalisation, the metal and mineworkers have continued to strike and to support national strikes.

Yet relations with the state are not the only feature external to the mining sector that affects social and political organisation within it. Highland industry coexists with a large rural sector, and most of the industrial workers are rural migrants. The continued existence of this large rural economy affects social organisation in the industrial sector and has been affected by limited industrial development.

Notes

[1] Bourricaud, F., 1970; Kruijt, D., and Vellinga, M., 1977.

[2] Laite, A. J., 1980.

[3] Mayer von Zulen, D., 1919.

[4] *El minero illustrado*, Cerro de Pasco newspaper.

[5] Colley, B., 1969.

[6] Sulmont, D., 1974, 1975.

[7] Billinghurst was president of Peru 1912–13.

[8] *El minero illustrado*.

[9] Colley, B., 1969.

[10] *El minero illustrado*.

[11] Sulmont, D., 1974, 1975.

[12] Colley, B., 1969.

[13] The following analysis draws on interviews with mineworkers, CdeP documents and newspaper reports in El Comercio, Unidad, La Voz de Huancayo.

[14] Pike, F., 1967.

[15] Ledesma, G., 1964.

[16] It is this view which is proposed by Bourricaud, F., 1970. In fact the situation was more complex than his discussion reveals, for again Communists and Apristas were vying for control of the negotiations. Indeed, the view of the CdeP Security Department was that the riot was a Communist plot (CdeP documents). However, Security saw Communist agitation in any union activities. The head of Security at this time was Chappers, an ex-Allied intelligence officer and (then) member of the American CIA.

[17] CdeP documents.

[18] Huizer, G., 1972.

[19] CdeP documents.

[20] 'The Left' here denotes Peruvian political parties of a Maoist or Trotskyist persuasion: MIR, Vanguardia, Bandera Roja, Frente de la Izquierda Revolucionaria.

[21] Ministerio de Trabajo, 1971.

[22] *El Comercio*, Lima newspaper.

[23] Instituto Nacional de Planificacion, 1970.

[24] In 1966 Chile, Colombia, Ecuador, Peru and Venezuela had signed the Declaration of Bogota, pledging a range of common economic policies.

[25] *El Comercio*.

[26] De Wind, A., 1977.

[27] Bourricaud, F., 1970.

5

The rural origins
of migrant labourers

Workers in the highland mining sector of Peru are only partially proletarianised. Two-thirds of the miners and four-fifths of the Oroya workers are migrants, and three-quarters of the Oroya *obreros* are of rural origin. These migrants retain their links with the rural sector and this factor profoundly influences industrial socio-economic organisation. A quarter of the migrant workers in Oroya come from the Mantaro valley. The relations between the industrial milieu and this rural area are reciprocal. Just as industrial development has affected the socio-economic structure of the valley, so the structure of social organisation and migration in the valley has affected social organisation in Oroya. Analysis of two villages in the valley, Ataura and Matahuasi, reveals these feedback relations between the industrial and rural sectors.

The relations between these two villages and the mining sector[1] show two general features. The first is that the villages in the valley are part of a wider capitalist economy. Much of village life is commercialised, owing to the fact that many villagers migrate into wage-labour and that many sell their agricultural and artisanal products on the open market. At the same time, however, the organisation of agricultural production within this capitalist framework still contains features characteristic of the peasantry, particularly in the owning and working of the land by the household. Just as the Oroya workers are partly proletarianised, so the valley agriculturalists are partly commercialised.

The second general feature is that the articulation of industrial and rural socio-economic structures is not a simple, direct one. Rather, those structures interact in a complex and cyclical manner. The major cycles are those of industrial organisation, peasant production and personal life. The latter two particularly are closely related, since peasant production and individuals' lives are linked through household structure. The response of individuals and groups at different moments in their lives to the pressures of the household and the requirements of industrial change is part of the indigenous response to industrial development.

Ataura and Matahuasi both lie on the left bank of the Mantaro river, some twenty kilometres from each other. As in most villages in the valley, the predominant activity is agriculture, practised on a household-based *minifundia* system. As is the case with other villages, migrants from Ataura and Matahuasi live and work in the mines and in Lima. Of all the valley villages Ataura has the highest percentage of its sons working in the mines, while Matahuasi has the largest number of villagers living and working outside the valley.

Ataura is a small village, with many of its houses perched on the valley sides overlooking other houses on the richer valley floor. Some 1,700 men, women and children live there,[2] and the village extends over some 600 hectares of land, 400 of which are suitable for crops or pasture. The inhabitants are mainly agriculturalists, four-fifths of them owning or working less than one hectare, while only two people own more than five hectares. All told, there are 107 adult men living and working in the village. Nearly all have some agricultural interest, it being rare to find men who do not own or work some land, but only one-third are solely peasants with no other supplementary occupations. Around half are artisans, with shoemakers, house-builders and drivers being the most common occupations. Shopkeepers and professionals each make up one-tenth of the resident males, the former often selling the products of their own fields, while the latter are schoolteachers or retired *empleados*.

Agriculture and semi-skilled trades thus account for most of the population, with construction, transport and the government sector accounting for one-tenth each. Almost half these men are semi-skilled – often a legacy of migration – and most are able to ply their trades around Ataura, where three-quarters of them work. One-tenth work in Jauja and Huancayo, while a further tenth travel to work in villages in the valley. Only a quarter are dependent labourers, hired by others, and two-thirds are independent workers. Around one-tenth are primarily independent but occasionally hire their services out to others. Of the dependent workers, one quarter work not for cash but as *partidarios*, splitting the cost and profit of cultivation with the owner of the land. The remainder are employed by small concerns, the government or private land-holders.

Matahuasi[3] is much larger than Ataura, contains some 3,000 inhabitants and extends over some 2,000 hectares, most of which is cultivable. Matahuasi is a recognised *comunidad* and so, within the village, there exists a group of some 120 households who have usufructory rights to around sixty hectares of communal land. Alongside these there is the private land-holding sector. Like Ataura, the system of production is *minifundia*, but unlike Ataura there exists in Matahuasi a large landless group, and a group of large land-holders. Around one-fifth of the Matahuasi population are landless, while another quarter own less than one hectare. Two-fifths, however, own between one and four hectares, while a significant one-sixth own more than four hectares. Thus there is much more land in Matahuasi and more people have access to it.

Again as with Ataura, the predominant occupation is agriculture. A little over half the population are peasant farmers, around one-tenth are shopkeepers, another tenth are craftsmen, and these are followed by teachers, traders and agricultural workers. Thus, in contrast to Ataura, agriculture is much more of a dominant single occupation for more people. And although non-agricultural occupational stratification seems similar to that of Ataura, there is in Matahuasi one group of people who have been able to undertake entrepreneurial activities on a large scale, something that has never occurred in Ataura. This group consists of the *transportistas* who own and run lorries from the Mantaro valley to other parts of the country. Overall, socio-economic differentiation is much more pronounced in Matahuasi than it is in Ataura. Broadly speaking, Ataura is comprised of poor peasants, whilst Matahuasi contains both poor and middle peasants.[4]

In that these two villages belong to a partly commercialised rural sector greatly affected by near-by industry, there are similarities between them. Limited industrial development has had a general impact on the rural sector. In terms of the organisation of peasant production, the history of outside contact, and the structures of land-holding, occupations and recreation, the villages are not unlike. However, closer inspection of these five dimensions of rural life shows that there are also significant differences both between the villages and between social classes in the villages. The importance of these differences is that they form the bases of differences in the industrial sector between groups of migrants from the villages.

Village similarities

The most significant resemblance between the villages lies in their contemporary organisation of peasant production and their history of external contact. The small-holding peasantry of the valley have been required by Incas, colonists and industrialists to work in the mines. At the same time the peasants have been increasingly drawn into the cash nexus of the capitalist economy as commercial relations have spread through the valley. The structures of land-holding, occupations and recreation rest on these general basic features.

Although in the two villages it is possible to distinguish between communally and privately owned land, between subsistence and market-oriented peasants, and between middle and poor peasants, yet persisting throughout these divisions is the basic unit of production which currently predominates in the Mantaro valley – the peasant household. Subsistence, household farming is common to both villages and important to both.

It is the peasant household[5] which controls property and organises production. Usually it consists of three-generation extended families, with the senior generations owning the resources while other members of the family work on them. So, whilst junior members of the household are 'landless', they do have access to land. Household property is transmitted by inheritance and there is a cycle of property dispersal and concentration. The organising principle of the household is that consumption needs must be met through the mobilisation of family labour. Labour is recruited and withdrawn by the cycles of birth, marriage and death, and so there is a constantly changing balance between the labour inputs of the household and its consumption needs.

No household can meet all its own needs, however, and attempts are made to mobilise external resources while maintaining its viability. These attempts may take the form of co-operation with other households, migration or the development of market orientations. Occasionally they lead to the breakdown of the household as external demands become too great.

Andean peasant culture includes a range of co-operative practices which can be used to sustain household farming. They range from the lending of tools to communal village work projects. Between individual households there is the practice of *uyay*, the exchange of household members at times of sowing and harvesting. Also between households are the systems of *minka* and *trueque* by which services and goods are paid for in kind. Between individuals there are the practices of *al partir* and *ipoteca*, the former being the sharing of cost and profit on land, the latter the pawning of land. At the village level is the *comunidad* itself, in which peasants may engage in common agricultural or construction tasks. Such larger-scale co-operation may be religiously based, when it is known as a *cofradia*. Underpinning and reinforcing these economic practices are the social systems of kinship, *compadrazgo* and neighbouring.

The history of external contacts with the two villages, giving rise to migration, is also somewhat similar. Both have long experience of such contacts and, in both, migration has been an aid to subsistence and a means of social mobility for some villagers. For both Ataura and Matahuasi relations with the mining sector have been particularly important.

During the Incan period[6] the valley was organised into *ayllus*, governed by *curacas*. An *ayllu* was a local corporate group, settled on an extension of land which usually included some high ground, some land on the valley bottom and some jungle. The *curaca* governed the *ayllu* for the Inca nobles. In the Mantaro region the Huanca nobles had in fact lost land to the Incas. In the *ayllu* individuals had rights to houses and to land around the houses, and the houses were often scattered throughout the *ayllu*.

There were several ways in which the valley *ayllus* were in touch with outside influences. The first was the *mitimye* system, through which the Incas moved populations from one region and settled them in another. Several Valley villages grew out of *mitimye* resettlements. The second way was the *mita* system, by which the *curacas* organised labour to work in the mines. During four months of the year peasants migrated from the valley to work in the mines for one month. The passage of Incan noblemen and their expropriation of agricultural surpluses for storage were other ways in which external contacts were made.

During the Spanish Conquest the Huanca *curacas* negotiated favourable treatment from Pizarro in return for men and provisions to help him overthrow the Incas. The *curacas* were granted large extensions of land in the highlands above the valley, which became *haciendas*, and they governed the valley populace on behalf of the *encomenderos*. At first the *curacas* supplied the mines with voluntary labour, but the increasing demand for mineworkers meant the reintroduction of a coercive *mita* system. Migrant labour flooded out of the rural sector either to die in the mines or to bring back epidemics to the valley. The rural population declined and the *ayllu* could no longer be maintained as a self-sufficient unit.

At the same time that the mining laws were changed to help recruit labour the *reducciones* were introduced into Peru. Under the *reducciones* the scattered *ayllu* populations were nucleated into villages in order to tax them, Catholicise them and establish reserves of manpower. The new villagers were given land which they were to hold collectively, and so became *comunidades*. As well as having rights to communal land, individuals also began to establish rights to private plots. In Ataura,[7] for example, a Spanish captain laid claim to some village land in 1749. He himself had moved to the other side of the river, and his claim was contested by some indigenous residents who pointed out that they had bought the land in 1694 and that they used its produce to support them while working in the mines.

The *reducciones*, the *mita* system and the population decline meant the end of the *ayllus*. The separate geographical parts of each *ayllu* began to split away as power was transferred to the villages and towns. Each different part began to specialise. The highland villages devoted themselves to livestock production and the valley-floor people to arable farming. This specialisation led to the growth of trade between the regions and villages, and groups of traders and intermediaries emerged. The bases for the commercialisation of rural life were being laid.

During the colonial period both Ataurinos and Matahuasinos were required to work away from their villages. As well as having to toil in the mines, Ataurinos had to do *faena* work in Jauja. *Faena* was labour tribute without payment, and they were expected to clean the streets or prepare the bull-ring. The Matahuasinos were required to do *faena* in Apata. If a man was working in the mines when his *faena* fell due, his son or wife went in his place, and if they could not go the family was fined.

The passage of Spanish, Chilean and nationalist armies through the villages during the nineteenth century brought the inhabitants into contact with the outside world. The villages were also resting and victualling places on the main road from Cajamarca to Cuzco, as the old Inca highway ran along the valley floor. With the growth of Lima and the several attempts to colonise the jungle even more migrants passed through, leading to the prosperous *pension* trade in Ataura and the emergence of several muleteers in Matahuasi.

The emigration of peasants to the mines also continued during the nineteenth century. Around 1900 this flow was quickened by the expansion of the mines and the recruiting activities of *enganchadores*. The *enganchadores* were often local notables such as mayors, heads of Spanish families or shopkeepers. They would persuade a mine owner to advance them money on the security of the land they held. Back in the village, armed with the mine owner's loan, they would persuade peasants to work in the mines. When contracting for CdeP the *enganchador* had to use his lands to raise his own cash, for the corporation did not make advance payments.

The effectiveness of the *enganchadores'* village recruiting was based on three factors. The first was the example of the successful mineworker turned *enganchador* himself, who provided evidence that fortunes could be made. The second was the status of the *enganchadores* or their 'front men' in the village. As landowners and council members they had enough authority to convince peasants that the work was neither too hard nor too risky and that contracts would be honoured. However, the danger and the high accident rate meant that it was the third basis of coercion that was more frequently used.

The *enganche* system was not so much a method of payment as a debt relation. As such it formed part of the other debt relations in which poor peasants were often trapped. *Enganchadores* who were also shopkeepers would allow them credit in the village store, or lend cash to help out at the life-crises of marriage, burial or *fiesta* finance. The *enganchador* would use the debt relation to coerce the peasants to work in the mines. If a migrant did not complete the necessary working days in the mines owing to illness or death the debt was passed on to his family, and children often spent years working off their father's debts. One way of cancelling the debt was to sell the family lands to the *enganchador*, many of whom became large landowners in this way. The seizure of land by *enganchadores* led to the bitterest family disputes.

In the first decades of the twentieth century emigration to the mines increased as American investment raised output dramatically and the railway network was extended to the valley. In Ataura these events led to the village's integration into the mining sector. By 1920 some Ataurinos had achieved white-collar status at the Oroya refinery. They were able to use their position as labour brokers to enable other Ataurinos to obtain posts. During the 1920s mining was the largest single employer of migrant Ataurinos,[8] although there were many others in government construction work and in offices, usually in Lima.

The outflow of men during the 1920s left a village of women, children and the elderly.

It was a similar story in Matahuasi, where the arrival of the railway in 1910 also led to migration on a larger scale. As well as poor peasants in debt to *enganchadores*, several small shopkeepers found they could not compete with the larger merchants who used the railway, and they too migrated. The Matahuasinos, however, more often went to the mines rather than to the refinery in Oroya, and did not take up white-collar work. As in Ataura, agricultural employment declined markedly during the 1920s owing to this exodus.

The depression of the 1930s meant the reversal of these migratory flows for both villages. The mining corporations, government and small employers all laid men off and they flooded back to their villages, once again becoming peasants on their own plots of land. This situation continued until the end of the depression, when employment in government and construction work began to expand. During the 1940s emigration increased again, and since the second world war the rate of migration from and to both villages has been high. However, the relative importance of the mines as a migrant work centre has declined. Migrants found that informal work in Lima paid better than mining, as well as being less arduous. So horizons have widened since the war, and Lima has become a relatively more important centre of employment.

In both the organisation of agriculture and the history of external contacts similar general features are to be found throughout the Mantaro valley. The arrival of colonial capitalism transformed the old *ayllu* system, established both private and communal rights to land, and led to specialisation in agricultural production. Migration has been a permanent feature of highland life, providing firstly coerced labour to the colonial mines and then wage-labour to the industrial centres of the highland and the urban centres on the coast. During the twentieth century villages in the valley have seen a high rate of emigration to the mines, large-scale immigration during the 1930s and then post-war emigration to a wider range of economic sectors than before.

Under the Incas the relationship between agricultural organisation and migration was one of balance. Colonialism and industrial development destroyed this stability and transformed agricultural life. Yet during both the Colonial era and the age of industrial development the existence of a *minifundia* peasant economy in the valley has enabled villagers to withstand many of the worst effects of contact with the outside world. Drawing on family structures and co-operation, they have been able to maintain themselves while in the mines and during fluctuations in external employment.

Peasant co-operative practices operate within an overall capitalist commercial framework established during the colonial era, however. They are an informal means of helping to organise commercialised agricultural work. The structures of land-holding, occupation and recreation show just how that commercialisation has taken place and how many aspects of village life have been brought into the cash arena. In both Ataura and Matahuasi the effects of these changes have been broadly similar.

The first dimension in which the impact of commercialisation has been felt is the structure of land-holding in the villages. From the nineteenth to the twentieth centuries land has increasingly been transformed into a commodity and brought into the cash arena. Much of it, of course, remains within families and never comes on to the market. But as families migrate or die out their land comes up for sale, and even within families the children purchase the inheritance from one another. Often it is with the money earned through migration that such acquisitions are made.

In Ataura during the second half of the nineteenth century there were four landholding entities – the Catholic Church, the *comunidad*, five Spanish families, and the indigenous peasants, owning small plots. Land was acquired and dispersed mainly through marriage and inheritance. In one instance most of the land controlled by the Spanish families became concentrated in the hands of two female cousins. The cousins were promptly married by two brothers, and so the land passed from the control of one Spanish family to that of another.

With the increase in migration at the end of the century this pattern changed as land was increasingly bought and sold. In Ataura the change was brought about by one man named Lucas. He was the illegitimate son of a Spanish descendant who at the turn of the century made a fortune in mining. He returned to the village and bought out the old Spanish families, their lands, houses and mill. By 1920 he owned twenty hectares and employed three full-time labourers. But although one of his sons continued as a farmer and added to the land, the others left Ataura and became professional men in Jauja and Lima. When the last son died, his sons in turn sold the lands and moved away. The estate was sold to returning migrants who bought not only Lucas's land but also that of potential emigrants and widows in debt to *enganchadores*.

The break-up of Lucas's estate was part of the fragmentation of the blocks of land owned by the Spanish families at the beginning of the century. During the 1930s this fragmentation was given fresh impetus in Ataura when the Church decided to sell its land. Again villagers who had built up savings in the mines were able to buy, and the Church property was divided into small plots. The *comunidad* land in Ataura came under the ownership of the village council and was rented out to individual villagers, since Ataura never registered as a *Comunidad Indigena*.

In Matahuasi the process of alienation took much the same course. Money from migration, or from commercial contracts with the mines and the metropolis, was used to purchase real estate. When in the 1930s the Church decided to sell its land in Matahuasi, a large block which had previously been worked by villagers and whose product had been used for village *fiestas* came on to the open market and passed into private hands. In fact the sale created a group of large land-holders and a group of landless agriculturalists in Matahuasi. This polarisation of the pattern of ownership contrasts with that of Ataura, an important difference which is taken up below.

The occupational structure of the two villages has also been influenced by migration and commercialisation. The effects have been felt on both the occupational and sexual division of labour in the valley. Migration and commercialisation have led to the rise of strata of shopkeepers and traders, providing them with capital finance and a cash market. They have also resulted in women controlling agricultural work in the absence of men, and using cash remitted by their migrant menfolk to hire labour in the village.

Undoubtedly there has always been some occupational differentiation in the two villages, owing to the presence of bakers, cobblers, muleteers and so on, but the greater range of occupations is a twentieth-century phenomenon. An example of the proliferation of commercial activities is provided by the shopkeepers of Ataura and illustrated in Fig. 5. The main block of shops flank the central square. They occupy the lower storeys of a house once owned by a man of Spanish descent. In the first decade of the twentieth century his sons divided it into three shops catering to travellers. On the marriages of their sons the house was divided again, and the process has been repeated until there are now seven shops in the old house. All the owners are the direct descendants of the original owner, and they either work in the shop themselves or let them to traders. In that the shops are now bought or rented, the relations established are commercial ones,

A HOUSE DIVIDED

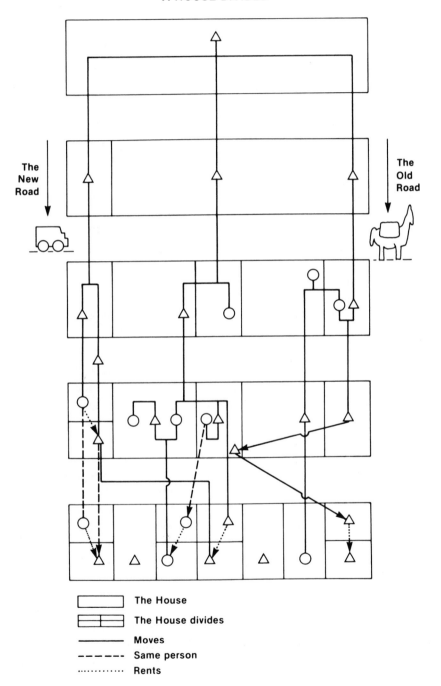

The New Road

The Old Road

| | The House |
| The House divides |
| Moves |
| Same person |
| Rents |

but the commercial relations are complemented by kinship structures.

In both Ataura and Matahuasi the people owning or working in shops all have a long history of migration. For many of them, setting up shop is a retirement occupation. Capital is accumulated from the earnings of migration and invested in stock. Sometimes the stock is partly financed by a bank loan or a forwarding loan from a wholesaler in Jauja looking for an outlet. Part of the stock may be grown on the trader's own land by himself or his wife while the other minds the store. Many of the shopkeepers gain experience of trading during migration, having run shops in the mining towns or Lima; others became friendly with traders there and took their advice about opening a village shop. Aiming to capture a share of an established market, the shops are all general stores, selling foodstuffs and beer. Their customers are people who themselves have cash, often due to the wages earned through migration.

Migration not only supports the rise of a commercial stratum, it also reinforces the sexual division of labour in valley villages.[9] It does this in three ways. Firstly, the absence of men means that it is the women who are called upon to perform communal tasks. In the nineteenth century women did *faena* when the men were away in the mines. In the twentieth century it was the women of Ataura who built the church tower and carried the stones to dam a spring. Secondly, the absence of men leads the women to turn more to their own company and kin. A women's world grows up in the village, organised around a whole range of local affairs from child-rearing to representation on the village council.

The third way in which male migration contributes to the sexual division of labour is probably the most important, however, and relates to land-holding and land use. When the men are away it is the women who work on the land. They do the manual work, or contract others to plough and harvest with the money remitted by their migrant husbands. At the same time, they can inherit land equally and occasionally amass property as the men are killed in mining accidents. Thus the world of women becomes closely related to the land, a feature that has certain consequences.

Although men may migrate, the women are reluctant to leave their settled world, and often have solid economic reasons for staying. Moreover their relation to the land distinguishes them from women from poorer highland areas. The valley women are a marriageable prospect, and alongside the returning migrants there is a marked influx of outsiders who have married village women. The outsiders are viewed with some suspicion by the residents, who joke cagily about these men who have married their sisters and taken over their land. For their part the outsiders recognise the suspicion and try not to aggravate it, since they are not on home ground.

The final dimension in which the villages are similar is in the recreational activities of the peasants, and again external contacts have intimately affected their habits. In both Ataura and Matahuasi *fiestas*[10] are held, either on the village saint's day or during a special week later in the year. The form of the *fiesta* is common to both villages, and is usually a *corta-monte*. A tree is cut down, decorated and set up in the main dancing area. A place for the dancing, a band, food and plenty of beer are provided by the *fiesta padrinos* who agree to finance one or other of these essentials.

The dancers circulate round the tree, occasionally chopping at it, and the one who finally cuts it down has to finance the *corta-monte* for the next year. The outcome is supposed to be due to chance, but in fact it is decided in advance between the families. They know who can afford to pay for a *fiesta*. In both villages the money often comes from the earnings of migration. It is migrants who dance round the tree: the *fiesta* is their holiday from wage-labour.

The effect of outside contact has thus been the commercialisation of peasant life in the valley, leading to agricultural specialisation, the alienation of land, capital accumulation, occupational differentiation and the secularisation of religious occasions. Household-based subsistence farming is contained within a web of capitalist commercial relations. Some co-operative practices continue, and the household is still the main unit of production and consumption. But to maintain the viability of the household the villagers have to migrate and operate on the open market. Thus the rural sector is not a 'traditional' sector in a 'dual' economy.[11] It is not the case that modern capitalism and traditional agriculture coexist relatively independently of one another, with the rural sector embodying 'obstacles' to its own modernisation, such as extended families or unfavourable attitudes to work. Rather, the rural and industrial sectors are part of Peru's capitalist development and are closely linked.

The effects of outside contact have been similar throughout the valley. Village economies, such as those of Ataura and Matahuasi, are alike in being based on subsistence farming households. Their migration histories are related in that the mines and Lima have been the main destinations, whilst the fluctuating levels of employment in both centres have led to the recycling of labour. Earnings from migration have enabled those returning to buy land and splinter holdings in the two villages. Their money has also led to the rise of commercial strata and supported the sexual division of labour. In the *fiestas* common throughout the valley, migrants take a holiday from urban work.

These process have occurred in other villages of the Mantaro valley. In Muquiyauyo,[12] across the river from Ataura, the history of external contacts has led to the differentiation of the social structure, transformed from an almost caste-like two-tier system of Spanish and Indians. Migration, education and political ideologies have provided the bases for a new stratification system. Indians have been able to acquire land, have become more educated and have used the money from migration to further individual and collective projects. Yet, despite the similarity of these effects at the general level, it is clear that there are still important differences between villages in the way their socio-economic structure has been affected by external relations, and between rural social classes in the way they relate to the wider world.

Village differences

The most important contrasts between Ataura and Matahuasi are in the structure of their village economies and their external relations. Differences in land-holding, occupations and recreation in turn stem from these basic dissimilarities. The sum of the differences is that whereas the poor peasants of Ataura have been integrated into a migratory way of life, in Matahuasi migration has been integrated into a commercial and agricultural way of life. In Ataura migration is a necessary and permanent adjunct of a small subsistence economy. In Matahuasi it is a source of finance on which middle peasants can capitalise, and through which some poor peasants can attain social mobility.

Today the economy of Ataura is small, divided and subsistence-oriented. It is an economy of poor peasants. Its small scale, plus the cultural devices available, support a migrant solution to the problems most households face. Women working the land are a common sight. The wives and mothers of migrants tend several small plots of land scattered around the village. At seed time and harvest they will call upon another female relative for hand-work, or engage a retired immigrant with a pair of oxen. As he ploughs the woman will bring him beer and food which they take together, gossiping. He receives a flat cash rate for the job and the woman helps him carry his implements home. This sort of operation does not provide a basis for diversification and so Ataurinos spend their working lives as migrants.

Matahuasi, in contrast, has more land and more middle peasants. The case of Saul illustrates this difference. He forms a link in the overall migration process from poor villages to valley emigration. Many of the able-bodied men in Matahuasi are away, and those who are left are working on their own land. So, to recruit hands, he hires a labour contractor. Together with the *contratista* Saul takes his lorry to a poorer village on the valley slopes and picks up a gang of six women. Their own sowing or harvesting period is over and they are free to work for him. He employs them on specialised tasks, such as reaping oats, for village children do the easier work. He pays the minimum of $1 per day per worker. The money goes to the *contratista*, while Saul himself gives the women $0·05 worth of *coca* per day, plus food and drink. On top of that, he pays the team one sack of whatever they have harvested, and the *contratista* an extra $0·12 per person per week.

Saul would prefer to use a combine harvester for some crops, such as wheat, as it would be cheaper. Six women take six days to harvest one hectare of wheat, which costs him $40, whereas a machine can do the job in a single day for only $20 hire. The problem is that the land is irrigated, with ridges across it, so that a combine harvester cannot be used on it. So Saul continues to contract labour. He engages the same team every year and gets to know their work, while they get to know their employer, the land, and the security of payment. Usually only women come, for their men are in small mines or construction work, but occasionally there is a man among them. He is put on a separate task, never joining the women in their work. Agricultural organisation on this scale can support independent, diverse ventures, and stands in contrast to the subsistence activity of Ataura.

The migration histories of the two villages also differ in a number of ways. Whereas Ataura has established labour contacts with external sectors, Matahuasi enjoys both labour and trading links. Secondly, for Ataura while such contacts have been dominated by the mines, and Lima has only lately come to prominence, for Matahuasi the capital has always been of great importance. Thirdly, Matahuasi's ability to support trading links has meant that its migrants do not take up dependent wage employment to the same extent as Ataurinos. Finally, whilst the depression of the 1930s resulted in Ataurinos taking up agricultural work in the village, some Matahuasinos were able to move into the transport sector, with profound repercussions on the local economy.

The parish records of Yauli, which include Oroya, show that between 1835 and 1850 seven Ataurinos were married in the town – the highest number from any of the valley villages. All were miners. There is no evidence of Ataurinos trading with the mining sector. In contrast, the first evidence of Matahuasinos in Oroya is provided by the town's *comunidad* records, which reveal that a Matahuasino was one of the seven outsiders buying up *comunidad* land. Present-day Matahuasinos recall their grandfathers travelling to the mines to open up shops and sell village produce there.

Overall, the incidence of migration is higher in Ataura than in Matahuasi. Nearly all the Ataurinos resident in Ataura have had some experience of migration, whereas only two-thirds of the Matahuasinos currently resident in their village have been away. Analysis of the life-histories[13] of migrants resident in the villages shows that whilst the Ataurinos have been either peasants or mineworkers all their life, the Matahuasinos have spent significantly more time as traders. Half the Ataurino migrants' lives were passed in dependent work in the mining sector, while most of the remainder was spent on the land. The Matahuasino migrants, however, have spent only two-fifths of their working lives in the mines, the balance being divided between self-employed agriculture, trading and transport. The scene of these last two activities has been not only the highland mining areas, but Lima as well. These historical differences between the villages are nowadays reinforced by the fact that whilst half the migrants from Matahuasi living in Oroya are traders, none of the Ataurino migrants is. The latter all work for CdeP or the municipality of Oroya.

The differences are further reflected in the work histories of migrants' brothers. Whereas half the brothers of migrants resident in Ataura have worked in Oroya, the main centre of mining work for Ataurinos, very few Matahuasino migrants' brothers have. Although one-third of the Matahuasino migrants' brothers have worked in Lima, only one-tenth of the Ataurino migrants' brothers can claim to have done so. And while four-fifths of the Ataurino migrants' brothers have worked for mining companies, the same is true of only a quarter of the Matahuasino migrants' brothers. Ataura migrants and their kin lead a peasant-worker existence, passing their days either in the rural or in the industrial sector. Matahuasi migrants and their kin are able to move into trading as well as working in the other two sectors.

One commercial activity that is now important among Matahuasinos is transport. The ground was prepared in the 1930s, although the real beginnings can probably be traced back to the muleteers who congregated at Matahuasi to take *colonos* down to the jungle. Whereas in Ataura returning migrants saw the depression out by taking up agricultural work, in Matahuasi some of those who came home diversified into transport, either buying a lorry themselves or in partnership, or working on lorries and buses. With the post-war boom, Matahuasinos consolidated this diversification away from mining and are now to be found in a variety of sectors such as transport. Ataurinos, on the other hand, re-established links with the white-collar migrants from their village who were working in the mines and had not been laid off, once more taking up industrial employment.

In both villages migration has contributed to land turnover and alienation. Whereas in Ataura the result has been fragmentation of holdings, in Matahuasi by contrast it has led to the concentration of ownership and sharp socio-economic differentiation. In Ataura there were several pressures towards fragmentation. The departure of Lucas's children and grandchildren in pursuance of professional occupations led to the breaking up of his estate. The property was divided among returning miners, the mill was bought by a miner's wife, and Lucas's big house was purchased by a retired refinery worker.

At the same time the forty hectares of communal land belonging to the village were lost. Refuse dumped into the Mantaro river by the Oroya refinery found its way into the valley. The communal land, on an island in midstream, was rendered completely useless by the pollution. This loss threw an even greater burden on to the land pertaining to Ataura at the bottom of the valley. In the 1930s the position was eased slightly by the sale of Church land, but so great was the pressure that this property was immediately broken up into small lots and sold off to migrants. Thus in Ataura there was fragmentation of holdings.

In Matahuasi the reverse was the case. There the sale of Church lands throughout the valley in the 1930s opened up opportunities for acquiring land on a large scale. A much larger hectarage was released in Matahuasi than in Ataura, and its disposal to private interests had a polarising effect on social stratification. Since the Church land had been communally worked and the produce communally distributed, the villagers felt that negotiations with the Church should proceed on a village basis. With many of those concerned working away, a group of representatives was elected to act on the villagers' behalf. Realising that organised opposition from the dispersed migrants would be sluggish, this group promptly bought the land for themselves. Much of the money for the purchase came from working in, or trading with, the mines and Lima. The response of the rest of the inhabitants was to form a committee to contest the deal, and it was out of this committee that the legally recognised *comunidad* of Matahuasi was formed.

Thus the combination of a sudden increase in the supply of land, the absence of many villagers and the availability of cash resources to a few meant that two of the most easily identifiable land-related strata in the village were created – the large private land-holders, and the members of the *comunidad*. Not only do these strata persist to the present day, but the effects of the original split are still expressed in hostility between the groups as they struggle for political office in the village.

In both Ataura and Matahuasi present-day returning migrants seek to buy land in their villages. However, there is a considerable difference of scale. In Matahuasi there is more land for purchase and sale and the properties themselves are usually in larger units. The opportunities are there for poor peasants to mobilise resources, through migration income or kin networks, and expand their agricultural production. While the produce of the land is similar in both villages – potatoes, maize, wheat, and some cows and sheep – it is the Matahuasinos who are more commercially oriented. They sell their crops on the open market, in fairs and stalls in Oroya and Huancayo, and a number of them have also developed pastoral activities. They attempt to raise sheep, and some have taken up dairy farming on securing a contract from CdeP to provide milk for the Oroya workers, following the STMO demand for meat, milk and rent subsidies.

In Matahuasi middle and poor peasants are clearly distinguishable; in Ataura the one or two middle peasants who can be identified are more akin to their subsistence neighbours than to the commercial farmers of Matahuasi. The middle peasants of Ataura are so because they have invested a lifetime's savings in land for their retirement. The middle peasants in Matahuasi are large agriculturalists. The crucial difference between the two, and between the two villages, is that not even the largest holdings in Ataura are enough in themselves to permit capital accumulation, whilst in Matahuasi farmers can use the products of their fields to finance further expansion.

Generally the middle peasants have obtained land by purchase to a greater extent than the poor peasants. Two-thirds of the middle peasants have bought land, compared to only two-fifths of the poor ones, while far more poor peasants than middle ones have only inherited land. Further, while the middle peasants have established land access through renting, the poor tend to use the mechanism of *al partir* or become members of the *comunidad*. At the same time it is the poor peasants who most frequently use the devices of *partidarios*, *minka*, *uyay* and kin to work land, while the middle peasants rely more on paid labour. In the disposal of produce it is the middle peasants who market their produce, whilst the poor consume theirs. Thus in both villages it is the middle peasants who enforce the processes of commercialisation of peasant life.

Differentiation has occurred in Matahuasi not only within the land-holding structure but also within the occupational structure. The rise of commercial strata linked to migration earnings has been much more marked than in Ataura. In Ataura the commercial stratum consists of petty, often part-time, shopkeepers. In Matahuasi significant commercial groups have emerged. Large shopkeepers flank the main highway, timber merchants flourish, and lorry-owning *transportistas* are an important group. Two case studies from each village illustrate the differences in occupational structure and the links between occupations and external relations.

In Ataura, during the late 1950s, Alfredo built a brick house with money he had earned working in Oroya. He decided to become a *transportista* and, having only a little land of his own, persuaded the elderly village priest to lend him the money for the lorry. The priest is a descendant of the old Spanish families of Ataura, and over the years he has increased his wealth by surreptitious acquisition of land in the village. He now rents it out and himself lives in Huancayo. He advanced Alfredo the money, but insisted that, since Alfredo had no land, the house be surety for the loan. Alfredo bought the lorry, but through lack of contacts and hence contracts the venture failed and the priest sued him for the money. Alfredo lost, was evicted, and the house now stands empty while Alfredo and his family are lodged in a small *adobe* dwelling near by.

A little later, in the early 1960s, Armando returned to Ataura from the mines of Tamboraque. With the savings he had put by, and a sum raised by putting their land in *ipoteca*, he and his brother Flavio scraped together enough to put down a deposit on a lorry. For three years they became *transportistas*, hiring a driver and carrying anything to and from

Lima and the valley. Again, however, the venture failed, and the brothers now shake their heads at the inexperienced way they went into the business without the necessary contacts. The problem, they pointed out, was that with their land in *ipoteca* they had no supplementary source of income to pay off the interest on the loan or even keep themselves during slack periods. Unable to repay their debts, they were evicted from their home and are now working in Oroya to earn enough to be able to redeem their land.

These examples are in marked contrast to the Matahuasino ones. The son of a large landowner in Matahuasi, Gonzalo studied in Lima before joining his brother's timber business in the jungle. Together they supplied wood to the mines and railway, but with timber prices falling and transport costs rising they could not compete with wood felled in the Mantaro valley itself. They sold the business and bought some land, a house and a lorry in Matahuasi. Gonzalo's brother opened a woodyard and Gonzalo became his transporter, taking timber to the mines, then minerals from the mines to Lima, then kerosene from Lima back to the valley. The brothers got the transport contract with the mines from their sister, who had a timber yard in Jauja. When Gonzalo crashed the lorry he was forced to look for wage-work. His brother-in-law, a chemical engineer in Oroya, offered him a job, and for five years he was an *empleado*. Eventually he returned to Matahuasi to work as a driver for his brother, who owns a wood yard in Concepcion, where he works today.

Another *transportista* in Matahuasi is Julio,[14] who uses his lorry to carry both timber and labour. His father established a timber mill in the 1940s and purchased land for farming. Both mill and land are now managed by Julio and his wife, though the father remains the owner. Three operatives, one a cousin, help Julio, but it is he who drives to the mines to negotiate timber contracts with contacts established by his father. The land is worked by his sister and her husband, and Julio markets some of their produce in return for a share of the profits.

Julio's parents-in-law were themselves successful *transportistas* and he is developing his business in association with them. He transports temporary labour to his mother-in-law's fields at harvest time, while she is the one with the market connections in Lima for the sale of the produce. In addition she allows Julio to use her lorry to take timber to the mines, enabling him to make several deliveries a week. Operating on this scale, Julio is now constantly on the look-out for timber, and his mother-in-law is able to put him in touch with local farmers.

Occasionally he is further helped by his affines, who, driving lorries under the direction of their mother, work with him at harvest time.

Gonzalo and Julio, then, contrast sharply with Alfredo and Armando. Through the availability of land and networks, middle peasants in Matahuasi have been able to build up independent trading relations with the mines and with Lima. Migration, resulting in money and contacts, has played a part in the establishment of those relations, but it has been complementary to viable household economies in Matahuasi. In Ataura, on the other hand, the peasant economy cannot underwrite the risks of commercial ventures and there has been no history of trading contacts that would help to give them a start.

The differentiation to be found within Matahuasi finds expression in the organisation of the *fiesta* there, for it is the means by which rich merchants can demonstrate their status and satisfy local business obligations. In Ataura, however, it is more of a holiday for the migrants. Although the history of the Ataura *fiesta* is one of division and conflict, occasionally between migrants and residents, the incorporation of Ataura into the wider national scene today means that it is the holiday function that dominates.

During the nineteenth century the *fiesta* dancing in Ataura was the province of two groups representing the two *barrios* of the village, and was led by the Spanish families. At the beginning of the twentieth, changes took place as a new *barrio* was formed, and returning miners paid for a band of their own. Tension between migrants and residents led to friction and brawling, exacerbated by dubious land deals concluded in the migrants' absence. The resulting fracas were so serious that dancing in the square was abandoned and each *barrio* withdrew to hold its own *fiesta*. However, as the *fiesta* has increasingly become a holiday for all participants friction has died away and the *barrios* finish their dancing together in the square.

The organisation of one of these *barrio* groups shows the importance of migration money in the Ataura *fiestas*. Of the twenty organisers who financed the *fiesta*, eight were *padrinos*, and of these three were currently working in the mines, two were professionals in Huancayo, one was a professional man in Lima, and one was a retired mineworker. Of the twelve *madrinas*, three were the wives and one the daughter-in-law of retired mineworkers, three lived in Jauja, two in mining centres, and only one in Ataura. The dancers themselves were mainly migrants and the *fiesta* was clearly a recreational moment for them.

In contrast is the *fiesta* of San Sebastian in Matahuasi.[15] San

Sebastian is the patron saint of the village, and in his name a club has been established there to organise *fiestas* on the saint's day. Its members are predominantly *transportistas* and businessmen, who either live in Matahuasi or keep in close touch. The club's main function is to serve as an arena in which certain types of relationships among entrepreneurs are defined and reinforced. As in Ataura, the *fiesta* itself takes up a week of dancing and drinking, but it is on a larger scale, with bull-fights, processions and horseback displays, as well as street dancing.

The *fiesta* is characterised by the attempt to project a 'good' image of the entrepreneurs and becomes an occasion on which they reward their clients and kinsmen by way of the feasting and dancing. A number of key roles in the celebrations are allocated to visiting migrants and townsmen, so the village club brings together urban and rural-based ties. It has connections with regional associations in Lima and the mines, and through these it organises contributions to village development projects such as the building of the new secondary school.

Analysis of its membership shows that persons of a certain entrepreneurial status are attracted to the club. Typically it consists of people whose principal economic activity necessitates the maintenance of strong rural–urban relations – such as traders and *transportistas*. To succeed in their businesses they have to build up a set of viable and trustworthy relations in the countryside, and this they do through the *fiestas*. The sponsorship of a *fiesta* is of special significance, as it becomes a public occasion for the reaffirmation of an entrepreneur's commitment to his home community and a way of improving his standing in it.

In Matahuasi the identification of the club with the patron saint helps to ensure good public relations at village level, a vital ingredient of local entrepreneurial success. The migrants have a network of local relations throughout the village and the valley for obtaining transport contracts, agricultural produce and livestock for sale in the urban markets of Lima and the mines. The structure of this network consists of a series of overlapping kinship and friendship bonds and includes a high proportion of people who are members of *fiestas* and/or migrant clubs. The Club of San Sebastian provides a crucial arena for the expression and operation of such bonds.

Socio-economic change in the Mantaro valley

The Mantaro valley has long been affected by external events which have influenced its economic and social structures. The twentieth century, although bringing the acceleration of some economic processes, did not witness the arrival of modernising forces acting on a traditional and passive peasantry living in a state of socio-economic equilibrium.[16] Once part of the Incan and Spanish empires, the valley is now an adjunct of the international capitalist system. The Spanish Conquest brought the valley into the world market and capitalist relations now enmesh the lives of those who live there.

External forces have had some general and similar effects throughout the valley. The demands of colonial Spaniards and industrial capitalists have resulted in large-scale emigration to the mining sector. Peasant life has been penetrated by commercial relations as land has been alienated, occupational differentiation increased, capital accumulated, and secularisation introduced. At the same time peasants have turned to their indigenous culture to cope with these processes. Utilising co-operative practices and maintaining the viability of household production, they now live partly commercialised lives just as in the industrial sector they are partly proletarianised.

Despite the similarity of these overall patterns of change, however, there are significant differences between valley villages and classes in the way they have been affected by, and have responded to, external pressures. In the small village of Ataura relations with sectors of the wider economy have led to commercialisation and migration. Land-holding has become fragmented, as has the occupational structure, which is characterised by small-time shopkeeping and subsistence farming. The religious *fiestas* have become industrial holidays. In the large village of Matahuasi important land-holding groups have emerged, at loggerheads with a large landless group. Strata of transporters, shopkeepers and timber merchants have established themselves, employing wage-labourers and migrants from other villages. The *fiesta* is an arena for the demonstration of their status. Ataura has become absorbed into a migrant system, while Matahuasi has capitalised on external contacts to establish independent relations with other sectors.

There are two dimensions to these village differences, one economic and one social. Economically, the village of Ataura consists of poor peasants whilst Matahuasi contains both middle and poor peasants.

Consequently the differences between them are not only village differences but also agrarian class differences. The migrant response of Ataura is in fact the response of the poor peasant class throughout the Mantaro valley. The commercial response of Matahuasinos is the response of middle peasants. Socially, however, village location does affect peasants' responses. The village milieu is a meaningful world for the peasant. Ataurinos have kin and village contacts with migrants in Oroya which Matahuasinos do not have, whilst Matahuasinos have kin and village links with both middle and poor peasants which Ataurinos do not have.

For both villages, relations with the mines have been crucial. For Ataura the relationship has been based on labour migration. For Matahuasi it has involved commerce as well as labour migration. In both villages the cycles of industrial employment have led to the migration of labour back and forth across the Highlands. The villages have responded to these fluctuations by taking up subsistence agriculture, and then either consolidating their links with the mining sector or venturing into independent work in other sectors, such as transport and construction.

The cycles of industrial production have thus profoundly affected the valley. But just as the effects have differed between villages, so too have the responses. Industrial development has not called forth a uniform stream of migrants. Rather, as agrarian and individual life cycles have evolved, so pressures have been brought to bear on people to emigrate from or immigrate to the valley, or to stay either in the industrial or in the rural sector. Industrial, agrarian and individual cycles interlock, producing complex inter-sectoral relations. Just as industrial development has affected the rural sector, so forces at work in the countryside affect socio-economic organisation in industry.

Notes

[1] Adams, R., 1959; Alberti, G., and Sanchez, P., 1974; Castro Pozo, H., 1946; Long, N., and Roberts, B., 1978; Maynard, E., 1964; Tschopik, H., 1947.

[2] Censo, 1961. Migrants not present in villages claim that they are village residents, which inflates the census figure.

[3] Some of this material was provided by Norman Long, University of Durham.

[4] Long, N., and Roberts, B., 1978, distinguish between rich, subsistence and poor peasants in the Mantaro valley. Rich peasants have sufficient land to produce a surplus for the market, use both household and paid labour and combine agricultural

production with trading. Around 15 per cent of the households in the valley are wealthy peasant households. Subsistence peasants comprise between 40 and 50 per cent of valley households. They produce enough for household necessities, but no more. To supplement their incomes they engage in craft work and migrate to urban work centres. Poor peasants either have small plots of land which do not meet their subsistence needs or are landless labourers. They work in the fields of others or migrate for long periods. They account for 35–40 per cent of valley peasant households. This definition of valley agrarian classes is adopted here, except that subsistence peasants are designated as middle peasants.

[5] Shanin, T., 1974.
[6] Long, N., and Roberts, B., 1978.
[7] Bullon, G., 1969.
[8] Life-history analysis, Laite, A., 1977.
[9] Harriss, O., 1978.
[10] Cancian, F., 1967.
[11] Higgins, B., 1956; Kilby, P., 1971.
[12] Adams, R., 1959.
[13] Laite, A., 1977.
[14] Long, N., 1972.
[15] *Ibid.*
[16] Holmberg, A., 1960.

6
The migrant response

While industrial development has affected the peasant sector, peasant socio-economic organisation in turn has affected the social structures that have emerged along with industrial development. Much of the feed-back between the rural and industrial sectors has been transmitted via the process of migration. In the work-place, migrants from particular villages have 'captured' certain departments. In the town, migrants from the same village re-establish relations with one another. In the village, potential migrants know that there are networks in both town and work-place that are prepared to receive them. Thus the migrants are a self-selected group,[1] deciding whether or not to migrate to the mining sector and then attempting to enter one kind of industrial work rather than another. That process of self-selection is grounded in village structures and networks.

The structure of contemporary migration[2]

Migration between the rural and industrial sectors has four major features. It is closely related to household needs and decisions. It occurs within a certain cultural milieu of relationships and expectations that support the move. The organisation of the move is around age-cohorts rather than between generations. Finally, migration is not a flight from the land by the landless but rather a means of maintaining work alternatives across a number of economic sectors.

Having to migrate because they owned no land at all was not put forward as an important reason by the migrants. Of course, being 'poor', supporting the family and looking for work opportunities are indicative of a situation in which there is little land and few work opportunities in the village. Yet these do not amount to massive alienation from the land. Migration is embarked upon for a variety of reasons, but not in most cases merely in order to subsist, for this is a condition that can be met in the rural sector.

Table 5. *All Ataurinos and Matahuasinos: reasons for migration from village*

Reason	% of respondents citing reason
To earn more money	39
To join kin already working	25
No work in the villages	12
Work opportunities presented themselves	11
Dislike of village life	11
To be near the village and family	11
To support the family	9
Poor	8
To pay for education	7
$N = 76 = C+D+F+G$	

[For C, D, F, G see appendix]

The role of the household is of great importance in the decision. Whether to migrate or not is decided in consultation with one's wife or mother and is related to household needs. With the father working away, it is the mother who spells out their family obligations to sons of working age as family subsistence and educational requirements are reviewed. The eldest brother often feels that, during the absence of a migrant father, the household responsibilities devolve upon him. Certainly several men – Armando from Ataura among them – are described as the 'father of the family' owing to their assumption of the burden of their younger siblings. Although the eldest moves first, his brothers often join him while the mother handles rural affairs. At her death, or before it, the brothers jointly decide whether to maintain or divide the household lands.

Migrating to be near family and village is a decision taken by two types of people. The first are those working in Lima or some other coastal town who take the opportunity to move to Oroya to be near ageing parents or to develop landed interests. The second are those who move to the mines from the village so that they can be at hand to maintain kin and village links. That is to say, for both these groups and other migrants, moving to the mining sector does not involve a break with kin or with the village. It is a move contained within a kin and village sphere of influence, supported by social networks. The decision to migrate often turns on news of a job in the corporation from a kinsman already working there. The fact that migrants readily take up these offers shows that migration is a normal part of highlanders' expectations.

Four-fifths of migrants know before moving that there are work opportunities at their destination and half actually have a specific job waiting for them on arrival. Some go chancing their luck – *a la ventura* – but often this will be with a friend to a work-centre that has advertised for labour. Again, nine-tenths go knowing that they can stay with someone for the first few nights: two-thirds had an offer of accommodation with kin and one-fifth of being put up by *paisanos*. Three-quarters knew about conditions in the mines and in Oroya either from visits or from information received, and so life in the mining sector did not generally come as a rude shock.

This information and these job opportunities are passed on by kinsmen and *paisanos*, not by fathers. Two sorts of people are involved – peers who have moved a short while previously, or established gatekeepers into the industrial labour force. The absence of fathers and the importance of peers in recruitment emphasises the difference between the mineworkers and a stable labour force in an industrialised country. In the latter, jobs are passed on from father to son, but in peripheral economies industrial employment is so uncertain and so limited that older men are rarely long enough in one job to be able to bequeath it.

The role of 'gatekeepers' is of great importance for village 'capture' and the establishment of village networks in the industrial situation. They are often older men, original village migrants who have reached a position of some importance in the labour force, perhaps as *empleados*. These men can use their position to place migrants from their village in certain departments within CdeP. As was noted above, one such gatekeeper is Arturo.

Arturo was born in Ataura and is now an *empleado* in the Research department. He became known in the village as having a good job in a good department and was approached by Ataurinos who wanted to work there too. The Ataurinos who approached him had some claim on him, for they were his kin or neighbours in the village. In return, Arturo could recommend them with some confidence, not only because he knew them but also because family pressure could be brought to bear if they did not work seriously. So Arturo has found work for six men and they in turn have brought in eight more. All fifteen are from Ataura and all are related, as fig. 6 shows. More than this, all work, or have worked, in Research, where the duties are not onerous. Indeed, over the years much of CdeP's routine research has been carried out by one family from one small Andean village. It is in this way that 'capture' occurs, and it is replicated by village and department throughout the corporation with Matahuasinos in Railways and valley migrants steering clear of the blast furnaces.

These village and kin networks thus establish the possibility of work for migrants and receive them when they move. Migrants travel alone at first, or with a friend, making arrangements about wives and children later. Very few actually 'doss' down wherever they can the first night, since most go direct to a known contact. Kinsmen and *paisanos* find room for him while he looks for work, so he has no rent to pay. They also feed him, although he meets his share of this. The arrangement usually works well: some two-thirds of migrants find work within a week and can then contribute rent and food until they find a place of their own. These successful ones usually have a job waiting for them, or are 'spoken for' by the employee they lodge with. For up to a quarter of migrants, however, the search can take three or four weeks and often these men become tense and desperate as they stretch their familial and financial credit to its limits.

For two-thirds of these valley migrants the first job they get is very often in CdeP itself. Having stayed in the village for a while, they go direct to CdeP. The rest find alternative employment and wait for an opening. Most valley migrants begin with the corporation as *obreros*, but they start as they mean to continue. They steer clear of the toxic areas of the refinery and take work which is not too dirty, noisy or heavy. They become apprentice mechanics and carpenters. If they have to start near the furnaces they make every effort to get into another section as soon as possible.

These features of migration are illustrated in individual migrants' life histories. Selected cases of ex-migrants in Ataura and Matahuasi, poor migrants, a trade unionist and a merchant, reveal the similarities in experience of migration and the different strategies adopted to cope with economic problems.

How ARTURO has helped

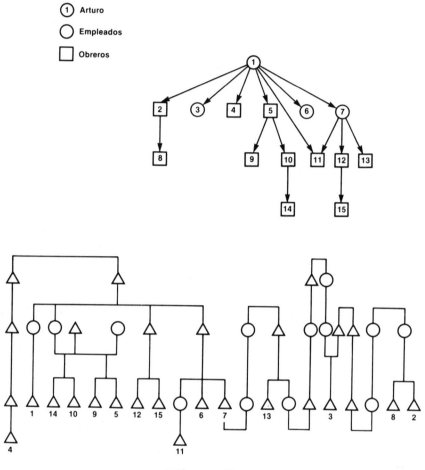

Migrant lives

Alido and Julio are now older men, living in Ataura. Both have worked long periods in the mines and Oroya. Alido was born in Ataura in 1905 and although his father died when he was three he managed to stay at primary school until third grade because his mother sold land to support the family. Just as his schooling was coming to an end a Czechoslovak arrived in the village, recruiting labour to work on the railway tunnel at Chosica, near Lima. The Czech was offering 1·80 *soles* per day: 0·80 *soles* for lodging and one *sole* per day wage. This was better than the 0·50 *soles* per day agricultural wage, so Alido and five other youths decided to go, accompanied by two adults.

During 1917 Alido and his *paisanos* worked on the tunnel. At the end of the year the work finished and Alido became an assistant chef in the railway hotel in Chosica, where he stayed for two years. In 1919 his mother fell ill and found it difficult to work in the fields, so Alido returned to Ataura to help her. He found it boring, and when Ataurinos heard that Isaias, the *enganchador* from neighbouring Huamali, was recruiting labour for the building of the refinery Alido went too. For three months in 1920 he was *enganchado* in Oroya. He found the cost of living very cheap and liked having money in his pocket, but since there were no cinemas and dance-halls it did not compare with Lima, and he went back to Ataura.

After working for a few months in the fields he decided to go and work on the new road from Chosica to Lima. This time he went alone, by train. Again, he was paid the same basic rates – one *sole* in wages and 0·80 *soles* for lodging – but the job did not last long, as the finance for it ran out in 1922. Unemployed, Alido began to make his way home, but a woman in Chosica had heard that he had worked in the hotel and asked him to be *major domo* in her house. After four years there he had to leave suddenly, for his mother was again complaining that she was too ill to cope. Alido stayed a while with her and then returned to the house in Chosica, where he was taken on as a chef, the previous one having since died.

In 1928 the manager of the Railway Hotel in Chosica recommended him as chef on the train from Lima to Huancayo. This suited Alido: not only was the job well paid but he could visit Ataura, which was one of the stops along the route. He was also able to do some trading on the side. When the train stopped at Ataura his wife would bring eggs, chickens and guinea-pigs (a culinary delicacy in Peru) for him to sell in Lima. On the return journey he would bring back flowers for sale in Huancayo. However, this job lasted only eight months, because he could not arrange stop-over lodgings in Lima. So Alido returned to Ataura and during 1929 and 1930 worked with his wife in his mother's fields.

When their first child was born in 1930 he sought employment in Casapalca. Despite the lay-offs, a *paisano* found him a job as a miner. The work was dangerous but the wages were good, and he stayed one year. On returning to Ataura for the *fiesta* he could not face the thought of going back to the mines. In 1933, with the revival in mining, labour contractors came to the village and Alido, his sister-in-law and her husband were all persuaded to go to Morococha. Alido earned the daily miner's wage-rate of $1. Morococha lies at 5,000 metres, and he disliked the cold, the headaches and the danger, so he returned to Ataura after six months and worked in the fields for a short while. He tried mining again in 1935, going alone to Huaron, but the only job he could get was pushing trucks in the mine. It was very dangerous, so he came back to Ataura.

But his family was larger now and it was not easy to keep them fed. In 1937 he went to Oroya. He and a friend originally meant to go to Huaron but stopped over in Oroya, joined a work queue and were offered a job with CdeP. He started as an assistant mechanic at $1 per day. Before long he brought his wife and children to join him and they lived in rooms in Old Oroya, paying $2 per month rent. After four years in rooms they moved into a CdeP barrack house which was rent-free.

Although he liked bringing home a regular wage and preferred Oroya to Ataura, Alido found that his lungs were beginning to give trouble and he was suffering from loss of appetite. When he was detailed to work in a section near the blast-furnaces he refused and returned to Ataura with his family in 1945. Now he is getting on in years, one daughter has married a retired *empleado* in the village and another sells clothes in Lima. Alido occupies himself with helping his children on the village land and taking bolts of cloth by train to his daughter in Lima.

During the afternoons he calls in at the shop of his cousin Julio. Julio also stayed in Ataura until he had completed his third year at primary school and then, in 1924, when he was fourteen, he and his brother decided to look for work in Morococha. They made their way on foot, carrying blankets and pots and pans. As they walked Julio's brother grew more and more dispirited. In the end he turned back, but Julio went on alone and got a job in Morococha.

On his first day at work he met an uncle on the way to the mine-shaft who upbraided him for coming to work so young but said he would help him. The first time they descended the shaft Julio was terrified, but he soon got used to it and was employed pushing the trucks for 2·50 *soles* per day. After some months at this, he asked his mother to come and cook for him, which she did. Four months later he had an argument with his overseer and was fired. That night there was a mining disaster, and hundreds of men were killed. Julio was immediately re-hired in the rescue operation and stayed on another two years.

In 1926 his brother-in-law came to Morococha from Ataura, looking for work. He told Julio, correctly as it turned out, that there was work to be had in the ore concentrator. Julio got a job as an office boy, which he preferred to the mines. Over the next two years he progressed to the rank of overseer. In 1929 a fall on to the conveyor belt broke his leg badly and he was taken to hospital in Morococha. The place was deserted, all the Americans and Europeans having fled after the events in Malpaso. He camped there with another man for two days until a doctor returned and set his leg.

Having been in hospital during the Oroya and Malpaso riots, Julio could not be placed on the CdeP black list, so he stayed at work during the 1930s, remaining an overseer on $1 per day. Then in 1938 he came to Ataura to visit his mother and to look over lands released by the Church. He had left without leave, however, and was fired. So he bought some of the land, prepared it for sowing, then took the train to Lima. His cousin had told him about work in the construction industry, and Julio lived with relatives and earned $·50 per day. The contract lasted two months. For a further three months he took on odd jobs around Lima.

Then his daughter fell ill and the doctor advised them to return to Jauja, where the air was purer. At the same time his old boss at CdeP wanted him back, so Julio went to Morococha and his family to Ataura. He was employed as an overseer throughout the second world war. In 1943 his brother died. This worried Julio, and he went for a medical check-up. The doctor told him that rheumatism had weakened his heart and he should not go on working at high altitudes. He went back to Ataura in 1944 to work on his land.

In 1949 the irrigation canal bringing water from the Mantaro river to the foot of the valley sides reached Ataura. Julio set up as a labour contractor, recruiting men from Ataura to dig the canal. At one point he had twenty men working for him and was making around $65 per week. After a year the canal had moved on and labour contractors from other villages were getting the contracts, so Julio gave up. Instead he and another Ataurino went to Lima and bought a lorry for $6,000. For six months they ran the lorry from Lima to the valley, carrying assorted goods, then they traded it in for a bus. After a few months the bus venture failed and Julio decided to set up shop in Ataura.

Julio now has the shop on the corner of the square, next to the road. Although the busiest shop in the village it provides him with only a modest living. To supplement his income he has his lands and he goes round the mining camps selling shirts and household goods. He used to deal with a middleman who came to the store, and took over the distribution himself when the middleman gave it up. Julio has worked all his life and is proud of the fact.

The elements in the life-histories of these two Ataurinos are to be found in nearly all such cases: the early loss of a father through death or desertion, the trek to the mines, the influence of pure chance, the dislike of rural work, the satisfaction of having cash, the fear of accidents, the perennial returns home, the obligations of family and the final settling in the village. These factors recur time and again. Yet there are also differences between the experiences of these two men and those of Ataurinos who work in the mines nowadays, as well as those of Matahuasinos. Contemporary Ataurino refinery workers migrate later, have a larger network to receive them, but have greater difficulty in acquiring land today than did successful migrants such as Julio.

The main difference between the ex-miners in Matahuasi and Julio and Alido is that the Matahuasinos are either part of a vigorous village economy or are engaged in larger-scale commerce, as the example of Gonzalo in the previous chapter showed, and as the experiences of Alejandro and Marcial also show. Alejandro is currently a farmer in Matahuasi, in the process of expanding his milk production, whilst Marcial is a mechanic who runs his own business servicing agricultural machinery throughout the valley.

Alejandro was born not in Matahuasi but in the town of Ayacucho, in 1918. When he was two his father left his wife and child to work as a tailor in Oroya. In 1928 Alejandro and his mother joined his father in Oroya and Alejandro continued his schooling until 1933. As a youth he remembered the riots in Oroya, the women marching at the front of the processions carrying banners, and the men storming the police station.

At school Alejandro had earned pocket money by carrying the bags of American and European women and by caddying on the golf course. Through a contact made while caddying he was able to start in the lead refinery in 1933. Getting work in this way was not unusual, for the CdeP labour office functioned only sporadically. Men would find work by slipping past the sleeping guard at night and approaching overseers direct. Throughout the 1930s Alejandro worked in the lead plant, then went to do his National Service.

He returned in 1941 to a job in the Chemicals department and was elected a shop-floor delegate. There being no union, it was his job to negotiate working conditions with the American and European staff. Rising prices and political party policies in 1943 increased the pressure for a trade union. Alejandro was one of the small group of Apristas and

Communists who met to form one. Although CdeP rejected their first attempts, the STMO was founded and Alejandro became one of its leaders.

During the first strikes of 1947 he helped raise funds and supplies for the miners. Both mining unions and regional entrepreneurs contributed. In 1951 he was involved in setting up the construction workers' union in Oroya. Throughout the 1950s he worked as a carpenter in the building department of CdeP and continued to be a trade-union leader. Then in 1962 the change of leadership in the STMO and the fluid national political situation led to the attack on the refinery. For two days the plant burned and hostages were held, until the army returned to restore order. Alejandro had taken part in the incidents and was rounded up with several others. They were taken to Tarma for interrogation and then to Lima, where they were imprisoned. After some days he was released and returned to Oroya, only to discover that he had been sacked. He took his indemnity money and left, never to return.

When he left he went to Matahuasi. His wife was from the village and had left to work in Lima, but she also had a sister in Oroya who told her about work there and so had come to work in a hotel in Oroya. There she had met Alejandro and they had married. Her parents owned land in Matahuasi, and when Alejandro was thrown out of work they gave over some of it to their daughter and son-in-law. Alejandro learned to work the land and began to develop commercial ventures. Owing to his political connections he was offered several jobs in agrarian reform agencies in Huancayo but he preferred to build up his farm and has been successfully specialising in breeding dairy cattle.

His experience as a dependent wage labourer in the formal economic sector in Oroya is complemented for Matahuasi by that of Marcial operating· quasi-independently between the formal and informal sectors. Marcial was born in Matahuasi in 1909 and completed his primary schooling there. He then went to Huancayo and studied until the second year of secondary school, learning to train as a mechanic. By working he would both be less of a burden to his parents and would have some cash for himself.

He worked in Huancayo for three years, earning around $0·80 per day and learning how to drive. When in 1935 the Yauricocha mine was being explored the opportunities there led two Matahuasinos who owned lorries to run them to Yauricocha. They needed a driver and contacted Marcial. Once in Yauricocha he took another driving job for

CdeP whilst still driving the Matahuasinos' lorries. He made about $1·50 per day at this, but the job only lasted one year, as the lorries broke down with use. So in 1936 he returned to Matahuasi and worked in his parents' fields for a short time.

He was quickly contacted by Manuel, the brother-in-law of the Matahuasino lorry owners. Manuel wanted to expand his commercial interests in Oroya, wished to borrow one of the lorries, and needed a driver. So Marcial took the lorry to Oroya and during 1936 worked for Manuel. However, the brother-in-law soon wanted his lorry back and Marcial again found himself in the fields at Matahuasi. Then Manuel alerted him to a job as private chauffer to an Italian businessman in Oroya.

Marcial became the Italian's chauffeur and whilst waiting for his employer would do odd repair jobs in the town's garages. From the Italian he received $30 per month and from the repair work another $50. Since his parents did not need his support, he lived quite well. Then the Italian moved to Lima, set up a motor repair shop, and took Marcial with him as head mechanic and lorry driver. Marcial would run goods in the lorry up to northern Peru. So he contacted Angel from Matahuasi to come and work in the shop while he was away.

The Italian died, the business was sold and Marcial became a mechanic in a Lima driving school. The business began to fail. At the same time, he had to return to Matahuasi to sort out family affairs on the death of his father. While he was there Manuel offered him a bus driver's job in Oroya. In 1938 he went to Oroya but the job lasted only a few months, so he moved on to Cerro de Pasco to work in road construction. He was put in charge of a levelling machine and contracted himself to work on a mileage basis. Some months he earned $200. This work lasted for two years until government financing ran out. Marcial returned to Matahuasi and with his savings bought a bus, which he ran from valley villages to Huancayo. Failing to make the bus pay, he placed it in storage. Acting on information from a *paisano*, he went back to Cerro de Pasco and engaged himself as service mechanic on CdeP lorries.

After two years Marcial's contract was undercut and he returned to work on his lands in Matahuasi. Some months passed, then in 1943 he obtained a job driving lorries carrying wood to Satipo. Displaying his skill as a mechanic, he became chief mechanic in the mechanic's shop in Satipo, earning $30 per month. Working in the jungle gave him malaria and in 1945 he returned to Matahuasi. A *paisano* he had known in Cerro de Pasco gave him the job of repairing the machines in a Matahuasi timber yard. He worked at this for three years, earning $20 per month. Then, in 1948, the timber merchant opened a new office in Tarma and Marcial went to work there. His wife was from Tarma, so they lived in her parent's house. After eleven years there Marcial was earning $60 per month but malaria again forced him to convalesce in Matahuasi. At the end of a year he returned to Tarma to work at the Ford agency, where he stayed eighteen months. He left the agency on applying for another job, but it fell through and he had to return to Matahuasi in 1961.

Marcial again worked on his lands and did contract agricultural work around the villages. He installed the petrol station in Matahuasi and then got a job with a large agricultural machinery hire and repair firm operating out of Huancayo. He was once more working on a contract basis, earning $35 per month. However, in 1968 the firm closed down its Peruvian branch, and Marcial has set up his own service agency to repair the machines the firm left behind. He knows, however, that this business will not last very long.

Unlike the Ataurinos Alido and Julio, the Matahuasinos Alejandro and Marcial are still working on commercial ventures that form the main source of their livelihood. For the Matahuasinos their land is either a commercial venture or the adjunct to one. For the Ataurinos it is a subsistence basis which allows them to engage in small-scale commercial activity. All four men were born in the same decade, but while Alejandro and Marcial are still busily at work Julio and Alido must pass the time at a slower pace.

Not only, then, are there differences between the life-histories of migrants now resident in the villages, but the experiences of Matahuasinos and Ataurinos in Oroya also differ. Again the same elements of village contacts, unstable work and the role of family are present in all lives, but the patterns of response have differed. Matahuasinos have been able to establish commercial ventures in Oroya, as well as gaining employment in CdeP. Ataurinos on the other hand have established their presence primarily in the corporation.

Nicolas, Feriol and Cancio are three brothers from Ataura who now live and work in Oroya. Nicolas is the eldest, born in 1935, whilst Feriol is the middle brother, born two years later, and Cancio the youngest, born in 1944. By the late 1940s the primary school in Ataura had been extended and it was possible for both Nicolas and Feriol to complete their primary schooling in Ataura. Nicolas knew that, with two younger brothers and two younger sisters at school, his parents could not support him at secondary school. Indeed, they were ageing and it was up to him to support them and his brothers and sisters. So when he was fifteen he went down to Tarma, where the road into the jungle was being built.

Nicolas knew that Alfredo, his father's friend, was a labour contractor on the road works. Alfredo took Nicolas on as a mason's labourer, paying him $1 per day. Nicolas lived in the same lodgings as Alfredo during the year that the work lasted. When it came to an end in 1951 he went back to Ataura to work in the fields. There Feriol finished his schooling and applied to the secondary school in Jauja. Although he was accepted he did not have the money to continue his studies and so he and his elder brother looked for work. Feriol wanted only to save up enough to pay for his schooling.

Alfredo was contracting labour to work in the mine of Cercapuquio, so in 1951 the two brothers went to work for him. However, Alfredo paid them only $.75 per day each and then began to default on their wages. They were a long way from Ataura and the two eldest boys were also uneasy about leaving their ageing parents and younger siblings. After only a month they decided to go back, but Alfredo raised Nicolas's wage to $1·60 per day, so he decided to stay while Feriol returned. Nicolas worked on in Cercapuquio for another nine months before going home in 1952.

Next year the two brothers worked in their own and other people's fields, earning $0·75 per day. Being still only eighteen and sixteen they were too young to get jobs in Oroya. Then in 1954 they heard from their uncle Felipe that there were posts vacant in the Research department. Felipe had been found work in the department some years earlier by his cousin Arturo. Nicolas and Feriol went to Oroya, stayed with Felipe and were taken on in Research.

Meanwhile the youngest brother, Cancio, was finishing his primary education in Ataura and wanted to go to the secondary school in Jauja. Having been denied this opportunity himself, Feriol was anxious to give his younger brother the chance he had missed, and so Feriol and Nicolas paid for Cancio's schooling. Cancio stayed on until he was eighteen, completing half his secondary school training. Then, in 1962, he went to Oroya to visit his brothers and look for work. On the way he was picked up by an army recruiting lorry and pressed into National Service.

He was demobbed in 1965, and Feriol managed to get him taken on in CdeP Plant Protection as a nightwatchman. Unused to the hours, Cancio fell asleep on the job and was fired after only six weeks. He then moved from one post to another in rapid succession. A friend in Plant Protection found him a job guarding machinery on a building site in Oroya. When the employer found he had been to secondary school he was moved to the office. After nine months the building contract ended, however, and Cancio was again unemployed. By this time he had met his wife, and the two went to live with her parents in Oroya. Cancio stayed on in Oroya looking for work because he knew there was nothing in the village and he felt that, with his education, something would turn up. Finally, in 1966, his father-in-law, who worked for the railway, got him a job in the railway consumers' co-operative.

After a year in the co-operative Cancio was made an *empleado* earning $3 per day. Compared to CdeP wages, however, the pay was low, and in 1968 Cancio went to work for an electrical sub-contractor to the corporation. During 1970, however, CdeP began to lay off all its contract workers and Cancio was once more out of a job. He had two children by this time, and sent his wife and family to stay with his sister in Ataura while he looked for work. He found a job on a building site in Oroya, and his wife and children moved back to join him. He knows that the job will not last very long.

Thus the three brothers have helped one another find work and lodgings. For the two older ones, Nicolas and Feriol, this mutual help has reinforced their family ties. This feeling is expressed in the fact that they have manoeuvred to live next door to each other. Nicolas moved to a corporation barrack to be nearer his work. Feriol waited until the barrack next door was empty and then he moved too. These two brothers are close and their wives get along well, but the latter do not like Cancio or his wife. They consider her 'common' and think that he is unstable and thriftless. When Cancio calls on his brothers on some pretext to go out for the evening the wives are clearly displeased.

Even though two of the brothers work at CdeP and one does not, all three, like the other Ataurinos in Oroya, are in dependent wage work. Not so the Matahuasinos. Perhaps the most prestigious Matahuasino in Oroya is Manuel. His life-history is a story of commerce and political influence centred on Oroya. Yet Manuel also maintains his village links, using village migrants in his own enterprises and placing them in the CdeP labour force.

Manuel was born in Matahuasi at the end of the last century and in 1913 left his village to work on the railway in Oroya, where a job had been arranged for him by his cousin. He was employed as assistant mechanic, waiter and coach cleaner until he had saved enough to return and buy land in Matahuasi. Changing his mind, he went instead to school in Jauja and then back to Oroya in 1919. He married in that year and took over his father-in-law's house, the lower half of which was a butcher's shop. With his wife came a dowry of fifteen beef cattle and Manuel became a butcher, for the refinery was being built and the labour force meant a demand for meat.

After two years' trading Manuel brought his nephew Teodormiro from Matahuasi, trained him as a butcher and installed him in the municipal market, where he worked for three years. The meat sold in the two shops came at first from the hills around Oroya, but as the smoke polluted the pastures Manuel had to travel to the markets of Junin, Cerro de Pasco and Huancayo. He would send his beef live by railway to Oroya. His brother in Matahuasi also supplied him with meat, which came up at first by rail and then by lorry.

At the end of three years Teodormiro became a butcher in the CdeP hotel in Oroya. In 1930 Manuel won the contract to supply meat for the workers in Malpaso, and so both Teodormiro and another nephew went with him to set up shop there. This enterprise came to an end with the troubles in Malpaso. While Teodormiro went to work for Manuel's brother in Yauricocha, Manuel branched out into other activities. He began both to send meat to Lima and in Oroya to sell eggs and butter. However, the Lima merchants did not pay as regularly as CdeP and so he once more concentrated his interests in Oroya. In 1935 his brother-in-law loaned him a lorry, the one Marcial brought from Matahuasi. At the same time Manuel recalled his nephew Teodormiro from Yauricocha and re-installed him in the municipal market. However, the depression continued and neither venture proved profitable. The lorry was returned to his brother-in-law and Teodormiro went back to his fields in Matahuasi.

Rising demand at the end of the 1930s and into the war years meant that Manuel was soon earning enough through his meat business to invest in buses and houses in Oroya. Again Teodormiro came up from Matahuasi to work in the market in Old Oroya. Manuel and his nephew not only obtained meat supplies from Matahuasi but also began to bring in milk from the village. Manuel persuaded his family to increase their milk production so that he could sell it in Oroya. He purchased two large houses in the town and turned them into apartments. One, in Old Oroya, was solely for tenants, the other was in

New Oroya and the ground floor was converted into a chicken restaurant. Manuel leased the restaurant to his brother-in-law, who brought chickens up from Lima. Occasionally Manuel would employ Matahuasinos in the restaurant while they were looking for work in Oroya.

Thus he became a prosperous entrepreneur. Yet his commercial activities were grounded in his village contacts. The rural location provided him with a supply of both products and reliable labour. So he had a position to safeguard in both Matahuasi and Oroya. He demonstrated his continued concern with village affairs by founding, with Alejandro, the Matahuasino village club in Oroya. Not only did the club provide a meeting-place for Matahuasinos, it raised funds for village projects, providing a roof for the school and a tower for the church. In Oroya, Manuel was appointed Governor of the town, a post which he held for twenty years and which he relinquished only to his son.

These histories of migrant labour were repeated among all the migrants in Oroya, Ataura and Matahuasi. Despite the differences between rich traders and poor peasant workers, there are basic similarities in all their stories. These common elements form the bases of other characteristics shared by the migrants. Faced with the universal problems of unstable work, dependent families and the vagaries of chance, they respond to some extent in similar ways.

Migrant characteristics and strategies

The forty-seven Ataurinos and Matahuasinos in Oroya are not only rural migrants, they are also stratified into *obrero, empleado* and commercial groups, as well as being differentiated by age. Consequently there are both similarities *and* differences in their characteristics and the strategies they adopt, depending upon the village they come from, occupation and age, among other factors.

One feature common to nearly all migrants is their maintenance of village interests. The most important interest is a continuing control over village land, and access to land is through either personal or family ownership. The ownership of land is a family affair, and for individual migrants it is access to land, rather than simple ownership, that is crucial. All the Ataurino and Matahuasino migrants were members of extensive families which embraced both rural and industrial locations.

Most of the families owned between half a hectare and two hectares, whilst some owned as much as ten. Some young migrants were 'landless', yet it was they who did the heavy work on their parents' land and they had an equal share in the product. Other young migrants did have a little land, but it was invariably a plot given to them when they married by their parents. The important lands to which these migrants had access were those of the senior household. Overall, three-fifths of the migrants from the villages who were *obreros* owned land, as against five-sixths of the village migrant *empleados* who did. The *empleados'* landholdings were larger than the *obreros'*. Since the *empleados* were older, they had inherited more property, and since they were better paid they had been able to buy more land. It was not the case that *empleados* came from landed families whilst *obreros* came from landless ones, but this is discussed below.

This ownership and access to land by nearly all the migrants had several immediate implications. It meant that land, land prices, food prices and the state of the weather were a constant preoccupation and topic of conversation. At harvesting and planting times they would be busy journeying back and forth to their village or recruiting labour by sending money to their wives. Some older men rented out their land and were always concerned about whether or not they would be paid. Indeed, such concerns touched all the men, who, although they sympathised with the expropriation of the *haciendas*, were afraid that any unworked land of their own might be affected by the agrarian reform laws.

Landed interests are maintained by wives and parents continuing to live in the village. Most migrants travel back to their village every weekend, or once a fortnight, in order to visit their families and look over the household property. When they return they bring cash and consumer goods such as shirts and shoes with them. The cash is either to help the family to buy the things like salt, oil and meat that it needs, or to recruit labour to help at planting and harvest time. This inflow of cash is more noticeable in Ataura than in Matahuasi. At the weekend Ataura is full of men and the women are able to do their weekly shopping in the small stores. In Matahuasi the shops are larger and there are always enough resident merchants and peasants to keep trade brisk all week.

Whereas both *empleados* and *obreros* in Oroya maintain village contacts, the *empleados* commercialise those contacts more than do the *obreros*. Having more money, they buy land more. They also purchase houses and shops. Nine-tenths of the *empleados* own houses in the villages, compared to only half the *obreros*, and they spent more on theirs, either purchasing them or building them themselves. The *empleados'* houses were for their retirement. Some have two houses, one in the village and one in Jauja, Huancayo or Lima. The town house is intended for retirement or for occupation while the children are in education, whereas the country house is kept on for village visiting. A few *empleados* sell their village houses to buy a house in a town.

Some *empleados* also maintain village links by purchasing a shop in the village or running a business there. The shop next door to Julio in the village square in Ataura is run by the wife of an *empleado* in Oroya. He also has a share in a bus which plies between Jauja and Huancayo. One migrant *empleado* from Matahuasi owns a lorry which his wife manages, as it is used for transport in the valley. These men are the exception, however. Usually, in both Ataura and Matahuasi, it is the wives of *empleados* who may rent a small shop in the village or a stall in the Jauja market, or the *empleados* themselves may have a small sideline in the village, such as bee-keeping or photography. These sidelines flourish more in the small-time economy of Ataura than in the more commercial environment of Matahuasi.

In contrast to these commercialising activities of the *empleados*, the *obreros* rely on non-commercial mechanisms for the maintenance of village links. When *obreros* are house-owners it is more likely that the house will have been inherited rather than bought. When *obreros* recruit labour they do so through the mechanisms of *al partir*, the *comunidad*, and the kin network. When *obreros* are landowners it is usually because they have assumed the responsibilities of the rural household, often on the death of the parents.

It is clear that the wider commercial activities of the migrant *empleados* are built up during their working lives rather than being due to the fact that *empleados* come from wealthier families. As the village histories showed, there were wealthy families in both villages and their children became professional people in Jauja, Huancayo and Lima. The bulk of the peasant population, however, are those owning a half to two hectares, and it is from them that *obreros* and *empleados* are drawn. There was no simple fit between rural and industrial social stratification so far as this mass of peasants was concerned. It was not simply that poorer peasants became *obreros* and richer peasants became *empleados*.

Analysis of the backgrounds of all the seventy-six migrants resident in Oroya and the two villages revealed no major predictors of *obrero* or *empleado* status. The parental families of both groups were the same size, and the educational levels of the parents were the same. The fathers of *empleados* and *obreros* held equal amounts of land and were similar in their ownership of houses. Nor did the fathers' occupations differ significantly. The fathers of both *obreros* and *empleados* held similar occupations for similar lengths of time. Around half the fathers had been *obreros* or miners for some years, while one-third had been peasants for many years. There was no correlation between the manual and non-manual status of fathers and the occupational achievement of their sons.

Clearly this lack of precise predictors is not the case for other Departments of Peru. As the analysis in Chapter 2 showed, the existence of better educational opportunities in Lima means that significantly more *empleados* are Limeños, while the presence of poor landless labourers on *haciendas* in other Departments may mean that they do not have the resources to gain anything more than elementary education. But the mass of peasants in the Mantaro valley do have a few resources and some education. Consequently their reasons for migrating vary from necessity to the search for education, whilst the fit between industrial and rural socio-economic structures is complex, depending on economic resources and social structures.

In these respects the mechanisms of occupational attainment differ from those found in the proletarianised labour forces of industrialised nations. Among an industrial proletariat the occupational status of a father is a good indicator of his son's occupational status. Manual-worker fathers often have manual-worker sons. Indeed, the links are much closer in that fathers often pass on their job, their experience and their tools to their son. It is fathers who introduce sons into working men's clubs. Such a close relation, however, occurs in situations where industrial employment is widespread and there are few alternatives.

In highland Peru industrial development is limited and dependent, so the migrant response of the indigenous peasantry gives rise to a reliance on intra-generational social relations, as in African migration,[3] rather than on inter-generational social relations, as under European industrialisation.[4] In African townships young male migrants re-establish similar bonds to those existing in the rural areas. These young men help one another find jobs, share their lodgings and spend their free time together. It is this cohort pattern of migrant relations that resembles the Peruvian situation, rather than the father–son pattern of

European industrial communities.

The similarities in the backgrounds of migrant *obreros* and *empleados* and the differences in their life-histories are revealed by analyses of the vertical and lateral social mobility accompanying migration. In industrialised societies, analyses of proletarian mobility focus mainly on vertical mobility, since there are few alternatives to industrial work. In societies with limited industrial development, however, lateral moves into other sectors, such as agricultural and commerce, must also be considered.

Table 6. *Ataurinos and Matahuasinos resident in Oroya: status change by occupational group*

Occupational group	% maintained status		% changed status	
			Low to Middle	Middle to Low
	Low	Middle		
Obreros	30	23	38	8
Empleados		25	75	
		N = 47 = F+G		

[For F, G see appendix]

The forty-seven Ataurino and Matahuasino *obreros* and *empleados* in Oroya were asked to assess whether moving into an industrial occupation had meant a change in their economic status (see table 6). The majority of *obreros* thought that to become an *obrero* was to maintain one's economic status as 'low' or 'middle'. Around one-third thought that the move had improved their status from 'low' to 'middle'. Three-quarters of the *empleados* thought that becoming an *empleado* was a rise in status from 'low' to 'middle', however. This confirms the finding that both groups are from similar backgrounds, since becoming an *empleado* is a move up.

Although the backgrounds of the two groups are similar, their careers have differed. Whereas the *empleados* have remained in one sector of the economy, working their way up the industrial occupational ladder, *obreros* have tended to move back and forth from sector to sector. Nine-tenths of *empleados'* working lives have been spent as *obreros* and *empleados*, whilst *obreros* in contrast have spent one-sixth of their working lives as peasants. *Obreros* tend to oscillate between industry and agriculture as industrial and life-cycles turn.

Table 7 shows that, on average, *obreros* change their occupations every five and a half years. The most striking feature of the figures is the high rate of geographic and occupational mobility. Second is the difference in rates between *obreros* and *empleados*. The average sectoral changes for the *obreros*, every 4·9 years, are very rapid and in marked contrast to the sectoral stability of the *empleados*. The different strategies of the two groups are quite clear. The *obreros* oscillate rapidly between jobs, employers and economic sectors as they establish a survival strategy, working where and when they can. The *empleados*, in contrast, although they may change jobs frequently, do so on account of a promotion within their specific economic sector. Again, the mobility characteristics of the *obreros* may be contrasted with the immobility of the industrial communities created by European industrialisation.[5]

Table 7.   *Ataurinos and Mathuasinos resident in Oroya: mobility rates by occupational group. The average empleado or obrero changes catagories 1–6 every N years of his working life*

Occupational group:	1	2	3	4	5	6
	Department	Province	Village	Occupation	Employer	Sector
	N	N	N	N	N	N
Empleados	16·4	7·0	6·4	6·1	7·4	12·2
Obreros	11·0	6·2	5·2	5·5	5·5	4·9
			N = 47 = F+G			

[For F, G see appendix]

The general mobility rates, although differing between *obreros* and *empleados*, do not differ between Ataurinos and Matahuasinos. The differences between the villagers, as has been shown, lie in the general availability of more land and economic opportunity in Matahuasi, and the particular strategies established by richer and poorer migrants, as shown by the life-histories. However, it is at this point, over differences in migrant strategies, that differences between the groups of villagers re-emerge alongside the *obrero–empleado* differences.

Among the villagers living in Oroya, the *obreros* did not want to stay long there. Over half of them wanted to stay less than another five years, in contrast to the *empleados*, three-quarters of whom wanted to stay longer than five years. The reasons for the difference are clear. *Obreros'* work is unstable, dangerous and difficult. It is also just one job within an overall migration strategy, so the *obrero* is always looking out for better opportunities. He cannot retire with pay until he is sixty and so he aims to accumulate savings to buy some tools, some land or a house. *Empleados'* work, however, is well paid and they can retire in their forties. So the *empleados* plan to stay on until they reach retirement age.

On leaving, all want to be independent workers, but whereas both *empleados* and *obreros* want to become peasants and traders in equal proportions, such is not the case for the village groups. Half the Matahuasinos want to return to farming, compared to only one-quarter of the Ataurinos. On the other hand, half the Ataurinos want to take up skilled practical trades, compared to only one-third of the Matahuasinos. Similarly, the destinations of different villagers diverged. Although, among both occupational groups, one half wished to return to their village, one-third to a highland town and one-tenth to Lima, the village groups differed. Two-thirds of the Matahuasinos wanted to go back to their village, but only two-fifths of the Ataurinos had this aim. Those who did wish to return to Ataura were the older men, on the point of retiring, but the younger Ataurinos opted for taking up jobs in Huancayo and Jauja, realising that the village economy could not support them.

Whether or not aspirations and strategies are realised cannot be predicted in each case. It is clear that many migrants become enmeshed in family obligations, dependent work and failing health, and their only hopes for the future lie with their children. Yet the presence of so much circular migration in the region indicates that men do go to the mining sector, do save cash and gain skills, and do then change their work and life styles. The opportunities for saving are there, through secondary occupations, 'time' money accumulated for years worked, high *empleado* earnings or subsisting on village products whilst saving the industrial wage. Most of the older men admitted that they had some savings put by, which in the end was a little more than they would have had if they had remained as peasants.

Migration is thus an attempt by highlanders to solve the problems of employment and cash accrual which confront them. The problems arise because of the growth of population on the land, the inability of household lands to provide for all the members of the household, and the change in expectations on the part of peasants who now want to accumulate some capital in the form of savings or consumer goods. The migration occurs within a context of limited and unstable dependent industrial development: it is a strategy of response to that development. Thus the elements of the migratory process are social networks covering different economic sectors, oscillation between sectors and limited involvement in any one sector. These elements are the characteristics of a migrant labour force, and as such they are in contrast to the characteristics of an industrially involved proletarianised labour force.

Notes

[1] Goldthorpe, J., 1968.

[2] The following analysis is based on interviews and discussions with migrants from Ataura and Matahuasi in Oroya and the two villages: Laite, A., 1977.

[3] Mayer, P., 1971.

[4] Willmott, P., and Young, M., 1957.

[5] Goldthorpe, J., 1968.

7
The social networks
of migrant labourers

Migration raises the question of how far there is a move from household and peasant bases for social interaction to occupational and class bases. This problem has been the subject of research into both historical working class formation and contemporary migrant labour situations. As we have seen, historically analyses of the development of the English[1] working class emphasise the importance of the work-place in the lives of industrial workers. Today studies of migration in Africa and Latin America reveal a shift from rural-based social relations to urban-based ones. Copper miners in Zambia[2] come from all over southern Africa. In the industrial situation, however, they form trade unions, develop occupational skills and join voluntary associations not found in the tribal areas. At the same time they actively deny the authority of their tribal elders and establish social relations across tribal boundaries. Migrants to Mexico City[3] also relate to one another in terms of economic rather than ethnic status and develop social networks to cope with unstable work in the informal economy. Again, in the *barriadas* of Mexico City, as in the copper mines of Zambia, new forms of associations are developed which contrast with those in the countryside.

At the same time, however, it is clear that in Africa as in Latin America migrants draw on elements of their rural culture to help cope with urban life. In Africa[4] a new 'urban tribalism' emerges which enables migrants to identify others from the same homelands and forms a first basis for social interaction. The former patterns of authority are not reproduced in the new tribalism, rather it is a means of identification and mutual aid. In Latin America[5] too, migrants use home backgrounds as a means of identifying one another, and establish *fiestas* and co-operative associations in the towns similar to those in the rural areas.

Thus in contemporary terms there are at least two bases for social interaction in the industrial milieu of countries like Peru. One is industrial and occupational, the other rural and peasant. There is some cultural continuity between the rural and industrial sectors, and migrants may, in different situations, turn to different relevant and legitimate social devices for coping with those situations. This cultural continuity and situational availability of a range of social mechanisms to contemporary migrant labour contrasts with the historical development of an industrial proletariat. In the English model there had been more of an historical break, both economically and culturally, between the migrants and their rural origins prior to industrialisation. Besides these two bases for group formation there are also the factors of age, residence and religious belief upon which social interaction can be founded.

In the Peruvian case migrants relate to one another in a number of ways, depending upon the situational relevance of each basis for group formation. In the work situation, *vis-à-vis* their employer, they relate to one another as workers, with similar economic and market interests. In the town they relate to one another as *paisanos* or family, seeking to co-operate in the face of difficult living conditions. In the village they relate to one another as peasants, concerned with family affairs and the control of land. And all these situations are linked by economic cycles and social networks.

So the migrants in Oroya from Ataura and Matahuasi have available to them alternative bases for group interaction. To assess the importance and situational relevance of these bases, the occupational and migrant characteristics of the men were compared, their networks of kin, friends, workmates and *paisanos* were established, and their participation in institutions and formal associations was analysed. It was found that as *obreros*, *empleados* or traders the men engaged in certain different patterns of activity, and that differences in activities were also discernible between them as Ataurinos and Matahuasinos.

Occupational and village characteristics

There were twenty-five men from Matahuasi living and working in

Oroya and twenty-two from Ataura. Twenty-seven of these forty-seven men were *obreros*, twenty-three of them working for the corporation and the remainder on the railways or in the building industry. The other twenty were of more 'middle-class' status, mainly *empleados* and traders. Twelve of the twenty were CdeP *empleados*, while the rest were railway *empleados*, butchers and carpenters. Hence, as we have seen, there were marked differences in life-style between these occupational groups, even though they came from the same villages. That of the *empleados* and traders was similar in many respects.

Of course, the *obreros* were younger than the *empleados* and had less formal education. But although the Ataurinos and Matahuasinos were of the same average age, the Ataurinos were better educated, as more of them had had some secondary schooling. And whilst all the Ataurinos were in dependent wage employment, with twenty out of twenty-two at CdeP, only fifteen of the twenty-five Matahuasinos, by contrast, were working for the corporation, a further four being in dependent wage employment on the railway. The other six Matahuasinos were butchers, carpenters or watchmakers.

Like the labour force at large, one-third of the twenty-seven *obreros* had been in Oroya for less than five years, and over half for less than ten years. The *empleados* had been resident considerably longer. These *obreros* earned between $4 and $5 per day, and the *empleados* $6–$9. With their higher income *empleados* could purchase cars, gas cookers and record-players. The *obreros* would have liked such luxuries but could only aspire to a sewing machine or a radio. Although the groups from each village had been living in Oroya for an average of fifteen years, there was a considerable difference in their earnings. Nearly two-thirds of the Matahuasinos earned less than $4·5 per day, but this was true of only a quarter of the Ataurinos. Conversely, while only one-third of the Matahuasinos earned more than $5 per day, half the Ataurinos could claim this level of income. Thus as well as being better educated the Ataurinos were also better paid.

One-third of both *obreros* and *empleados* had a second occupation. The *obreros* who were carpenters and mechanics would be busy in Oroya during evenings and weekends at lathes installed in their homes, or in garages. The *empleados* rented shops or lorries in their villages. Both Ataurinos and Matahuasinos had spare-time occupations which not only supplemented their daily income by $1–$3 per day but also provided for their retirement or an alternative to dependent wage-labour. Often the second job would be a joint activity with wives, who would run the rented store in the village or bring up sacks of family produce to sell in the streets.

The *obreros*, being younger than the *empleados*, tended to go out in the evenings, when the *empleados* spent more time reading or listening to the radio. Some opportunities for further education are to be found in Oroya, at municipal night schools or CdeP's further education classes. The Ataurinos pursued these opportunities, hoping to gain a formal qualification which could help them advance within the corporation. The Matahuasinos, however, spent their evenings in garages or carpenter's shops, trying to learn a trade which they could then ply independently. All the migrants, however, wanted their children to pursue their educational opportunities as far as they could.

Thus these men formed groups of *obreros* and *empleados*, Ataurinos and Matahuasinos, and as such engaged in different strategies and activities in the industrial situation. The patterns become clearer when the social networks of the groups are outlined.

Occupational and village social networks

The major networks[6] of the migrants are those of kin, friends, workmates and *paisanos*. It is the kinship network that is the most important and which overlaps the other networks. Like the development of the trade union to deal with industrial market interests, the kinship network is maintained to ease the problems of a migrant labour way of life. Other relations, such as those of friendship and common village origins, are also esablished, but it is perhaps the all-pervasiveness of kinship relations that is of greatest significance. Such relations are found both in the household and in the social links between the rural and industrial sectors.

At the general level of the overall labour force in Oroya there were differences between *obreros* and *empleados* as regards family structure. Significantly more *obreros* were married or cohabiting, and they tended to have more children. Statistical analysis shows that, when age, income and education are controlled for, the men between the ages of twenty and forty-five who were *obreros* with lower incomes and less education had more children. Why *obreros* had more children than *empleados* is partly explained by the overlap between the variables, in that those with a high level of education were also those with high incomes, and partly by other factors.

A higher income frees the *empleado* from the necessity of having children as 'social security' for his retirement. More money also brings within reach consumption goods that can lift him out of an *obrero* lifestyle in which unrelieved daily oppression can lead to unpredictable sexual relations. The superior education of the *empleados* gives them access to contraceptive advice and greater ability to understand it. Moreover the status of *empleado* is in itself an influence. *Empleados* are concerned to establish social distance between themselves and the *obreros*, who have large families, and to emulate the Western staff, with their small families.

The occupational groups differed not only over nuclear family structure, however, but also over household composition. These differences are revealed at the level of the forty-seven village migrants in Oroya. Tables 8 and 9 show that the household composition of the *empleados* is more nuclear than that of the *obreros*, and day-to-day contact with people confirmed this. Whereas *empleados* occasionally have a niece or nephew living with them, the *obreros'* houses were always full of uncles, aunts, cousins, nephews and nieces either living with them or passing through in search of work. The age structure of the households of the two occupational groups also differed. The *obreros* have more young children, but fewer adolescents, living with them than do the *empleados*. They also have more people of the same age as themselves living with them than the *empleados*.

These differences in household composition did not apply between the village groups and so they are occupationally grounded. *Obreros* tend to live in extended family units in the industrial situation, whilst *empleados* tend to live in nuclear family units. Such tendencies seem to be similar to those found among the proletariat in industrialised societies. On the one hand, traditional working-class communities contain extended families which regroup even when the communities are broken up;[7] on the other, occupational groups which are geographically and socially mobile tend to restrict the number of dependants.[8]

Yet there are two important differences between this migrant labour force and a traditional working-class community. In the traditional working-class community the extended family is intergenerational, whereas the *obrero's* extended family in this situation is intragenerational. The people living with him are of the same working age as he. *Obreros'* grandparents and adolescent children do not live with them in Oroya. The second difference is the maintained

Table 8.　*Ataurinos and Matahuasinos resident in Oroya: household composition in Oroya, by occupational group*

Household composition	Obreros	Empleados
Number in household	116	61
Average household size	5.3	4.1
Nuclear family members*	90	58
Nuclear family as % of household	78	95
Distribution of nuclear family between obreros and empleados	$x^2 = 9$ $\quad$ N = 47 = F+G = Highly significant	
* Nuclear family = respondent, partner, children		

[For F, G and significance tests see appendix]

Table 9.　*Ataurinos and Matahuasinos resident in Oroya: household age composition in Oroya, by occupational group*

Age in years	Obreros Household members	%	Empleados Household members	%
1–11	59	51	21	35
12–21	13	11	15	24
22–41	37	32	13	22
42+	7	6	12	19
	$x^2 = 16$ = Highly significant		N = 47 = F+G	

[For F, G and significance tests see appendix]

link between these workers and their rural origins. It means that the family structure in the industrial sector cannot be regarded as isolated from that in the rural sector. They must be considered together. Analysis of the family structures of all seventy-six respondents living in Oroya, Ataura and Matahuasi reveals the linkages. (See table 10.)

The families of people who live in the rural areas are more extended than those in the industrial areas. As in other periods of industrialisation,[9] it would seem that there is a move from the rural extended family to the urban nuclear family, whilst in the urban industrial situation it is the working class who tend to re-form extended families. But the kin category and age composition of the rural and urban households show that this transitional model is not appropriate for a migrant labour force.

Table 10. *All Ataurinos and Matahuasinos: household composition, by rural and urban*

Household composition	Rural	Urban
Number in household	135	177
Average household size	5.7	4.8
Nuclear family members	100	148
Nuclear family as % of household	74	84
Distribution of nuclear family between urban and rural	$x^2 = 4.3$	N = 76+C +D+F+G = Probably significant

[For C, D, F, G and significance tests see appendix]

Table 11 reveals clear differences between the rural and urban households. Whereas 46 per cent and 12 per cent of the extended kin living with respondents in the rural areas were, respectively, grandchildren and grandparents or parents, this inter-generational spread was not found in the town. Living with respondents in Oroya were siblings and cousins – the respondents' peers – and nieces and nephews, often not far removed in age from the respondent. The differences in age structure are shown by table 12. The households of Oroya are made up of people of working age and the very young. The households in the countryside comprise the old and the adolescents.

Table 11. *All Ataurinos and Matahuasinos: categories of household extended kin, by rural and urban*

Extended kin living with respondent*	% of total extended kin living with respondent	
	Rural %	Urban %
Grandparents, parents	12	
Aunts, uncles	3	7
Siblings, cousins, in-laws	9	24
Nieces, nephews	9	52
Grandchildren	46	
	N = 76 = C+D+F+G	

* Extended family = non-nuclear kin of respondent

[For C, D, F, G see appendix]

Table 12. *All Ataurinos and Matahuasinos: household age composition, by rural and urban*

Age in years	Rural Household members	%	Urban Household members	%
1–11	39	29	80	45
12–21	31	23	28	16
22–41	23	17	51	29
42+	42	31	18	10

$$\chi^2 = 29 = \text{Highly significant} \quad N = 76 = C+D+F+G$$

[For C, D, F, G and significance tests see appendix]

These differences between rural and urban households are explained not by a transition from the rural extended to the urban nuclear family, but rather by the fact that rural and urban family structures are complementary. The relevant structure for the migrants is not solely the rural or the industrial one, but both. The family structures of the migrants extend across the rural *and* industrial sectors. To understand familial organisation in one sector it is necessary to analyse both the households that make up the overall family.

The explanation for these complementary households is clear. In a situation of economic instability there is a need for mobility on the part of migrants striving to keep work alternatives open. The need is met by the nucleated urban household. The urban household contains those who are mobile – working adults and very young children. As far as the *obreros* are concerned, when the urban household extends it does so laterally, to include others of working age; not vertically. The *obrero* household continues to be geared to mobility and so differs from the extended family of the traditional working class which is geared to stability.

It is in the rural areas that the family structure extends inter-generationally; that people of pre- and post-working age are to be found. The parents and grandparents of Oroya workers live in the countryside and manage the family affairs there. One such concern is the land, worked by older generations, its products the subsistence basis of the family's income. Another is the children and their education. Often the grandparents act as their guardians while they are at school and the parents are away working.

Complementary households are maintained simultaneously. In both there is constant coming and going. In Oroya, cousins and nephews looking for work are lodged whilst children are sent off to be educated or go of their own accord to be married or employed. In the valley, occasional migrants are to be found as they look for a new job, but the preponderance of the young and the old in the villages is quite marked. The complementary household system is a crucial means of managing a migrant way of life.

The importance of kin for these migrant workers is not confined to their immediate household organisation, but permeates wider spheres of their lives as well. Most of the migrants from the two villages have some relatives in Oroya and most had some contact with them. The amount of contact varies, from the case of the two Ataurino brothers Nicolas and Feriol who live next door and see one another constantly, to the occasional visits of migrants to newly arrived nephews or cousins who might be able to help them with a particular problem. Contact with kin also varies between the occupational groups and the village groups.

The *obreros*, and the *empleados* and traders, regularly visited about three members of their kin network in Oroya. Statistical analysis of visiting patterns showed that the men interact regularly with kinsmen of similar occupational status. *Obreros* clearly interact mainly with other *obreros*, although *empleados* regularly visit both *obreros* and *empleados* in their network. Occupational status also influences the type of visits made. *Obreros* will return each others visits, and *empleados* will do the same, but the groups do not reciprocate across occupational categories. Reciprocal visiting occurs within each occupational status rather than between them.

Occupational status differentiation within families can, of course, lead to strain, as the example of a birthday party shows. Flavio and his brother Armando came to Oroya from Ataura, as described in chapter five, and are now *empleados* there. Flavio's son had a birthday and the wives of the two brothers organised a party for all their children. The children of Juan, Flavio's younger brother, were not invited. Juan is an *obrero* and his wife was very annoyed at their exclusion, making references to their difference in status. In general, the relative importance of occupational and familial statuses is situationally resolved.

The village groups also exhibited different visiting patterns. The Ataurinos call on each other and return the compliment much more often than the Matahuasinos. The Ataurinos are constantly visiting one another for a variety of reasons, but the Matahuasinos will only go to see their kin on a particular occasion, perhaps when advice or help is needed. The kin visiting of the Ataurinos covers both occupational groups. That is to say, their kinship network is more solidaristic than that of the Matahuasinos. Evidence adduced later will support this conclusion. The solidarity of the Ataurino network is that of kin and village, part of a migrant strategy for handling the exigencies of industrial work.

Within the kin network, solidarity is reinforced by the numerous exchanges that occur. Ataurinos and Matahuasinos would exchange gifts, money or help. Within each situation the exchange is reciprocal. For example, in Oroya cousins will help one another, whilst in the village in-laws may co-operate. Between the industrial and rural locations, however, the net flow of assistance is from the former to the latter. The rural areas do reciprocate through the provision of foodstuffs, but their main contribution is in providing subsistence to dependants and a guarantee against lay-offs and retirement.

The second major network in which migrants are involved is that of friends. Peruvians distinguish between *amigos*, who are really acquaintances, and *amigos de confianza*, who are trusted friends. Most of the migrants in Oroya drew a sharp line between the two, and most had very few trusted friends. The average number cited by the migrants was only one or two and several said that they had no trusted friends. These latter felt that the friendship commitment, alongside that to the family, was just too great. For those who did have trusted friends, however, occupational status was clearly very important. Statistical analysis revealed that *obreros* have *obreros* for close friends, and when they visit their friends those friends will be *obreros*. Similarly, the friends who are cited and visited by *empleados* are also *empleados*. *Obreros* visit friends more often than do the *empleados*, and the friends are more likely to return the visit. Occasionally *obreros* have *empleados* for friends, and will visit them, but such visits are rarely reciprocated.

Again, visiting patterns differed between the two village groups. It was the Ataurinos who visited their friends often and who were visited in turn. The Matahuasinos tended to see their friends a lot less often. The Ataurino friendship network is the more solidaristic of the two. The influence of village ties on friendship networks was felt in a second way, too. Although the trusted friends of the migrants were *obreros* and *empleados*, they were also their *paisanos*, from the same village. In fact, two-fifths of the migrants' close friends were from the same village. This proportion did not differ between the occupational or the village groups. Further, when friends were also *paisanos* they were visited more often than when they were not *paisanos*, a feature particularly marked among the *obreros*.

The third network is that of migrants' workmates, and the influence of village links was apparent here as well. Workmates were taken to be the men currently in the same work group as the migrant, so it followed that *obreros* had mainly other *obreros* for workmates, while *empleados* usually had other *empleados*. At work these men interacted with one another, exchanged tools and assistance and relayed information about jobs, work-rates and union meetings. Outside the work-place, however, the work groups dissolved. There was very little visiting of workmates in their homes or in beer-houses. The work group as such did not form the basis of social groups outside work, unlike the situation with a traditional working class.

What little visiting of workmates there was outside the place of work was usually due to the fact that the workmate was also a *paisano*. Owing to the way in which departments and sections of the corporation were 'captured' by particular villages, the men with whom the migrants work are often their *paisanos*. For these Ataurinos and Matahuasinos one third of their *obrero* workmates in the same group are also their *paisanos*. At the same time, statistical analysis revealed that it was mostly the *obreros* who counted *paisanos* amongst their work-friends. The *empleados* made friends at work who were not from the same village as themselves.

In terms of the move from rurally grounded to industrially class-based social relations, it emerges that the *empleados* and traders are mainly the ones who experience such a transition. It is the *empleados* who establish trust relationships with friends at work and who are more likely to interact outside the work-place with people who are only colleagues. The *obreros*, on the other hand, continue to base industrial relations on kin and village networks, making friends with *paisanos* both inside and outside the work-place.

The *paisano* network itself provided a basis for group interaction in Oroya. Again, significant differences emerged between the *paisano* networks of the two village groups. The Ataurino migrants know of their *paisanos* in the town and interact with them. Both Ataurino *empleados* and *obreros* know about each other and nearly all of them could name the other Ataurinos in Oroya. Among the Matahuasinos things are quite different. Although the Matahuasi *empleados* know one another, and are known to the *obreros*, the latter did not know each other.

Further, the Ataurinos visit their *paisanos* more than do the Matahuasinos. Ataurinos see each other often, and not only within occupational groups. Ataurino *empleados* visit *paisanos* who are *obreros*, and receive visits from them. Matahuasino visiting is much lower overall than that of the Ataurinos. *Empleados* visit *paisanos* who are also *empleados*, and *obreros* visit *obreros*, but the occupational divide is rarely bridged.

These patterns of knowledge and visiting support previous findings. The Ataurinos as a village group are more solidaristic than the Matahuasinos. They nearly all know one another, and this acquaintance exists each side of, and across, the occupational divide. By contrast, the Matahuasinos know one another less well. Not only is their general awareness of each other less than that of the Ataurinos, but there are two distinct occupational groups among them. These groups visit one another much less than do the Ataurinos. The higher incidence of visiting among the latter shows how their *paisano* network is continually deployed.

Reinforcing the visiting and exchanging that takes place within the Ataurinos' *paisano* network is the fact that many of their *paisanos* are also their kin. Villages in the Highlands are to a great extent loose kin agglomerations, and these groupings are reproduced in the industrial milieu through the process of 'capture'. Thus *paisanos* in Oroya also tend to be kin. The tendency is more marked among Ataurinos than among Matahuasinos. On average, each Ataurino has five relatives among his *paisanos* in the town, compared to only one for the Matahuasinos. For the Ataurinos, village solidarity is reinforced by kinship.

Hence, for both the occupational and the village groups, kin are of great importance for coping with limited industrial development. The migrants grew up with their cousins and future in-laws in the village and contacted them when they moved to the industrial sector. Yet kin are more important for some groups than for others. For the Ataurinos they are crucial, and nearly all the visits Ataurinos make in Oroya are to recognised kin members. The migrants from Matahuasi come from a larger village containing more families, and so only half their visiting is to recognised kin members. Similarly, the *obreros* tend to rely on kin more than do the *empleados*.

Occupational and village institutions and associations

Alongside the informal networks established by the highlanders are the social institutions and formal associations to be found in Peru. Migrants take part in them as another way of helping to cope with the exigencies of their way of life. Consequently their participation is oriented both to affairs within each economic sector and to relations between those sectors. Again, the degree of participation varies between occupational and village groups.

One important social institution in Hispanic culture is that of *compadrazgo*,[10] or ritual co-fatherhood. *Compadrazgo* relations are established at turning points in the life-cycle. Baptism and marriage are the most common occasions, but such moments can range from ritual hair-cutting to the opening of a new shop. At times like this one man asks another to be *padrino*, or godfather, to his child, and *compadre*, or co-father with himself. The child becomes the *ahijado* or godchild of the *padrino*.

Becoming a *padrino* involves some expense, for it means helping to pay for the wedding or baptism. It also entails a lengthy commitment, as the *padrino* is expected to help his *ahijado* throughout his life. For this reason the *empleados* have twice as many *compadres* as the *obreros*. They take the commitment seriously, sending birthday gifts to their *ahijados* and trying to find them jobs. For the *obreros*, however, the *compadre* may well be a now forgotten companion who helped celebrate the birth of a child. For the *empleados*, *compadrazgo* is a means of reinforcing an extra-familial relationship; for the *obreros* it is a means of selecting one member from the kin network and raising the importance of that particular relationship. Participation in this institution did not vary between the village groups.

As well as being more involved in *compadrazgo*, *empleados* are also more involved in formal associations than the *obreros*. In Oroya there abound a variety of associations, from sports clubs to parent–teacher associations to religious associations, and all the migrants belong to at least one. The younger *obreros* usually join football clubs, playing either in Oroya or in the valley. The Matahuasinos are quite renowned players and would occasionally be sought out by the more prestigious clubs of Tarma and Oroya for the occasional game. The *empleados*, being older, do not join sports clubs, tending instead to belong to parent–teacher associations or savings co-operatives. It is the *empleados* who are more likely to be on the committee of such bodies, the *obreros* to be ordinary members. Some men of both occupational statuses join religious groups. If Catholic, these are devoted to the establishment of a saint; if Protestant, to proselytising.

Participation in most clubs does not vary between the two village groups, but there was one that does distinguish the Ataurinos from the Matahuasinos, and that is the village club. In urban work centres such as Oroya and Lima migrants from the same village or region will get together to form a club.[11] These clubs have been seen as arenas for urban activities, their function to introduce new migrants to urban life and provide a meeting place for people with a common background. It seems more likely, however, that they are a means of handling migrants' urban *and* rural interests. The migrant is introduced to urban life through his own social networks rather than through his club, and it is the older, established urban migrants who belong to them rather than those who are younger and newly arrived. The older men have continuing interests back in the village – children being educated there, or some land.

The Matahuasinos in Oroya once had a village club, but it had become defunct. It was founded in 1945 by Manuel and Alejandro in order to raise funds for the new church roof. With this project in view the club functioned well and at one time had around a hundred members, including wives and friends, who supported dances and *fiestas*. Once the roof was provided, however, its *raison d'être* was undermined. People could no longer see what their subscriptions were paying for, or where the money was going, and the club folded up.

The Ataurino village club is still functioning. It is run by an *empleado* and through dances and subscriptions has raised money for the school roof and school books in Ataura. Between projects it becomes dormant but does not disband. The migrants are reluctant to pay fees except for a specific project, but they have no intention of letting the club fade away. The records are intact, the migrants still claim membership and the three-to-four-man committee still meets occasionally to discuss whether there are any worthwhile projects. On such occasions the talk soon turns to village affairs and problems.

Just as the village clubs are activated to deal with specific problems, when other problems arise other institutions and networks are called upon. Two such crises are illness and financial stringency, and whereas the village groups respond similarly to them, the occupational groups react differently. If illness or accident strikes, all the men turn first to the corporation for medical treatment. During convalescence, however, *obreros* turn to their kin network, whilst *empleados* have other alternatives. *Obreros* stay with their parents or in-laws; *empleados*, partly because they are older, convalesce with brothers, or *compadres*, or draw on their savings at the co-operative. In times of financial crisis, too, the *empleados* have their savings, whereas the *obreros* turn to their kin. The *empleados* are reluctant, when in difficulties, to depend on family relations which might be open-ended and might, in the long run, be very costly to them.

So, a number of different bases are available upon which migrant workers can build social networks. They derive from both the rural and the industrial sectors and are used to cope with diverse interests in both sectors. In the industrial situation it is possible to identify village and occupational groups not only in terms of ascribed characteristics but also as interacting entities. The village and occupational bases for social interaction are complementary to one another and are deployed situationally.

The most important network is that of kin, which extends across economic sectors. Household composition in one sector is complementary to that in another, kinsmen provide support and information, workmates and friends are related, and relatives are turned to in times of crisis. Alongside and overlapping the kinship network is the village network, providing similar support. *Paisanos* recognise the common problem of working in an industrial centre whilst maintaining home ties. The institutions and clubs they are involved in are also oriented to that multi-sectoral problem. Certain clubs, such as sports and school associations, are at hand to provide recreation and education in the industrial situation. Others, like the village clubs, are used to maintain a village presence. *Compadres* are drawn from both the town and the village as a relationship is established which will help a child gain an education in the valley or a job in Oroya.

The prevalence of extended kin, *paisano* networks and village clubs shows that there is much cultural continuity in the migrant labour situation. It is not so much that there is a move from a peasant-based system of social relations to an industrial class-based system, but that there is a range of bases for social interaction which are complementary. This cultural continuity contrasts with the situation in which the English working class, after drawing on its former rural culture,[12] developed a working class culture, in which lodges and clubs were oriented to an alternative political order. The alternative with which migrants' clubs are concerned is a rural one.

The groups that most markedly reveal a move from peasant to industrial social organisation are the white-collar-workers and traders, seeking trust relations at work and commercialising village links through the purchase of land and houses. *Obreros*, in contrast, continually resort to kin and village ties to maintain a migrant life-style. Yet to draw attention to the differences between *obreros* and *empleados* is not to argue that, in a context of limited industrial development, industrially based class relations will come to dominate.

On the one hand these migrants have occupational interests which constitute the bases of group formation. The trade union, work groups and work clubs are examples. On the other, the migrants also form village groups with different characteristics and strategies. Whereas the Ataurinos are solidaristic, calling their kin and *paisano* networks into operation more frequently, the Matahuasinos are more individualistic, attempting to establish instrumentally relations with people who are in a position to help them. Such strategies are consistent with the social structures of the villages they come from. Ataura is smaller and less differentiated; a village of poor peasants. Its migrants know and help one another. Matahuasi, on the other hand, is large and has polarised. Poor peasants from one part of the village may not know migrants from another part, but all have heard of the Matahuasi merchants who have prospered in Oroya.

Given the differences in the village backgrounds of these migrants, it is not surprising that they should adopt different industrial strategies. Since the analysis so far has concentrated on migrant groups, it is not surprising either that village interests have figured large. In order to counteract this bias, attention now switches away to three different work groups in order to assess the impact of technology in the industrial sector.

Notes

[1] Hobsbawm, E., 1975; Marx, K., 1957; Thompson, E., 1965; Dennis, N., *et al.*, 1956; Scott, W., *et al.*, 1956; Liverpool, 1956; Blauner, R., 1964.

[2] Epstein, A., 1968; Kapferer, B., 1972.

[3] Lewis, O., 1952.

[4] Gluckmann, M., 1960.

[5] Mangin, W., 1970.

[6] Mitchell, J., 1969.

[7] Willmott, P., and Young, M., 1957.
[8] Parsons, T., 1949.
[9] Anderson, M., 1971.
[10] Wolf, E., 1950.
[11] Doughty, P., 1970; Long, N., 1973; Mangin, W., 1959.
[12] Thompson, E., 1965.

8
Work groups and age groups

The importance of technology for the structuring of social relations in an industrial milieu has long been recognised.[1] The factory system itself is seen as an influence, in that it draws the labouring masses closer together and provides them with a common work experience. Attitudes to work and proclivities to strike have been correlated with different types of technology: the more alienating, the greater the propensity to strike. Different technologies are deemed to require different managerial and authority structures. Changing technology is seen as inducing a move from solidaristic to associational forms of industrial co-operation. At the lowest level, technological differences are described in terms of machine size, pacing and spacing, which affect the ability of men to form solidary or satisfactory work groups. At the highest level, technological similarities are viewed as demanding similar social requirements of different political systems.

A first sight of the Oroya refinery high in the Andes seems to confirm the importance of technology. The chimneys and sheds stand starkly against a desolate background. Smoke drifts on to the slums huddled at their base. The refinery is an epitome of industrialism, dominating the landscape and the labour force. The contrast with the green Mantaro valley could not be more dramatic. There is undoubtedly an enormous technological gulf between the wooden agricultural implements of the valley and the industrial machine that is the refinery.

But while technology clearly does influence workers' attitudes and social relations, the directness of the influence has been called into question.[2] Certain features of workers' lives and experience mediate between the demands of technology and their behaviour at work. These features derive partly from the work situation itself but mainly from outside it. Indeed, many aspects of behaviour at work, including attitudes and group formation, can be understood only in terms of factors extraneous to the work situation.

At work, the role of technology may be mediated by managerial policy as regards work routines. Outside it, personal and societal factors may generate orientations which tend to reduce the effect of work technology on social relations and heighten other elements, such as pay. Personal features stem from age, the point an individual has reached in his life-cycle. Young men, for instance, may be prepared to take up arduous work. Older, family men may establish affective social relations with their family rather than with their work group. Societal features include the break-up of traditional working class communities and an increase in geographic mobility. So, for example, men may be prepared to work with different machines for a short time.

Several personal and societal features affecting attitudes and strategies towards work have already been outlined. Life-cycle position influences the decision to migrate, whilst the coexistence of rural and industrial sectors affects overall migration patterns. In order to assess the influence of technology and age on group formation in the industrial location, three different work groups in the refinery were studied. They were quite distinct from the migrant groups previously examined, but migration again emerged as an important feature.

Altogether there were ninety-three men in these work groups, thirty-four process workers, twenty-seven carpenters and thirty-two mechanics. All were *obreros*. As well as forming three work groups, they were divided into three age-sets. The average ages of the three work groups were the same – forty years – and their age-ranges were similar. The limits for the age-sets, or peer groups, were put at twenty-nine years for the fifteen 'young' men, thirty to forty-five years for the forty-eight 'middle-aged' men, and forty-six years and above for the thirty 'old' men. Since the aim was to separate out the influences of technology and life-cycle position, it was important that the two types of group did not overlap. In fact, on most major factors there was little overlap.

Educationally the work groups did not differ. All were *obreros* with primary or some secondary education; their skills were learned on the job and were not a function of education. The peer groups did have different educational levels, however, with the 'middle-aged' men having most schooling, owing to the night-school and day-release opportunities available in Oroya. Nor did the work groups differ in terms of the number of children they had, each worker in each group averaging four. The age-groups clearly differed here, of course, with one-third of the 'young' having no children, four-fifths of the 'middle-aged' having more than two, and half the 'old' group having six or more. On educational and family variables, then, the peer groups differed but the work groups did not.

The differences were reversed with respect to industrial rather than social characteristics. In terms of unionisation there were no differences between the peer groups, around four-fifths of them belonging to a union. Between the work groups, however, union differences were marked. The mechanics and the process workers were significantly more unionised than the carpenters, only about half of whom had joined. Industrial experience also varied between the work groups. The mechanics and carpenters had worked longer in Oroya than the process workers, only one-fifth of the former having worked there for less than ten years, compared to nearly half of the latter. There were variations in income, too. The mechanics were the best paid, with nearly all earning over $5 per day; the carpenters came next, with half earning over $4 per day; and the process workers were the most poorly paid, with four-fifths earning less than $4 per day. Income and industrial experience both increased with age.

Despite the overlap between the two types of group on some industrial characteristics, there were enough social and industrial differences between them to separate out the influences of technology and life-cycle position. The three forms of technology used by the men were similar to those distinguished for analysis in other industrial studies.[3] The carpenters were craftsmen, shaping wood with their hands; the process workers were unskilled or semi-skilled operatives engaged in repetitive tasks with intermediate technology; the mechanics were highly skilled, working in their own time with complex machinery.

The twenty-seven carpenters operated as a resident work group, housed in a long hut. They worked, on their own or in groups of two or three, at benches placed near to one another and under the general guidance of an *obrero* supervisor. They were occupied in making things like door-frames, chairs or machine models, and followed the job through from sorting the timber to handing in the finished product. They took tea breaks together, without leaving the warmth of the hut. Their work was clean, quiet, not strenuous and they were allowed to work at their own pace.

The conditions of the process workers were quite different. The thirty-four men in this group worked either in pairs or in teams of six. The teams were concentrated at particular points in the production process or strung out alongside the machines. Thus one team worked in the open, using long metal poles to prise compressed ore dust out of railway hoppers. On days of sleet and snow the dust would be frozen and the poles could only be handled with gloves. Another team patrolled the conveyor transporting the dust from the hoppers up a slope to the spreaders. They removed pieces of wood and stone from the belt, running constantly up and down a slippery ramp. One pair of men raked over the slag inside the burning ovens, and exposure to the heat had burst the smaller blood vessels of their faces. Another pair spent their working lives tipping cold slag from large disposal buckets. Management as well as men agreed that this group carried out the dirtiest, most monotonous, most onerous and most dangerous work in the refinery.

The thirty-two mechanics worked on their own, or with two or three helpers – mechanics of the second and third grades. Unlike the process workers they were not closely supervised, nor did they work in teams. Their repair tasks took them all over the refinery, so they saw one another only when picking up tools from a central depot or when a job required two of them. Whereas the process workers took their lunch together in a hut, the mechanics either ate on the job, or crossed into Old Oroya for something to eat when it was finished. They took their own time over tasks each of which constituted a problem that had to be solved in its own way.

In terms of job satisfaction and attitudes one would expect the groups to differ. The carpenters enjoyed conditions that seemed congenial and conducive to group solidarity and job satisfaction. The process workers laboured in arduous circumstances, enough to alienate them from their work and from the corporation. The mechanics had an interesting and engaging job. In terms of skill and mobility they seemed most like modern industrial workers, tending advanced machinery and being masters of their own time. Differences in working conditions such as these necessarily affect the men's attitudes to their jobs.

Although there is a close relationship between working conditions and immediate feelings about the job, it is not easily broadened into a generalisation about technology and work behaviour. The concept of 'technology' is difficult to operationalise. Although at first glance a refinery seems to fall into the same general category of intermediate technology as a car plant or a cotton mill, it embraces so many different occupations that the exact point at which comparison may be made is hard to find. The more general the category, the more difficult it is to isolate the technological variable from other factors such as managerial organisation or the political milieu.

Nor is it easy to identify 'technology' at a particular level. Similar machines may be run at different speeds, and may be so close that the noise makes it difficult to communicate or so far apart that the operatives may not see much of one another. Indeed, the important intervening variable here is managerial policy. The pacing and spacing of machines depend upon management decisions, and it becomes impossible to isolate the relative influences of management and technology. In the Peruvian situation statistical analysis of the relational and normative[4] aspects of the lives of these ninety-seven workers reveals other factors influencing behaviour both at work and outside it which are more important than technology.

Work-group and age-group social networks

As with the village migrants, the networks of friends, companions and family were investigated with respect to type of contact, occupational difference and residence. The way in which the men took part in formal associations was also considered. Kinship again emerged as being of great importance for all the groups, forming the basis of both non-work and trust relations. Occupational differentiation was evident too, for it was the skilled men, particularly the mechanics, whose relations were most work-centred. The unskilled tended to rely more on kin and village networks, as observed among the *obreros* from Ataura and Matahuasi.

In associational terms the work groups disintegrate outside the refinery. No two of the ninety-seven men had the same trusted friend, while only one-tenth had a trusted friend in the same work group. All again emphasised the importance of trust relations, commenting that it took years to really get to know a man, and they all restricted such confidence to one or two close friends. The unskilled process workers made friends with other *obreros*, but the skilled mechanics and carpenters were more likely to be friends with corporation *empleados* or independent people like traders. These work group differences persist into specific occupations. The carpenters' friends, in particular, tended to be other carpenters, not necessarily from the same work group and quite often self-employed craftsmen in the town who would help the CdeP man with timber for his secondary occupation or pass on business gossip.

Young men at first find friends in the corporation, but as they get older the pattern changes and friends are sought outside CdeP. The younger men also tend to make more close friends among their work group than do the older ones. A quarter of the friends of the 'young' and 'middle-aged' men were members of the same work group, whereas the 'old' men had very few friends working with them.

In all cases, however, friendships were established with others who lived near by. Oroya is bisected by the Mantaro river, and to the people on each bank the other side is *la banda*. Going *la banda* is something of a journey, for it involves taking a mini-bus, and paying the fare, or walking in the cold and dark over an unlit wooden bridge. For all the men, two-thirds of their friends lived on the same side of the river as they did, a proportion which varied with neither age nor work group. To visit them is to go 'neighbouring'. They are geographically as well as socially close and meet often. Even though not all are from the place of work, the networks are solidary. These men have one or two good friends whom they see a lot of.

However, not only are these friends from outside the work group, they are more than just friends. Only one-fifth of them were first met in the work-place, while over half of them were also the workers' kinsmen. The close friends of the unskilled process workers were more likely to be relatives than those of the skilled men, for two-thirds of the former's friends were kin, compared with under half of the latter's. As with the valley migrants, it is the upper strata of the labour force that base social relations in the work-place and the lower strata who rely more on kin.

This difference was borne out in respect to the second network of these men, that of their companions. Defined as men with whom the workers chatted or occasionally drank with, it emerged that three-quarters of them were also *obreros* who again lived on the same side of the river. Although the occupational status of these colleagues did not vary between the groups of workers, their specific occupations did. Once more, mechanics sought out other mechanics and carpenters sought out carpenters, in order to keep up with information about jobs and pay.

Striking up acquaintances is much more grounded in work than is the establishment of trust relations. For all the men, around half of their companions were members of their work group, while only a quarter of them were kinsmen. Yet the extent to which the companions were interacting groups was limited. It is very rare to visit acquaintances. Colleagues are met in the beer-shop, at the works club or at the football match, but they are never invited home. Also, such meetings may be a matter of chance, as the workers tend to go to such places with their kinsmen or *paisanos*. The importance of colleagues declines with age, for it is mainly the young men who fraternise with their workmates; the older ones become increasingly kin-centred.

The kinship network of these workers showed that family was as important for them as it was for the valley migrants. Nearly all of them had some extended kin in Oroya; over half had three there and one-third had over four. Such kin were mainly peers – brothers, brothers-in-law, cousins and nephews – falling roughly within the same age-group as the workers. Very few had fathers also resident in the town. Many of the extended kin of all these workers were employed in the corporation and a quarter of them had three or more kin working for CdeP in Oroya. This high figure was the result of 'capture', which also influenced the distribution of those kin. The process workers laboured in the refinery itself, and owing to 'capture' so did two-thirds of their kinsmen in the corporation. The carpenters, however, worked away from the central refining process and the mechanics met foremen from a variety of departments. Hence three-quarters of the kinsmen of these skilled groups did not work in the refinery but elsewhere in the corporation. Thus, even though it is work-place and life-cycle considerations that are under scrutiny, these men emerge as members of family groups in Oroya.

The clubs and associations to which they belonged were similar to those of the valley migrants. The younger men joined sports clubs while the older ones were members of parents' associations and village clubs, reinforcing the view that such clubs are arenas for the pursuit of village interests. The type of club did not differ between the work groups, but the nature of the membership did. The mechanics were more likely to be among the leaders than the process workers and carpenters. Nine-tenths of the process workers and carpenters were ordinary members, while one-third of the mechanics were on the committee.

This readiness of the mechanics to take on responsibility was similar to that of the valley *empleados* and was reflected in discussions with them. They were interested in my research, discussed the wider issues of Peruvian development, talked earnestly of their own and their children's future, and commented intelligently on the nature and organisation of their work. This difference between them and the other *obreros* was not due to the technology they worked with, nor to psychological factors. Rather, it was a result partly of the process of self-selection and partly of the limited alternatives open to them.

Individuals and groups establish themselves in different corporation departments and occupations and work with the technologies in them. They engage in strategies ranging from a focus on industrial work to balancing industrial and rural interests. Consequently the differences between different work groups are due not only to the technology involved but also to the range of factors influencing membership of those groups[5] – factors such as personal characteristics, family decisions and village resources which structure the flows of migration to Oroya and the intake into particular departments. In the case of the mechanics, migrants have learnt a skill which they can put to good use in the industrial sector and which has led them to become involved in it. The process workers have not learnt such a skill, because skilled jobs are limited, because they had no network entry into that work group, or even because some men prefer to work sporadically in Oroya and the rest of the time in the rural sector. Analysis of the experience and attitudes of these workers brings to light the differences and strategies.

Work-group and age-group experiences and attitudes

Like the Ataurinos and Matahuasinos, the refinery employees were migrants. Two-thirds of them were of rural origin, a proportion that did not vary between the groups. During their working lives they had been highly mobile, moving frequently between jobs, sectors and employers (table 13). They had spent between five and eight years in one job, and only five to seven with one employer. Although they switched readily from one sector to another they tended to stay in one Department, that of Junin.

It was the mechanics who were most mobile. They had had to migrate to learn their skill and were now in a position to look for highly paid work. Although less skilled, the carpenters' craft can be learned and practised in the rural areas. In consequence most of them have remained in the same Department of Junin, but have moved around from village to town within it. The process workers too have been

Table 13. *CdeP Oroya work-groups: mobility rates, by work-group. The average worker changes categories 1–6 every N years of his working life.*

	1 Department N	2 Province N	3 Village N	4 Occupation N	5 Employer N	6 Sector N
Work-group						
Mechanics	14·4	8·7	7·6	5·7	5·7	6
Process	17·7	10·5	10	6·4	6	7·4
Carpenters	23·6	10·8	9	8·7	7·2	7·2
			N = 97 = L			

[For L see appendix]

mobile, but they have gone wherever job opportunities arose, in contrast to the skilled men who had sought out high returns for their skills.

The differences in the options open are reflected in their work histories.[6] The process workers oscillate between mining and agricultural work. One-fifth of their working lives has been spent as peasants, compared to around one-tenth or less for the mechanics and carpenters. The latter groups have spent more time in skilled work, preferring to remain as *obreros* and artisans when faced with economic change rather than return to the land. If the skilled men are unable to remain employed in the mining sector, or if they think pay is higher elsewhere, they move into commerce, transport and construction work. Around one-fifth of the skilled men's working lives have been spent in these sectors.

So it is the process workers who have been in mining longer, even though less of their time has been passed in Oroya. The demand for mechanics and carpenters is much higher in the refinery than in the mines themselves, so these groups come straight to the town. The process workers, however, have been *obreros* in the mines as well as in Oroya, and have spent some two-thirds of their working lives in mining. Most of that time saw them in dependent wage-labour for CdeP. The skilled workers, on the other hand, have only been in mining half their working lives and so have known longer periods as independent artisans. One-sixth of their working lives has been in independent work.

Clearly, then, not just industrial technology but industrial work itself are only a part of the work experiences of these men. They seek out industrial work, and so group formation in the industrial sector is not only influenced by factors such as technology, internal to that sector, but must be related to the limits of and opportunities in that search. They bring to their work attitudes which relate to their wider situation and which mediate between their working conditions and their work behaviour.

Like the valley migrants, they came to work in Oroya because they needed the money. It was not a subsistence need; rather, it was related to the migrants' life-cycle requirements of marriage, support for children and helping aging parents. As with the valley migrants, these men did not come looking for work because they were landless. Like the Ataurinos and Matahuasinos, they had access to family lands and produce.

Migrating from the village through 'need', they came to Oroya because they had kin there, because employment was available, to learn a trade or to be near the village. As with the valley migrants again, some had come from the coast so that they could be closer to their family and village lands. It was the process workers, however, who most revealed the 'need' motive. For them, migration was necessary because they were poor or had family commitments. The skilled workers, on the other hand, emphasised the 'target' aspects. They had migrated in order to save, to learn a trade or to take up a job that had been offered them. Once they have found skilled or unskilled work these differences between the men are compounded, since skilled workers can go on to other work opportunities whereas unskilled men are constrained to come and go with fluctuations in the industrial sector.

Table 14. *CdeP Oroya work-groups: reasons for migration from village*

Reason	% of workers mentioning reason
Needed the money; poor, orphan	52
Work available/better paid in Oroya	40
No work elsewhere	30
To support family	33
Kin already working in CdeP	20
To be near the village	25
To save; learn a trade	12
No land	10
N = 97 = L	

[For L see appendix]

The 'target' reasoning of the skilled workers is also reflected in the fact that over half of them originally intended to stay less than five years. They meant to learn a skill and then move on. For the process workers, on the other hand, it was more often a case of having to solve a life-crisis, and they arrived with less certainty about how long they would stay. Only one-third of them thought their problems could be resolved in under five years, and the rest had expected to stay longer than that at the beginning. Once in Oroya aspirations tend to change. The carpenters wanted to stay on, most of them for longer than the next five years. In this they are similar to the process workers who have not overcome their personal difficulties and have to remain. However, only one-tenth of the mechanics wanted to stay more than five years. There were no differences between the age-groups on these past and present expectations, suggesting that mobility is related to skill as well as to age.

The men continue working in Oroya for much the same reasons: to support their wives, children and parents. The mechanics were saving up to finance their next move. They were planning to buy a lathe, some tools or some land for a mechanics' shop. They were not the only ones, however, who wanted to be independent. All the men would have preferred to be their own master. Around one-third would have liked to be farmers, one-quarter traders and one-quarter artisans. It was the process workers who were most attracted to independent work on the land, and the skilled men who wanted to be self-employed traders or artisans. Consequently it was the process workers who intended to return to their villages when they left Oroya. The mechanics preferred to work in the towns of the Highlands, setting up small workshops to service the large highland transport sector. The carpenters wanted to retire to Lima, where the construction industry would require their skills.

These aspirations for the future influenced current job preferences. Even though working conditions in the refinery are dirty and dangerous, both the mechanics and the process workers liked to be near the industrial process. The reason was not money, since the income range of *obreros* is not great and does not compensate for the danger. Rather, both groups wanted to get into, or to stay in, the engineering section. It is there that a trade can be learnt, since it means working with electrical equipment or learning how to dismantle diesel and steam engines. A trade can provide a basis for self-employment. Already proficient in a trade, and with comfortable working conditions, the carpenters preferred the section they were in.

Emphasising past experience and future aspirations with respect to work attitudes, however, is not to negate the influence of current working conditions. The latter varied markedly between the different groups and affected people's feelings about their job. The process workers most disliked the work they were doing. Most of them hated it. They were plainly alienated from the labour process itself. Their only source of satisfaction was that the pay was regular and the employment fairly secure in the short run. These men simply needed the money.

The carpenters and mechanics, in contrast, were more involved. They liked working in wood or with machines, making models or servicing equipment, and engaging in intricate tasks. They found it congenial to tackle a problem and see the job through. They could work at their own pace and most found some satisfaction in having assistants to help them. In addition the skilled workers knew that they were well paid and that their jobs were secure.

Notwithstanding these positive aspects, the skilled men, like the process workers, were aware of the drawbacks of life in Oroya. They disliked the cold, the dust and the damp. The mechanics and the process men in particular objected to the dirt, the noise and the heat in the plant itself. They resented having to work in an old refinery where the machines were constantly breaking down and there were few spare parts. They were all concerned about their health, and accidents and disease were a constant worry.

They had strong feelings about the organisation of the work-place as well. Alienation[7] has several dimensions, and alienation from the labour process itself is only one of them. There was dislike of the way authority was organised in the corporation. This resentment did not manifest the anti-imperialist overtones to be found in trade union policy, nor was it often personalised. Rather, there was a permanent feeling of dissatisfaction with the system of authority.

The most important pivot of the corporation's hierarchy was the divide between *obreros* and *empleados*. In the work-place it signified a division between those who did manual labour and those who did not, between those who got their hands dirty and those who sat in offices, between those who received orders and those who gave them. All the *obreros* strongly resented this sharp division. Not only the process workers, enjoying very little autonomy, felt that authority was a persistent rub, with *empleados* appearing briefly to yell instructions over the noise of the machines before returning to their office. The skilled men shared the same sentiments, since *empleados* would criticise the results of their efforts or blame them for machinery breakdowns.

The *obreros* did not legitimate the authority of the *empleados*. The process workers thought they were too abrupt and did not understand the difficulty of the conditions in which they laboured. The skilled men knew that the *empleados* could not do the work they did and were resentful of desk-bound clerks sheltering behind paper qualifications. All the *obreros* felt the divide as an artificial one which served only to generate hostility and conflict. They argued that all were Peruvians, working for the same corporation, and all should be treated on the basis of effort and merit rather than slotted into an arbitrary system of command.

These feelings were no less apparent among the more senior *obreros* who were closest to the *empleados*: first-grade mechanics and carpenters with one or two assistants under them. As other industrial studies have demonstrated,[8] such men are in a position with difficulties of its own. They are intercalary, standing between a higher authority and the labour force. They are assessed by supervisors on the basis of jobs completed and have to win the co-operation of their assistants if they are to get anything done. The senior *obrero* must continually placate and cajole both sides of the authority divide. In the refinery it was not uncommon for mechanics to berate their assistants and in their next breath criticise the *empleados*.

Resentment was not often personalised, however. Most men had good working relationships with their immediate supervisors, Peruvian or foreign. When *obreros* were promoted to *empleado* it was an occasion for congratulation, though it was accepted by all that their future work relations would be modified. Some *empleados* and foreign staff were known to be capricious and were personally disliked. Other staff, by contrast, played football with the men and organised sweepstakes. It was not occasional caprice on the part of individuals that gave rise to the general dislike of authority so much as the arbitrary way in which the system was organised.

Despite their satisfactory working conditions the carpenters were affected by it too. They were as critical of those in authority as the mechanics and process workers. Hence the lower level of unionisation among them, noted above, cannot be explained by their better working conditions. Rather, it was a result of union activities. The carpenters were in a different trade union from the process workers and mechanics, one which did not campaign militantly to include all workers, like the STMO.

There was thus no direct relationship between the technology the men worked with and their general behaviour and attitudes. Differences in working conditions did not account for their overall dislike of the corporation's authority system. Clearly, however, conditions did influence immediate feelings about work. The problem is that no generalisation either to type of technology or to syndromes of attitudes is possible. Rather, at the general level, the influence of technology is felt through the way production is organised. The corporation is a productive system embodying certain technical processes which influence the patterning of social relations. As such, it has to have groups of men operating with certain types of technology.

On one hand, the corporation requires groups of workers. On the other, men with certain skills and strategies come together to form those groups. Group membership is a product both of the corporation's needs and technology, and of the structure and strategies of the wider highland situation. The achievement of the system of production is that it brings these features together. Consequently, mechanics in Oroya know one another and interact with one another, even though mechanics in Peru are as rare as, say, thatchers in an industrialised country. The interaction of such men is not solidaristic, grounded in a refinery work group. It is associational, in that men with common skills meet occasionally to pass on information.

Although these workers were selected for study specifically to counteract the bias towards migrational characteristics and to emphasise their involvement in industrial work, they nevertheless emerge as essentially migrant workers. In their expectations and the strategies they adopt they have more in common with the valley migrants than with a traditional working class. The industrial work group is not a basis for continuing, solidary social relations. It does not give rise to relationships of trust, which, instead, are contained within kinship networks. Companions may be drawn from the work group, but in many cases these companions are also kin. Social relations are not work-centred to the same extent as in a traditional working class. Those who do ground some social relations in work are the skilled men. They fraternise with others of the same skill in order to discuss jobs and rates of pay.

Moreover it is not merely the case that social groups outside the place of work fail to reflect relations inside it: associations may not even be oriented to the industrial situation. Clubs and beer-shops are partly places for relaxation where a colleague may be encountered and the latest work or union developments discussed. But they are also places in which to pursue other interests. Older men will spend time on the local parent–teacher association, helping their children, or at their village club, furthering their rural interests, rather than in the company of their workmates. Young men prefer to relax with their friends, playing football and going to the cinema and dances.

Thus intervening between technical organisation and work behaviour are the point a man has reached in his life cycle and his migration strategy. The fact that these people are migrants is confirmed by their everyday interaction. At first glance the barracks of New Oroya seem to house a typical industrial proletariat. On sunny days the doors are open and children stream in and out. Their mothers sit at the doorsteps and spin wool, or congregate round the communal laundry sinks. Their common status as workers' wives appears to provide the basis of this interaction.

As one talks and passes the days with these people, however, other patterns and interactional bases become apparent. Although the children rush from barrack to barrack, the women will cross a threshold only on a specific pretext, e.g. to ask if they can borrow some small item. Their 'neighbouring' needs to be legitimised. At the same time, 'neighbouring' is usually confined to kinswomen. The groups around the washbasins or sitting spinning are kin groups. In-laws, aunts and nieces, the women are from the same village and have contrived to move near one another in the barracks. After work the men rarely visit. They will call on a friend and go to the village club or the beer-shop.

The status of these workers as migrant labourers is evidenced both through the networks they employ and through their strategies towards industrial work. An integral part of those strategies is their orientation to industrial work, and it was possible only to touch on the subject with these process workers, mechanics and carpenters. With the valley migrants it was possible to discuss attitudes to work and trade unionism in greater depth. They are examined in the following chapter.

Notes

[1] Blauner, R., 1964; Kapferer, B., 1969; Kerr, C., 1962; Marx, K., 1957; Scott, W., 1956; Walker, C., and Guest, R., 1952, 1956; Woodward, J., 1958.
[2] Goldthorpe, J., 1968; Etzioni, A., 1961.
[3] Blauner, R., 1964; Woodward, J., 1958.

[4] Goldthorpe, J., 1968.
[5] *Ibid.*
[6] Laite, A., 1977.
[7] Lukes, A., 1967.
[8] Walker, C., and Guest, R., 1956.

9

The orientations of
migrant labourers

These Peruvian workers have orientations[1] to industrial work which form part of a wider migrant career, and which embrace attitudes to the work itself, promotion prospects, the organisation of authority, and the role of trade unionism. Generally, three types of orientation may be characterised: solidaristic, instrumental and bureaucratic.

Solidaristic orientations are characteristic of a traditional working class. Industrial employees expect to find affective and satisfactory social relations with their colleagues both in and outside work; the trade union is an expression of that solidaristic feeling. Instrumental orientations characterise modern industrial workers. They see work as a means of satisfying other, often familial, ends and do not place great importance on workplace relationships. The trade union is an instrumental device for gaining (usually monetary) advantages. Bureaucratic orientations are typical of white-collar employees, who wish to make a career of their work and who ground some important social relations in the workplace.

The concept of orientations to work replaces here the concept of work commitment adopted in other studies of industrial development. With respect to trade unionism, orientations allow some discussion of the class consciousness of the workers we are concerned with. That discussion is developed more fully in the conclusion. In the Peruvian industrial situation the orientations of the migrant workers are mainly instrumental, although the *empleados* do exhibit some bureaucratic attitudes. Those instrumental orientations result in different projects on the part of the migrants, depending on the resources available to them.

Orientations to industrial work

Previous studies of industrial development have analysed the 'commitment' of workers to their industrial work.[2] Stages of non-commitment, semi-commitment and full commitment have been identified and the obstacles to full commitment in contemporary industrialising economies analysed. Such obstacles are usually found in workers' rural links, bucolic behaviour and leisure orientations. In other Peruvian studies they have been found to stem not from the workers but from management policies of labour turn-over in a context of limited industrial development.

One problem with the notion of commitment is that it implies workers' acceptance of the norms and exigencies of industrial work. It is extremely difficult not only to establish this psychologically, but also to reconcile workers' commitment with their frequent expressions of dissatisfaction. A second problem is the difficulty of establishing the strength of commitment. These problems have led some authors to reject the idea of commitment and adopt other concepts, such as industrial discipline[3] or work orientations. The usefulness of the concept of orientations is that it allows different strategies to be related to different orientations and resources, rather than to variations in the strength of one factor.

Orientations to industrial work were elicited from the thirty-five migrants from Ataura and Matahuasi working for CdeP in Oroya. Twenty of the Ataurinos worked for the corporation, as did fifteen of the Matahuasinos, stratified in turn into twenty-three *obreros* and twelve *empleados*. These groups' relations with supervisors, attitudes to promotion, preferences for CdeP or non-CdeP work, and attitudes to wages and working conditions, were all systematically analysed.

On the whole, these men had an instrumental orientation to their work which resulted in different tactics on the part of Matahuasinos and Ataurinos, given their different resources. The lack of a viable village alternative on the part of the Ataurinos meant that they saw industrial work as a long-term necessity. The greater rural and commercial opportunities open to Matahuasinos meant that they regarded industrial work as a short-term means to a non-industrial end. At the same time, the *empleados* were involved in their career to a greater extent than the *obreros* and displayed work attitudes and preferences typified by a bureaucratic orientation.

As a result of their different strategies the characteristics of the

Ataura and Matahuasi groups in the corporation also differed. Owing to the 'capture' process the two groups of villagers worked in different departments, and the Ataurinos had managed to avoid the more unpleasant work-places. Only one of them was employed in the refinery itself, compared to half the Matahuasinos. One-third of the Ataurinos worked in Research, but none of the Matahuasinos did. The Matahuasinos have tended to congregate in the Railways department, owing to the skill of certain individuals as telegraphists (passed on to them in Matahuasi by the stationmaster who once worked there).

Since two-fifths of the Ataurinos are *empleados*, as against only a quarter of the Matahuasinos, industrial life for them is on the whole less tiring and cleaner than for the Matahuasinos. Overall, like other valley migrants, they worked in less unpleasant conditions than men from other regions. Moreover there were no Ataurinos on night shifts, in contrast to two-fifths of the Matahuasinos. Even though there was a bonus for night-shift work, the Ataurinos were well pleased at being able to avoid it.

As a consequence of this different distribution between departments the Ataurinos worked in smaller groups than the Matahuasinos. In the Research department the Ataurino *obreros* were to be found in a small laboratory in groups of two or three. This contrasted sharply with the large groups to which the Matahuasinos belonged, toiling in the shadow of the furnaces or in the railway sheds. The *empleados* who supervised the Ataurinos were also from Ataura and had originally secured them their jobs, so that work relations for this village group were harmonious. Although the Matahuasino *obreros* did not have *paisanos* for supervisors, they too had good relations with these supervisors, and, like the previous workers researched, did not personalise their general attitudes to authority.

So for these village migrants, as for the workers previously investigated, it is not the characteristics of their working conditions that determine their job preferences and attitudes to industrial work. Rather, the attitudes brought to industrial work by migrant workers partly influence the types of employment they take up and thus their working conditions. Again, whereas immediate attitudes to particular tasks are influenced by the nature of the tasks, yet general attitudes and preferences are influenced by wider considerations.

The marked difference between *obrero* and *empleado* working conditions meant that nearly all these men wanted promotion. The advantages were clear enough. The ceiling on *obreros'* wages was low, even with bonus schemes and danger money. *Empleado* work meant higher pay, less heavy work, less dirt and danger, and probably a desk job. They saw promotion as more money for less work. The increase in responsibility it entailed did not alter their feelings, in contrast to the evidence of blue-collar workers' aspirations in other studies.[4]

If promotion was a common objective it was not a common expectation. Over half the Matahuasinos thought the possibilities remote. They saw promotion as depending on education, and since many of them had no secondary schooling and were not prepared to follow a policy of acquiring it they discounted their chances. Three-quarters of the Ataurinos, on the other hand, thought the possibilities were good. Their experience suggested that if they were diligent, worked long enough and built up the right contacts, then promotion was probable. They judged their prospects over a longer period.

Meanwhile the alternative to long-term vertical promotion was short-term lateral movement within the corporation. Here again the villagers differed. All the Ataurinos had at some time held other posts in CdeP, but this was true of only half the Matahuasinos. Moreover the Ataurinos' moves had been a definite search for improved conditions. They preferred their present jobs to their previous ones and explained how they had manoeuvred to get them. The Matahuasinos had not moved about so much, half of them still being in their original corporation job. The ones who had moved had been transferred as much by the corporation as by their own planning. They had no network of contacts to assist them in making such lateral moves; the Ataurinos did.

It is on job preference within corporation work that the influence of working conditions is most felt.[5] The small differences in *obreros'* wages do not compensate for the marked variation in conditions throughout CdeP. The men aimed to steer clear of the dirty and dangerous jobs. The only consideration that could compensate for working in the refinery itself was the chance of learning a trade. Like the workers analysed earlier, the men were prepared to trade off danger and dirt for the acquisition of a skill.

On the other hand, it is on preferences for corporation as against other employment that the influence of wider factors is felt. Such preferences differed between village as well as occupational groups. The Ataurinos liked working for CdeP because it was near their village, the work was fairly secure and earnings were high. Some Matahuasinos, too, found the security and the earnings attractive, but half of them strongly disliked being in dependent wage-labour, preferring to be their own master. In assessing whether pay or working conditions were more important the Matahuasinos focused on the short-term trade off between dependent work and regular earnings; the Ataurinos concentrated on the long-term problems of health hazards and pension arrangements.

The differences were even more marked between the occupational groups. Some *obreros* liked the relative security of corporation work, the fact that they had training opportunities, the regular wages and the proximity of their work to their home village. But they all thought there were bad as well as good points. They disliked their dependent status, found little satisfaction in the labour process and accused the corporation of flagrantly attacking their trade union. Although their earnings were higher than in other sectors of the Highland economy they knew that wages were better in Lima and in other mining companies. Some had taken a reduction in earnings, moving from independent artisan work in the capital to dependent wage labour in Oroya so as to be near their families. Others continually encountered migrants in the town and in their village and were aware of the opportunities elsewhere.

The *empleados*, however, liked working for the corporation; nearly all preferred it to other employment. The few who did not thought that there were possibilities of opening a shop or running a profitable farm. The *empleados* liked CdeP because it offered good salaries, stable work and excellent fringe benefits. The corporation hospital in Oroya was one of the best in Peru and could be used by workers' dependants. They knew their salaries were higher than would have been the case elsewhere in the Highlands, in Lima or with other large companies. Their retirement arrangements were good and working conditions not unpleasant.

More than this, however, the *empleados* liked the work for its own sake. It was good to be part of a modern concern with efficient and professional work relations. They admired well organised routines, analytical discussions and firm decisions. They felt that relationships at work were polite and civilised and they legitimised the role of foreign staff, both in terms of technical expertise and in moral terms as stemming from a more ordered culture. In turn, they liked having people under them who would follow orders and respect decisions. They saw themselves as part of an organisation and planned their careers within it.

These differences in the preferences and attitudes of the two occupational groups towards industrial work were accordingly reflected in their response to authority in the corporation. Like the men discussed in the previous chapter, they had strong reservations about the system, and as before the main bone of contention was the *obrero–empleado* divide. The *obreros* intensely disliked the difference in status from which they suffered. Several were quite vehement in denouncing what they regarded as an arbitrary distinction, and a quarter of them maintained that they 'carried' the *empleados*, who could not do practical work. However, the hostility was not manifest at a personal level, and most of them had good working relationships with their *empleados*.

In their turn the *empleados* resented the division between themselves and 'staff'. The number of Peruvians on the 'staff' payroll was increasing, and they felt the distinction between such fellow countrymen and themselves was an artificial one. Again, however, their feelings were not personalised. On the other hand they saw the gap between themselves and the *obreros* as quite justified. They had superior education and training and had worked longer in the corporation. And was not such a distinction necessary if the orders crucial to the running of an efficient enterprise were to be given and obeyed?

Thus the reservations about the corporation's authority structure were held by subordinate groups about superior groups. The hostility was directed at a set-up which was considered artificial, imposed and divisive. Attitudes to authority did not vary with village groups, work-group size, income levels or working conditions. They depended much more upon position within the system. There was a general negative response to what was felt to be an unjust hierarchy.

Hence the characteristics, preferences and attitudes of the workers formed part of their orientation towards industrial work. For the *obreros* it was instrumental, for the *empleados* it was partly bureaucratic and partly instrumental. These orientations resulted in different strategies on the part of different village groups as a consequence of the differing resources and opportunities available to them.

Obreros use industrial work as a means to an end – to learn a skill, amass savings, complement village subsistence, support a family or further an education. It is not seen as intrinsically satisfying and the corporation is viewed as capricious and occasionally hostile. The advantages of being with CdeP are that it is at least a job and the pay is regular. The satisfaction of such employment often comes from meeting non-industrial needs. The usual tactic is to work with other *paisanos* and away from the industrial processes themselves. The attitude of most *obreros* is that they would prefer to be self-employed. This instrumental orientation is in contrast to the solidaristic one of a traditional working class.

The *empleados* have a bureaucratic orientation. They approve of official practices and authority. They like the work itself, identify with the aims of the organisation and plan their career within it. Yet their position remains to some extent instrumental. They too are planning to retire to the rural sector and their aims were as instrumental as the *obreros'* when they first came to Oroya. Bureaucratic work engenders a bureaucratic orientation.

Despite the similar attitudes of the Ataura and Matahuasi *obreros*, it is clear that their tactics differ. The former are more involved in industrial work in that they develop longer-term and more elaborate work-place strategies. In the short-term they move from department to department, building up contacts and improving their working conditions. In the long run they gain more educational qualifications, work hard and await promotion. The Matahuasinos are engaged in a shorter-term strategy of learning a skill or putting some savings by. They are prepared to stay with the job they have until their short-term non-industrial aim has been met.

The reasons for the difference lie within and outside the industrial sector. The Ataurinos are more involved because their village resources offer few alternatives. They are concerned with long-term industrial manoeuvring because they will be migrant labourers all their lives. The main alternative is subsistence farming. The Matahuasinos, in contrast, do have a viable alternative. The greater resources and opportunities in their village mean that migrants can stay in the industrial sector for short periods and then set up as commercial farmers or petty traders.

Within the work-place Ataurinos can engage in lateral moves and long-term strategies because there is a network of Ataurinos in the corporation. As previous analysis has shown, the network is solidaristic in that there is constant interaction between the Ataurinos. What is now clear is that the network figures largely in their strategy. They know and are prepared to help one another within the industrial milieu because their other resources are limited. As Ataurinos become members of the network and in turn help fellow villagers so the network is reproduced and its success demonstrated.

This instrumentalism on the part of these *obreros* does not imply an acceptance of authority. As industrial workers they resent their subordinate position in an arbitrary system of authority. Their preference for regular work near the village and good wages neither blunts their criticisms of the corporation as an employer nor makes them acquiescent in wage negotiations. As previous analysis has shown, such negotiations can be protracted and bitter, supported by an instrumental desire for higher wages. Yet that instrumentalism does have repercussions on attitudes towards trade unionism and union involvement.

Orientations to trade unionism

Previous studies of industrial workers have analysed their 'class consciousness'.[6] In underdeveloped as in developed economies, stages of workers' consciousness are identified. At first, there is a perception of interests in common, then a realisation that these interests are in opposition to those of another class. There follows the understanding that they must rely only on themselves in political action, and finally they develop ideas about an alternative social order. Between the first stage and the last there is a move from 'trade union' to 'class' consciousness, a move that is made possible by the role of political leadership.

As with the concept of 'commitment', the notion of 'class consciousness' has certain drawbacks. Firstly, it is extremely difficult to operationalise.[7] Discussion of consciousness is often carried on at a level which is not susceptible to empirical validation or refutation. Secondly, the 'stages' model of class consciousness is not readily applicable to situations of limited industrial development. Analyses of the attitudes of mineworkers in Peru[8] and Chile,[9] whilst providing useful insights into their political aspirations, are less successful in trying to fit those attitudes into a European model of the development of *class* consciousness. In Europe, owing to sustained industrialisation and the proletarianisation of the industrial labour force, both trade unionism and the development of workers' political attitudes were stages in the development of class consciousness. The position under limited industrial development, however, differs significantly. Class analysis cannot proceed by comparing the trade union institutions of European and Latin American workers and deducing that they represent similar stages of class development – a point taken up in the final chapter.

Before moving on to consider class consciousness it is necessary to identify the workers' orientations and attitudes towards trade unionism and political issues. Their political institutions exhibit two important features: the level of unionisation is high, and there are variations in union participation by different groups.

Both the *obreros* and the *empleados* are highly unionised. Among the *obreros* union membership is 86 per cent and among the *empleados* 67 per cent. The reason for such high levels is clear. Large groups of workers are concentrated in one place and it is evident to them that as wage-labourers they have similar interests *vis-à-vis* their single employer. Besides, they feel that this employer is aggressive and they need protection from it. Further, their trade unions are themselves aggressive in defence of the workers and are seen to be successful. Added to this, new workers automatically become members of a union and must make the effort of contracting out if they wish.

What is also clear about unionisation, however, is that there are variations between groups. The reasons are twofold. Firstly, they stem from the recruitment policy of the trade unions, particularly the STMO, which leads to different corporation departments being unionised to varying degrees. Secondly the variations may be described as a 'logic of alternatives'. Analysis of the total labour force shows that men of different ages, different family status, with different levels of industrial experience, and different education, exhibit different levels of unionisation. Among the village groups in Oroya, although the level of unionisation did not vary between villagers, the extent of involvement in union activities did.

Different corporation departments display significantly different levels of unionisation. It is the industrial departments, comprising the refining process itself, that are the most highly unionised compared with the non-industrial ones. The Railways department has its own trade union. Closer inspection reveals more marked differences. *Obrero* unionisation in Personnel and Administration is only three-fifths, compared to nine-tenths in the refinery itself. Such differences also exist among the *empleados*. In Industrial Relations and Research union membership is down to one-fifth, whilst in Railways and Accounting it rises to nine-tenths.

Previous analyses adduced above suggest that there may be other variables intervening between department and unionisation which explain these variations. The distribution of workers between

Table 15. *1971 CdeP Oroya work-force: obrero unionisation by corporation department*

Corporation department[10]	Obreros unionised		Obreros non-unionised	
	N	%	N	%
Industrial	3,124	92	285	8
Non-industrial	267	85	49	15
Railways	581	69	257	31
Industrial:Non-industrial $\chi^2 = 18$ = Highly significant			N = 4,563 = B	

[For B and significance tests see appendix]

departments is non-random and so two important intervening variables would be the worker's age or his place of origin. However, secondary analyses show that these variables do not interpose. As regards age, men of the same age in different departments were differently unionised, while men of different ages in the same department displayed the same level of unionisation. With respect to place of origin, men from different Peruvian Departments, provinces and villages working in the same sections of the corporation were unionised to the same extent, as were workers from towns and from rural areas. In terms of industrial work there were no 'politicised' villages, but there were 'politicised' corporation departments.

Previous analysis has also shown that whereas some work attitudes can be related directly to work conditions, the latter are not enough to explain general variations in behaviour. Rather, variations in departmental unionisation depend upon union policy.[11] During the 1950s and 1960s union activity was in the doldrums. After 1968 the STMO began to win large wage claims and workers were attracted back to its ranks. Capitalising on the momentum, the STMO began to strengthen its organisation inside the corporation. The thrust of the recruitment drive was within the refinery itself, among the industrial workers. The recruiting was carried out by cadres of enthusiastic shop stewards. During the early 1970s the shop stewards' morale was high, owing to the success of their efforts, and at one point they even threatened to wrest control of the collective wage negotiations from the STMO leadership and conduct negotiations themselves. This union activity is the principal explanation of the varying departmental unionisation.

The second set of reasons for the varying degrees of unionisation are those comprising the 'logic of alternatives'. It was a popular myth in

Oroya, shared by the union leaders, that the older workers were difficult to recruit. The younger workers were seen as the most highly unionised, 'young turks' similar to the union leaders themselves. In reality however, it was the older men who were unionised. For the *empleados* unionisation rises with age from just over half to over three-quarters of the *empleados*. For the *obreros* it rises with age from around 80 to nearly 90 per cent. More detailed analysis shows that unionisation increases significantly with age, rising to 92 per cent for *obreros* over fifty-three years old.

Table 16. *1971 CdeP Oroya work-force: unionisation: age group by occupational group*

Age	Empleados				Age	Obreros			
	Unionised		Non-unionised			Unionised		Non-unionised	
	N	%	N	%		N	%	N	%
18–34	214	52	201	48	18–25	592	81	135	19
35+	521	78	146	22	26+	3,380	88	456	12
	$x^2 = 83$ = Highly significant					$x^2 = 24$ = Highly significant			
	N = 1,082 = A					N = 4,563 = B			

[For A, B and significance tests see appendix]

Age, as an indicator of life-cycle stage, has implications for both marital status and occupational history. Further statistical analysis shows that for both the *obreros* and the *empleados* it was significantly the married men rather than the bachelors who were more unionised. Whereas nine-tenths of the *obreros* with dependants belonged to a union, this was true of only four-fifths of the bachelors. Similarly, for both *obreros* and *empleados*, unionisation was significantly lower during the first five years in the corporation, standing at only one-third for the *empleados*. Subsequently, for both occupational groups, it increased steadily, until the unionisation of *empleados* with more than twenty years' service was 86 per cent. During both these analyses the variable of age was controlled for.

The different levels of unionisation displayed by men of different ages, marital status and industrial experience reflect the differences in alternatives open to them. As workers become older their family commitments increase and mobility becomes more of a problem. Employers are reluctant to take on older men and so short-term plans become long-term ones. Retirement becomes a distinct possibility and the high proportion of older, unionised *empleados* reflects their worry that they may lose their job and their pension rights just before retirement. The worker feels increasingly vulnerable in the face of an aggressive employer and turns to the union for protection. At the same time his industrial experience teaches him that the union is efficacious in that it protects its members and wins pay increases, so his inclination to join is reinforced.

The relationship between the alternatives open to workers and their tendency to unionise is perhaps best expressed through the link between education and union membership. For the *obreros*, statistical analysis controlling for age showed that the level of unionisation did not vary with level of education. The reasons are that the educational differences between them were small and the secondary education which some *obreros* had did not open alternative avenues of employment. So most of them adopt the trade union alternative for dealing with industrial life.

For the *empleados*, however, there is a clear inverse relation between education and unionisation, even when age is held constant. The more educated the *empleados*, the less they have recourse to trade unionism. The reason is plain. Well educated *empleados* do not need a union to conduct their industrial affairs. Their educational qualifications are an alternative to unionism. Their professional qualifications do open up alternative avenues, both within industrial work and between it and other forms of employment. At the same time, unionisation would be stigmatising to more educated *empleados* intent on promotion to 'staff'. Non-participation is a means of expressing social distance between themselves and less educated colleagues. The foreign staff see trade unionism of any sort as 'red bolshevism'. The use of education to further occupational interests is successful for the *empleados*, since the more educated receive higher incomes, explaining the second inverse relation between *empleado* income and unionisation. The *obreros*, homogeneous with respect to both education and income, do not vary with income as regards unionisation.

Thus, at the general level of the overall labour force, the logic of alternatives helps explain the variations in the degree of unionisation between different groups. That logic operates at the lower level of village groupings also. The attitudes to trade unionism of the thirty-five Ataurinos and Matahuasinos differed. Although there were no differences in the level of unionisation of the two village groups, nine-tenths of both groups being unionised, their attitudes to and involvement in trade unionism were dissimilar. There were also differences in orientations to trade unionism between the *obreros* and *empleados* among these men.

For three-quarters of the twenty-three *obreros*, the STMO was the first union to which they had ever been affiliated. Yet this was significantly more the case with the Matahuasinos than with the Ataurinos. Half the Ataurino *obreros* had belonged to a union before joining the STMO, usually building workers' unions in Lima or Oroya. The reason for this difference was that the Ataurinos had spent longer in dependent work outside the agricultural sector than the Matahuasinos. Since unions in Peru are employer-specific, these previously unionised workers had to leave their union in order to join the STMO. Both *obreros* and *empleados* joined their unions in Oroya mainly for protection from CdeP. Some had joined the STMO when it was founded, others had joined after the change of leadership in 1968. They looked to the union to make economic gains for them.

Involvement in union affairs did not differ between the occupational groups. Around one-third of the men went often to union meetings, one-third went occasionally and one-third hardly ever. The main occasions for participation were strike meetings, when nearly everyone went, including wives. Then the union hall was packed with some 2,000 workers who argued policy until the small hours of the morning. The only absences from such meetings are due to people being on night shift, or the meeting being held on a Sunday. In the latter case men wait in their villages for news of a strike call to see whether the return trip to Oroya is worth while.

Nor did the occupational groups differ in their assessment of the proper objectives of their unions. In the main, most workers considered the union's role a defensive one, its function being to protect workers' interests. About one-third of them also pointed out that it was the union's duty to further workers' economic interests through improvements in pay and conditions. Some also felt that supporting other unions was part of legitimate trade union activity. As for strikes, most men thought that the legitimate grounds for strike action were salary claims and to defend their interests.

However, involvement in union affairs and the assessment of union objectives did differ between the village groups. The Ataurinos went far less often to union meetings. Two-thirds of them hardly ever went. The Matahuasinos discussed work and union matters with their shop stewards more than they did. The *empleados* hardly bothered with their shop stewards, but around three-fifths of the *obreros* regularly talked to theirs and felt that they had some influence in the work-place. It was the Matahuasinos, however, who engaged in such discussions. Nearly all of them talked regularly to their shop-steward and two-thirds thought he could effect changes. In contrast, two-thirds of the Ataurinos neither discussed matters with their shop-steward nor considered him effective.

At the same time the Matahuasinos were more enthusiastic about strike action. The Ataurinos tended to feel that strikes should be called only in pursuit of salary claims or to defend victimised workers. Few of them agreed with strikes in sympathy with other unions and several thought that most stoppages were unjustified and politically motivated. The Matahuasinos overwhelmingly supported strikes for wage claims and in support of other unions, while some agreed with action to defend particular workers. None criticised the use of strike action.

When a strike occurred most migrants went back to their villages. Some stayed behind in Oroya, for example, the *empleados*, who could afford to live off their savings, or skilled workers who plied their secondary occupation during a strike. Some workers were called on for picket duty. In the village the migrant has access to family assistance and may even take up work there. It is not that village production can be turned on to keep him afloat, rather that the village is a more familiar milieu in which to mobilise resources. Both the migrant and his creditworthiness are known, and he can rely on credit in the local shops until the crisis is over. The debts are eventually repaid with village products and industrial wages.

Attitudes to the union did not vary with factors specific to the industrial situation, such as income, work-group size, industrial experience or education. Nor was there any simple relationship between them and characteristics based in the rural sector. There was, for example no correlation between land ownership, or the lack of it, and unionisation. It is not simply the 'landless' who become a unionised proletariat. Rather, the men separate the rural from the industrial situation, seeing themselves as operating in linked sectors, and their position and interests in one complementary to their postion and interests in the other. That is, as far as orientations to trade unionism are concerned, the relation between the rural and industrial sectors forms part of the logic of alternatives.

Although the Matahuasinos are more involved in union activities, the Ataurinos are dependent on industrial work to a greater degree. The reasons are twofold. The Ataurinos, with their long-term involvement in industrial work, have established other means than the trade union for handling affairs in that sphere. In the work-place they have a close-knit village network and well placed *empleados*. Further education is another option, as are lateral departmental moves. The Matahuasinos, with shorter-term strategies, do not have the help of such networks and so look to the trade union to win them wage increases and protect them against victimisation.

The second reason stems from the extent to which non-industrial resources are available. Matahuasinos can fall back on village production or assisting in Matahuasino commercial enterprises. They can pursue industrial union action to the full not only because it will benefit them but also because they have viable alternatives in the meantime. For the Ataurinos things are different. During a strike they can finish off a few tasks in the village but very quickly find themselves killing time, a burden to their families and frequent visitors to the beer-shop.

The coherence of the workers' orientations to industrial work and to trade unionism, matters which were of immediate concern to them, was in marked contrast to their somewhat vague attitudes towards social class and the politics of the Peruvian military government. Very few of the Matahuasinos and Ataurinos in Oroya had a clear-cut class model of Peruvian social structure. Most identified a number of groups in society, including rich, middle, poor, workers, peasants, clerics and several others. The *obreros* classified themselves as workers, poor or peasants, whilst the *empleados* saw themselves as either poor or middle, but never as peasants. The outstanding feature of these attitudes, however, was that they were varied and inchoate.

The migrants' views on the army's policies were equally mixed. Most felt that the new government's reforms had not affected them very much. They supported the take-over of the large *haciendas* but were fearful that agrarian reform might affect their own land. They were suspicious of the new mining community and felt that it was aimed against their trade unions. Most of them, in fact, had grown disillusioned with the Revolution and complained about food scarcities and attacks on their industrial rights. They were becoming resigned to the idea that political changes in Lima did little to help the people of the Highlands.

There was, then, a high degree of unionisation in Oroya overall but considerable variation in the extent of union membership between different groups. As wage-labourers the men had similar interests in opposition to a large employer, and they sought protection in the form of a well organised and successful union. Variations in the level of unionisation were due to union policies and the logic of alternatives. Joining the trade union is one of several possibilities. The union is seen as effective in the pursuit of certain goals, but other means may be better for other ends. Young men have their youth and mobility. Older men with family commitments are more vulnerable and join a union. Educated ones know that their qualifications will raise their income whereas trade union activity might jeopardise promotion. Villagers with few alternatives to industrial work do not want to be laid off because of strikes. They look to alternative industrial strategies, such as establishing cohesive village networks, making lateral moves and learning trade skills.

For the most part the alternatives complement one another, since they are oriented to different ends. Ataurino unionisation is an example. Not only are Ataurinos unionised but they also have a close-knit village network. They see the union as increasing their wages while the village network helps to ameliorate working conditions. This explains their limited involvement in union affairs. Sometimes, however, there are conflicting ways of gaining a particular objective. Thus on occasion, the workers may resort to direct action instead of union negotiation. So far, direct action has been used as a sharp, short-term alternative to prolonged bargaining. As the history of workers' conflicts shows, however, it provides a political alternative even when their institutions are suppressed over long periods.

The logic of alternatives is an instrumental logic. These migrants have instrumental orientations not only to industrial work but also towards trade unionism. They turn to their union because it is an organisation geared to the achievement of specific objectives. They use it to defend their interests and to win higher wages. Those who have other industrial alternatives join but rarely attend meetings and criticise it when it becomes too politicised. Others with some rural alternatives become involved in union affairs and push their wage claims to the limit. Both sets of workers see the union as a means to an end. Certainly, STMO strike meetings and marches of sacrifice were moments of moral cohesion vis-a-vis employers and government.

In as much as these workers recognise that they have common interests and use their trade union to defend their living standards their orientation is akin to a 'trade union consciousness'. However, there are pitfalls in generalising this to a class consciousness. In a situation of limited industrial development such an orientation is not in itself evidence of a nascent working class whose class consciousness will ultimately crystallise. Indeed, the political and class attitudes of the migrants were notable for their variety and vagueness.

The instrumental orientation of the Oroya workers posed problems for the union leaders. Many of the latter believed that the miners' attitudes could be transmuted into class consciousness. They were persuaded that the miners were a nascent working class whose self-awareness could be increased by political conflict. To this end they engaged in the politics of confrontation with the corporation and the government. The aim of the strikes of the 1970s was to heighten political awareness and prepare the way for a major struggle over the issue of nationalisation.

Despite their efforts, the union leaders met only with disappointment. It became increasingly clear that the miners viewed the economic goals as more realistic than the political ones, and the government was able to prevail through the use of force and the offer of financial inducements. The union leaders had miscalculated. The miners may be industrial workers for the moment, but that does not make them a solidaristic working *class*. In the Highlands it appears one of the great strengths of industrial action that it is supported by the agricultural sector. During a prolonged strike the workers retreat into the countryside, where they wait for the heat of the furnaces and managerial opposition alike to cool. However, the retreat is symbolic of the limits to working class formation.

Political action by the miners is based on an identity of market interests. It is not an expression of working class consciousness. The move from that identity of interests to class opposition is undermined by relations with other sectors. It is the sectoral interdependence of industry, agriculture and commerce which characterises this situation. There are alternatives to class formation both within the industrial sector and between that sector and others. The alternatives are maintained precisely because the industrial sector is limited and unstable. That is the fundamental difference between migrant labour in Peru and the rise of a traditional working class under fully fledged industrialisation.

Notes

[1] Goldthorpe, J., 1968; Etzioni, A., 1961.

[2] Chaplin, D., 1967; Kerr, C., *et al.*, 1962; Moore, W., and Feldman, A., 1960.

[3] Schofer, L., 1975; Thompson, E., 1967.

[4] Goldthorpe, J., 1968.

[5] Daniel, W., 1969.

[6] Foster, J., 1974; Giddens, A., 1973; Hyman, R., 1977; Mann, M., 1973; Thompson, E. P., 1965.

[7] Goldthorpe, J., 1968.

[8] Bourricaud, F., 1970.

[9] Di Tella, T., *et al.*, 1967; Petras, J., and Zeitlin, M., 1968.

[10] The industrial departments were the Foundry, Engineering, Electricians. The non-industrial section was Administration.

[11] Beynon, H., 1973.

10
Industrial development and migrant labour

International capitalist development has created different types of workers. Coexisting within capitalism are industrial, rural and 'lumpen' proletarians, artisans and agricultural petty commodity producers, and migrant labourers. Various factors affect the emergence of these types. Where industrial proletarians and migrant labourers are concerned they include the nature and extent of industrial development, agricultural structures, the role of the State and worker organisation. Complementing them are the influences exerted by the relationship between national and international economic sectors.

The effect of these factors on the formation of worker types in Peru is now clear. Industrial development has been limited, unstable and dependent on foreign finance.[1] It has been limited to metal mining, fishing, some manufacturing and construction, and the agricultural commodities of cotton and sugar. It has been unstable in that the volume of investment has fluctuated and its direction has been switched between sectors by a national bourgeoisie with a variety of economic interests. Much investment has been by multinational corporations and international finance agencies, upon whom Peru is dependent. That dependency results in the import of capital intensive technology.

Limited investment has resulted in a small industrial labour force, only one-fifth of the total work-force, which is splintered into groups of textile workers, dockers and miners. Unstable development produced fluctuations in employment such that these workers have had to find ways of alleviating the distress of periodic unemployment. Dependency has led both to capital-intensive technology reinforcing the limits to industrial employment and to the disciplining of workers in the interests of foreign investors.

Peruvian agriculture contains three major forms of production – *hacienda, minifundia* and *comunidad*. All are part of capitalist development and are interdependent with industry. However, the extent of capitalist relations varies within and between them, as do the relations between each form and industry. *Haciendas* sell products and supply landless labourers to industry. *Minifundistas* and *comuneros* work in industry but continue to participate in subsistence agriculture. Among these agrarian structures variations in land ownership and the levels of commercialisation and wages also affect the relations between industry and agriculture.

Government industrial policies have varied during the twentieth century. Generally, the State has not been an effective vehicle for industrialisation. It has not always favoured industrial development and even when it has there have been planning problems. The government's readiness to act in concert with foreign capital led to economic enclaves and a flow of funds out of the economy. The State and the industrial unions have confronted one another in hostile postures. Recognition has been offered to organised labour but at the price of the control and eventual dissolution of the union movement.

The trade unions of the miners and textile workers are among the strongest in the country. The miners, in particular, exert considerable political pressure owing to their strategic position in the economy and their high level of unionisation. Their leaders espouse class ideologies and have political goals and affiliations. Miners support and use their unions, engaging in both strikes and shop-floor discussions.

The case study of the central mining region shows how such elements have influenced the emergence of different types of workers. The commercialisation of agriculture, the expansion of *haciendas* and the arrival of the railways were beginning to change social and economic relations in the Highlands during the nineteenth century. The transformation of the region came with the industrial development of the mining sector, however, which entailed four major processes conducive of working class formation: capitalisation, monopolisation, proletarianisation and unionisation.

The capitalisation and monopolisation of mining occurred simultaneously as CdeP bought the region's mines and introduced machinery. Capitalisation generated sharp increases in production which in turn necessitated more investment and so the Oroya refinery was built. Monopolisation and the refinery's operations brought the corporation into conflict with agricultural interests in the region as a result of which CdeP eventually came to control much of highland agriculture. The proletarianisation of the workers migrating from agriculture occurred both in and outside the place of work. Pay and tasks were standardised, and the labourers were housed in common barracks. CdeP treated labour as a commodity, increasing and reducing it as the metals market fluctuated. One response by the workers was unionisation. When legally permitted, the miners organised themselves into powerful unions and confronted the corporation and the government. Their leaders employed the rhetoric of class struggle and attempted to encourage class consciousness.

Influential as these processes were, the limits on the development of this enclave meant that the workers in the mines were not 'free' labour. Many of them came from a smallholding peasantry and retained links with the land. Highland agriculture is part of the capitalist framework of the central region but it is not completely commercialised. Subsistence production is still an important activity for many households. Mineworkers are not encapsulated within industry, in that their behaviour and interests are affected by rural factors. They have established other responses to industrial development alongside that of unionisation, responses which are often based in the rural sector. Two such are 'self-selection' and 'capture'. In the countryside some men decide to migrate to the mines whilst others may go off to Lima or other towns. The reasons for migrating vary, but they include the influence of 'capture'. Certain villages have come to dominate particular corporation departments as one man gains a position of influence and then recruits fellow villagers.

However, the most important of the other responses is that of migration itself. There has been alternative work available to highland migrants besides mining, and agricultural links are retained as a form of social security. Consequently the highlanders have established complex and wide-ranging patterns of migration, one of which is circulatory as people periodically return to their villages.

In the countryside industrial development has had several repercussions. Early migrants began to buy and sell land, breaking up the blocks once held by Spanish families. Occupational strata have emerged in the form of shopkeepers, entrepreneurs, transporters and timber merchants, people engaged in trade with the mines who have often set up on their own with savings from mine work. Migration by men and continued residence in the village on the part of women has led to the consolidation of women's role in village life as they organise peasant production and maintain migrants' landed interests.

Subsistence agriculture is household-based, as are many commercial agricultural ventures. Access to land, and land use, are household affairs. The household provides continuity of land ownership for migrants who may be away for long periods. Decisions regarding migration and the distribution of products are made in the light of household structures, including both resident and migrant members of the family. Rural households co-operate with one another. One ubiquitous basis for co-operation is kinship, since some villages are loose kin agglomerations. Other bases derive from highland peasant culture, ranging from helping a neighbour to the *comunidad* itself. At the same time, many households do produce commodities for sale and are part of a wider capitalist framework.

Class differences within agriculture affect relations between the industrial and rural sectors. Middle peasants and rich farmers are able to use their agricultural production and credit to buy lorries or shops and trade with the mines. This has occurred in Matahuasi as wealthier farmers have capitalised on the commercial opportunities offered by industrial development. Poor peasants on the other hand use subsistence production to supplement a migrant way of life. Their relations with the mines are relations of labour rather than trade. They are found in Matahuasi, but constitute most of Ataura, which has little more than a subsistence economy.

Within the class of poor peasants there are also important differences between villages. For example, Ataura built up migration links with the mines and with Oroya in particular, where there is now an influential group of Ataura *empleados*. Villages such as Matahuasi establish links with Lima as well as the mines, and have commercial and industrial contacts. A village network which contains poor peasants, richer farmers and entrepreneurs influences the mobility patterns of Matahuasi migrants. Poor peasant-workers approach wealthier village contacts for assistance. The presence of poor peasants and white-collar workers in the Ataura network influences their mobility patterns. Poor peasant-workers approach Ataurino *empleados* for assistance. These village differences are expressed in day-to-day rural activities. In Ataura the picture is of women working in the fields, whilst in Matahuasi prosperous farmers and entrepreneurs drive tractors and lorries. In Ataura the *fiesta* is a recreational moment for migrants, in Matahuasi it is an occasion for entrepreneurs to meet their obligations.

In Oroya the influence of these rural links and differences is marked. At work the labour force is divided into *obreros* and *empleados*, and this distinction is most important in terms of income, job content and life-style. Yet outside work there are social relations which cut across these occupational divisions and are grounded in village networks.

Household and kin dominate social relations in the town. The industrial households are intra-generational and are complementary to inter-generational rural households. The former are geared to mobility, whilst the latter are organised to meet subsistence needs. Both *obreros* and *empleados* operate this complementary form. Friends were mainly kinsmen and relations of trust were kin-based. Workmates were often kin, owing to the process of 'capture'. Occasionally even neighbours were kin as migrant families regrouped near one another. Kin helped migrants find jobs and lodgings, and leisure time was frequently spent with family.

A second important network was that of village colleagues, or *paisanos*. Often *paisanos* were kin and would help migrants find jobs and lodgings. Some *paisano* groups established village clubs in the town in order to spend their leisure time there and to provide help to their village. The village networks varied in their cohesiveness, the Ataurinos being more close-knit than the Matahuasinos.

At the same time, occupational differentiation was also important. *Empleados* grounded trust relations in the work-place more than did *obreros*. Men in different work-groups, although not making friends among their colleagues, did seek one another out after work to exchange occupational gossip. Young men spent their free time with their workmates, whilst for all workers the trade union was an important institution and a meeting-place.

The orientations of these workers to industrial work and trade unionism are instrumental. They view industrial work as a means to an end which is often non-industrial. Migration is due to a variety of reasons, including 'need', the desire to save or acquire a skill, and the wish to be near family and lands. Industrial work is seen as a means of solving these problems and achieving these aims. Its instability has made the men cautious of committing themselves to the industrial sector.

Such instrumentalism gives rise to different tactics on the part of migrants with different objectives and resources. Poor peasants, such as Ataurinos, may engage in long-run industrial strategies. Theirs is a migrant way of life and so they develop tactics which improve their industrial situation. They manipulate kinship and village links over a long time in order to secure better promotional and working conditions. Middle peasants, some of the Matahuasinos for instance, may have shorter-term objectives, and are oriented to saving, learning a trade and achieving independent employment. Thus they establish commercial contacts that will be useful to them when they leave industrial work.

With respect to trade unionism, instrumentalism is expressed as a logic of alternatives. The high level of unionisation in the mines is due to the workers' identity of interests. Variations in that level are attributable to a number of factors. Older men with families join the union to protect their vulnerability. Men with long industrial experience realise the efficacy of the union. More educated ones rely on their qualifications and so do not join. Village groups vary in their degree of involvement in union affairs. The Ataurinos have extensive networks in the industrial sector and are able to better their working conditions without union help. When on strike, they are reduced to sitting it out back at the village. Accordingly they are less concerned with union matters and are unenthusiastic about strikes. The Matahuasinos, in contrast, use the union to further their monetary aims and during a strike find work in Matahuasi. Clearly, behaviour and attitudes in industry are influenced by non-industrial ends and resources.

At this point the two problems posed at the beginning of this study may now be addressed. The first is the extent to which these Peruvian workers, and others like them, are being proletarianised and are forming a working class. The second is the extent to which contemporary capitalist industrial development in the Third World requires proletarianisation. This in turn raises the questions whether such workers are of transitional status and how sections of the international industrial economy articulate with one another. The first problem involves issues of class definition, and the class position of migrant workers may be considered in three ways – in terms of their social and economic characteristics; in terms of their relation to the labour market[2] and the means of production and reproduction;[3] and in terms of the political struggles in which they are engaged.[4]

As regards social and economic characteristics, the Peruvian mineworkers differ from the working class that formed in the mines and factories of England during the industrial revolution, although they are somewhat similar to workers involved in early European industrial development. The English response to industrialisation was solidaristic in that occupational communities with occupational cultures emerged. Shared experiences of work provided the basis of a culture outside the factory. The social structure of Oroya, however, is not that of a working class community. Households are complementary rather than three-generational. Work-groups do not form the basis of social relations outside work. Clubs are village clubs rather than working men's clubs, and are oriented to village affairs. In the working class community jobs were often passed on from father to son, but highland migrants gain employment through contacts with peers. Their instrumental orientations differ from the solidaristic ones of a traditional working class. Peruvian mineworkers see industrial work as a means to an end which is often non-industrial. They do not expect to find affective social relations in the work-place.

Rather, their characteristics are those of other migrant labourers. The maintained links with the land, the establishment of urban associations oriented to rural affairs and the circulation of labour between sectors are all to be found in Africa. Although there are no tribes in the Latin American mines, interwoven *paisano* and kinship networks are similar to 'urban tribalism', as villagers in the town have a means of identifying and relating to one another. As in Peru, African migrants know that there are limits to their industrial employment and they too use that employment as a means to an end. Migrant workers in Europe[5] and America[6] also display these characteristics. Algerians, Portugese and Mexicans all retain links with their places of origin. Their families are outside the industrial centres and they work to meet familial needs and goals. If the camps and barracks of migrants in Europe and America differ from urban Oroya, they are yet similar to the barracks around the mines of Peru. Billeted in single-sex camps, with little family life, and relatively isolated, both European migrants and those in underdeveloped countries have similar living conditions.

In terms of their relation to the labour market migrants are in the same position as industrial proletarians. Both sell their labour to multinational corporations, and as dependent wage labourers all are members of the international working class. Within this overall grouping, however, important differences do exist. Unlike a proletariat, migrants operate in labour processes without alienating their own labour and in labour markets where they employ others. In Peru they work in subsistence agriculture, where they control the work process and consume the product. In commerce, ex-industrial workers use savings to employ assistants in their shops or garages. In West Africa[7] industrial workers have secondary jobs in the informal sector and maintain their rural links. The Arabs in Europe[8] come from poor rural areas and participate in agriculture there. Mexicans in America remain involved in subsistence production. Of course, there are limits to the access to different sectors. The large numbers of migrants in Europe and the frequency of return migration show that their access to the commercial sector in their place of origin is limited.

In terms of their relation to the means of industrial production, migrant workers are similar to an industrial working class. Both types of workers combine with capital which they do not own. However, in terms of their relation to other means of production there are differences. Migrants own, or have access to, the means of agricultural production and in the Peruvian case they occasionally become successful artisans and entrepreneurs, themselves owning capital.

It is the relation of migrant labour to the means of reproduction that clearly distinguishes it from an industrial working class.[9] The industrial proletariat reproduces physically and culturally within the industrial sector, supported by the State and by wages that are high enough for both the labourer and his family to subsist and reproduce. The reproduction of a migrant labour force, in contrast, occurs outside the industrial sector. Industrial wages do not necessarily cover the subsistence costs of either the worker or his family. Workers must organise their own subsistence in the agricultural sector. The difference has important implications for wage levels, social organisation and the articulation of economic modes.

In underdeveloped countries multinational corporations are aware that agricultural production subsidises workers' wages and have set wage levels accordingly. In South Africa wages were deliberately fixed below the subsistence level. Hence the labour supply was cheapened not only by low wages but also by the costs of family housing and sustenance being borne by the rural sector. In Peru miners' wages did not guarantee subsistence for a man and his family, although they were usually sufficient for a worker alone. Today miners' families who depend solely on the wage have a hard time – though, again, it is enough for a single man. However, while the subsistence subsidy is one element in wage levels, it is not the only one. Wages have to be high enough to attract labour, and so relative wage levels are very important. In Peru, where *minifundia* agriculture continues and work has been available elsewhere, this consideration has been extremely important. Political factors too influence wage levels. Multinational corporations may set rates of pay but labour opposition may alter them. The final wage level emerges from the political process.[10]

In Europe and America the low wages paid to migrants are enough for their subsistence. Indeed, they migrate in order to save and remit cash home. It is doubtful, however, whether such low wages would cover the cost of the reproduction of the labour force in the industrialised economy. This is one reason why indigenous workers do not want the jobs which are offered to migrants. The subsistence subsidy in this case goes to the migrant's family rather than to the migrant himself, whilst the level of wages is affected by a range of factors, including State intervention and occasionally trade union action.

In as much as the level of industrial wages does not provide for the reproduction of the migrant labour force, workers must organise their family lives accordingly. It is this which helps explain the complementary family system and continued migratory labour. Maintaining access to the subsistence sector becomes crucial not only during a migrant's working life but even more when he can no longer work in industry. The village-based family may be his only form of social security.

Thus there are both similarities and differences between migrant labourers and industrial proletarians in their relation to the market and to the means of production and reproduction. They both participate in an international industrial economy in which they sell their labour and do not own the means of industrial production. Migrant labourers are a 'market' class.[11] The two groups differ, however, in their relations to non-industrial labour processes and the means of reproduction. Migrant labourers may own the means of subsistence and reproduction.

In terms of their political institutions and struggles there are equally points of resemblance and divergence. The most striking similarity is in trade union organisation. The mining unions of Peru are like any other mining unions around the world. They arose in response to difficult and dangerous conditions and from visible, shared occupational experiences. Throughout the world, miners have been subject to political control, often on account of their strategic importance in the economy, and have confronted government with organised resistance.

In Peru the unionisation of the mines was stimulated by a number of factors. Monopolisation of the central mining region faced the men with a single employer, whilst proletarianisation made them homogeneous in terms of pay and working conditions. The corporation's and the government's aggressive stance reinforced their sense of a common identity. Attempts by political parties to organise them led to the emergence of capable and articulate leaders who developed union structures and secured notable victories. The importance of the mines strengthened their political power. In these respects the history of the unions in Peru[12] is similar to that of mining unions in Chile,[13] Europe, America and South Africa.

In contrast, the migrant labourers of Europe and America are not well unionised. They rarely form unions of their own, have not been enthusiastically approached by indigenous unions and, even when approached, have proved difficult, if not impossible, to recruit. Their long-term interests lie outside the industrial economy and their wages seem relatively better than those at home. Perhaps most important, they are politically vulnerable in that they are subject to strict legal and political controls, which makes them fearful of trade union participation. However, that vulnerability is shared by mining unions throughout the Third World, where miners are subjected to political regulation. In Peru the unions were prohibited for three decades of the twentieth century. Each time miners have become too active politically they have been harshly repressed. In South Africa they are not allowed trade unions, whilst in Chile they are subject to the same sort of control as in Peru.

One reason for their vulnerability is that workers in Third World industry are not part of a wider working class spread throughout the country. The strength of the trade unions lies in the tactical pressure they can bring to bear on an underdeveloped economy. Their weakness is in the pressure the State can bring to bear on an enclave sector. The miners can be isolated from the other splintered working class groups. In Europe, by contrast, miners form part of the largest social class in society. There, the history of trade union organisation among the miners is also the story of the emergence of mass-based social democratic parties. Differences like these in the economic and political situation of industrial workers at the periphery and the centre of the international economy mean that trade unionism in underdeveloped countries cannot be taken as a simple index of working class formation.

The final way in which the class position of migrant workers can be considered is in terms of the political struggles they are engaged in. Through struggle, these workers may be constituting themselves as a working class. Space here does not permit a review of all migrant workers' political conflicts, but one major issue can be addressed. This is whether or not industrial workers in the Third World form a labour aristocracy in conflict with the peasantry for the furtherance of their own interests.[14]

The labour aristocracy thesis has been applied to industrial development in Africa. Multinational corporations allied with local bourgeoisies expropriate surplus from the peasantry which is used to subsidise industrial development. Some of that subsidy goes to industrial workers, who receive higher wages than peasants and so collaborate with capitalists in the exploitation of the peasantry. Industrial capital is accumulated not so much by exploitation within industry as at the expense of the peasant sector. A similar process took place in France during the mid-nineteenth century. A working class can be born of political struggle not only against the employers, as in the British case, but against other classes, including the peasantry.

Further evidence from African countries has led to modification of the thesis.[15] It is clear that industrial workers establish links with other workers and identify with them rather than with multinational managements. This applies in Peru but, even more, the industrial situation there is one in which political divisions are complex and class formation remains fluid. On different occasions the industrial workers have both fought against and combined with other major groups in society.

Although it was peasant labour that dug the mines and built the refinery, much investment also came from abroad and was not extracted from the peasantry. When peasants have engaged in political struggle, as in 1962, they have had the miners' support. Many miners are worker-peasants who supplement their wages with subsistence production. Thus they have not seen themselves as a class whose interests conflict with those of the peasantry. Rather, they have been doubly exploited by their employers. As industrial workers they do not receive the full value of their labour and as subsistence producers they subsidise their own industrial wages.

The main political battles have been against the local bourgeoisie, the corporation and the State. The bourgeoisie extracts surplus from them in the form of profits and rents. The miners are aware of this and try, not very successfully, to get their representatives into positions of municipal power. Yet miners and entrepreneurs have joined forces against the corporation. During the first strikes in the late 1940s traders allowed the men credit in their shops and organised fleets of lorries to bring in food supplies. This support was probably based on expectations of early repayment following a successful strike and of more spending from the higher wages. In addition the entrepreneurs were members of APRA, which supported the mining unions. Today rents invariably rise with each increase in miners' pay.

At the local and national levels the miners' most consistent conflict has been with the corporation. Yet it has been a struggle against international capital, controlled from New York, and the men have often felt they were shadow-boxing with the managers in Peru. They acknowledge too that the corporation ran the *haciendas* more successfully than the government now does, and there were fears that nationalisation of the mines might lead to inefficiency and failure. The government in its turn has sometimes supported and sometimes repressed the miners. Relations with the government have been mainly a story of oppression, but in the end it was the government that nationalised the mines in the name of the people.

Nationally, the political struggle has been a complex one. In the long run it has been against multinational capital and a hostile State, but changing alliances have complicated short-term class crystallisation. These complexities were reflected in political practice. The Communists wanted an alliance of all the mining unions, for they saw the miners as a proletarian vanguard. They supported the military government. The left, however, tried to associate the miners with peasant aspirations, peasant federations and agricultural workers' unions. It opposed the military government. Nationally the process of working class political constitution is limited and confused.

Internationally these workers are clearly part of a world-wide industrial labour force under multinational capital. The struggle of Third World workers for better wages and conditions parallels that of workers in Europe and America. Yet it is also clear that establishing the international aspects of class struggle is a very difficult task for union leaders. Their members are concerned mainly with short-term economic issues and not with their place in a world political process. This is the case with industrial workers in Peru and migrant labourers in the industrialised nations alike.

Thus, politically, the vulnerability of Third World workers and their complex struggles limit working class crystallisation. Migration, as a solution to instability, reinforces the confusion as workers switch their interests and involvement between sectors rather than committing themselves to industrial life and struggle. In this they differ markedly from the proletariat of the first industrial revolution. For the English working class the alternative to industrialism lay in another form of society, a utopian order in a religious dimension.[16] For migrants the alternatives are rural life and commercial life, which are cleaner, safer, less alienating, and do not have to be won by political organisation.

The second major problem which arises with respect to labourers is the extent to which contemporary capitalist industrial development requires a proletarianised labour force. Historically, extensive proletarianisation was a necessary part of capitalist industrial development. Alienating workers from the product of their labours and paying them less than its market value aided capital accumulation in the industrial sector. Early labour-intensive technology required a proletarian army disciplined to work at the pace set by the machines, and a reserve army ready to take its place. The first industrial revolution was part of wider capitalist development and absorbed the free labourers being created in the rural sector.

In our own day capitalist industrial development profits from cheap labour and requires both skilled and unskilled workers, but extensive proletarianisation has its costs as well as its benefits. Initial investment often comes from multinational corporations. Industrial capital accumulation is not generated locally by worker-peasants, although they underwrite its continuation. The advantages of proletarianisation to the multinational are that industrial discipline and skills can be instilled in the labour force. The workers also provide a market for the output of food and consumer goods. The drawbacks are that they must be housed and their families educated. They need wages high enough to cover the cost of subsistence and reproduction for a man and his family. Proletarianisation leads to the recognition of common interests among people who will organise on that basis. Ethnic and racial ideologies help to keep them divided. Politically, a migrant labour force is vulnerable and liable to control.

Under conditions of limited industrial development, multinationals need not automatically support extensive proletarianisation but will weigh the costs and benefits. When industrial employment is unstable, and labour is supplied by a peasantry, it benefits employers to have the costs of unemployment borne by that peasantry. Indeed, in such situations the pressures for the creation of free labour come as much from the expansion of capitalism in the countryside as they do from factors internal to the industrial sector. Thus, in as much as industrial development involving migrant labourers is limited and unstable, and there are advantages in not fully proletarianising them, and they themselves actively resist full proletarianisation, then the transitional status of migrants must be seriously questioned. Development may not require extensive proletarianisation; equally, migrant labourers are not transforming themselves into a working class.

The dominant characteristic of such people is that they maintain interests across a range of economic sectors. They do so in order to protect themselves against the uncertainties of capitalist development. The institutions and practices by which they keep other options open are drawn from their indigenous culture and from industrial situations. Trade unions defend industrial interests, whilst family structures, village clubs and friendship networks link and further interests in agriculture, commerce and industry. Unlike the devices employed by the European working class to cope with industrialisation, those of contemporary migrants are not transformational. They do not integrate them even further into industrial life. Rather, they are instrumentally established to limit such an involvement. Migrant labourers form migrant status groups,[17] with their life-style organised around themes and values of their indigenous culture, not around peculiarly industrial concerns.

Of course, however much they may wish to maintain access to a range of sectors, it is occasionally denied to them. Unstable capitalist development in the industrialised economies has resulted in large-scale unemployment and a decreased demand for migrants. In Switzerland they have been repatriated, whilst immigration to England is strictly limited. Moreover development in the Third World is not expanding industrial employment very rapidly, so that labour forces there may be stabilising.

Such tendencies in capitalist development are, however, long-term. In the short run it is clear that industrial capitalism still benefits from cheap migrant labour, and millions of such workers remain in the industrialised and the underdeveloped economies alike. It is also evident that the tendency under capitalism for the peasantry to decay is not without some resistance.[18] Smallholding peasants often show a tenacious desire to maintain their hold on land, despite intensive economic and political pressures to remove them. Nor is it the policy of all governments to support the dissolution of the peasantry. Following the Chinese example, some actively encourage peasant organisation and agricultural development. Although they are outside international industrial capitalism, such countries are often seen as a model by underdeveloped nations.

Thus migrant labour and a partly commercialised peasant sector can be efficient features of capitalist industrial development. The articulation of agriculture with industry is not that of a 'traditional' sector with a 'modern' one,[19] nor that of a 'feudal' sector with a 'capitalist' one.[20] Peasant subsistence production subsidises industry and is an efficient part of capitalist development. As the system expands the relative efficiency of this articulation changes and encapsulation of the labour force within the industrial sector may become more effective. Such is the case in South Africa.

The mechanisms of rural-industrial interdependence in an overall framework of capitalism are many and varied. Politically, there are the labour supply arrangements agreed at one level between industrialised and underdeveloped nations and at another between mining companies and village headmen. Economically, agriculture supplies industry with labour and products in exchange for cash and consumer goods. Socially, there are complementary family systems, village networks and clubs. Generally, articulation occurs at the local, national and international levels.

A cyclical dimension is also apparent. As production follows the rise and fall of demand, so industry absorbs and releases labour. Instability reinforces the migrant response. At the same time subsistence production has its own peaks and troughs as household composition changes, altering the relation between production and consumption. Migration is designed to meet household needs, with people leaving or returning to the agrarian household as circumstances dictate. And there is the personal life-cycle. People migrate in order to resolve the turning-points of marriage, rearing children or death in the family. Articulation is thus processual as well as structural.

The relation between the international industrial economy and a partly commercialised peasantry is, however, only part of the wider articulation of different productive forms. Industry may be organised formally or informally, whilst agriculture may be organised into small plots, large farms or communities. Each organisational form gives rise to different types of workers, wage labourers or artisans in industry, peasants or landless labourers in agriculture. Depending upon the articulation of these forms, and which workers migrate to which sectors, migrants may be transformed into an industrial proletariat or may remain as migrants.

In other words, social and economic mobility are central to the problem. The social groups to which the combination of different productive forms gives rise, cannot be understood in terms of their relation to one form alone. Among existing categories of workers they are inter-categorical. Both peasants and workers, independent and dependent labourers, their status can only be identified in the context of the wider situation that brought them into being. That situation includes the organisation of international economies, the role of States and the relations between economic forms.

Drawing attention to the persistence of migrant labour, and the particular conditions which give rise to it, has implications for understanding the emergence of 'free' labour and the growth of industrial working classes. The formation of a traditional working class such as England and Europe experienced may itself be due to specific historical features. Neither industrialisation itself nor that type of working class is being reproduced on a large scale around the world. Thus, it is not simply the case that underdeveloped countries are following in the footsteps of the industrialised ones, and will eventually come to have social systems similar to theirs. Both alike are developing simultaneously, linked by an international economy which generates free as well as migrant labour.

Notes

[1] Thorp, R., and Bertram, J., 1978.
[2] Weber, M., 1968.
[3] Marx, K., 1957.
[4] Poulantzas, N., 1973.
[5] Berger, J., and Mohr, J., 1975.
[6] Portes, A., 1977.
[7] Hart, K., 1973; Peace, A., 1975.
[8] Trebous, M., 1976.
[9] Burawoy, M., 1976; Meillassoux, C., 1972; Wolpe, H., 1972.
[10] Arrighi, G., 1973; Wolpe, H., 1972.
[11] Weber, M., 1968.
[12] Bourricaud, F., 1970.
[13] Di Tella, T., *et al.*, 1967; Petras, J., and Zeitlin, M., 1968.
[14] Arrighi, G., and Saul, J., 1973.
[15] Sandbrook, R., and Cohen, R., 1975.
[16] Thompson, E., 1965.
[17] Weber, M., 1968.
[18] Hobsbawm, E., 1974; Shanin, T., 1972.
[19] Higgins, B., 1956; Kilby, P., 1971.
[20] Laclau, E., 1971.

Appendix

Statistical notes

1. The source of the statistics and tables is Laite, A., 1977.
2. *Significance.* The significance tests used in the analysis are those given by Spiegel, 1961. Spiegel observes that statisticians usually refer to two levels of significance in relation to the X^2 test. The first is the 1 per cent level, which is called Highly significant, noted here as HS. The second is the 5 per cent level, called Probably significant, noted here as PS. Wherever the word 'significant' is used in the text it means that a statistical test has been carried out on the variables under discussion.
3. *Computations.* There were two major sets of computations. (i) Life histories: investigated and analysed using a life-history programme from the University of Texas which was modified by S. Pursehouse, Manchester University. (ii) Interviews: analysed using the Statistical Package for Social Sciences, Mark 6.
4. *Samples.* In each table in the text the sample size is given as N, and the computation of N is given as the sum of the samples to which it refers. For example, all the migrants interviewed in depth are samples $C + D + F + G = N = 76$. All the respondents interviewed formally were males, and the statistics in the tables refer only to males. This was for two reasons. Firstly, 97 per cent of the workers in Oroya were men. Secondly, as a consequence, the migration which was of immediate concern was male migration.

   Samples:

A. Total male corporation *empleados* in Oroya	= 1,082
B. Total male corporation *obreros* in Oroya	= 4,563
C. Males, now resident in Ataura, with migration experience. These are a 1:7 sample of all males in Ataura	= 15
D. Males, now resident in Matahuasi, with migration experience. These are a 1:10 sample of all males resident in Matahuasi with migration experience	= 14
E. Males resident in Ataura, including C	= 107
F. Ataurino males, resident in Oroya. These are all known Ataurino males in Oroya	= 22
G. Matahuasino males, resident in Oroya. These are all known Matahuasino males in Oroya	= 25
H. Ataurinos, resident in Oroya, working for the corporation	= 20

I. Matahuasinos, resident in Oroya, working for the
corporation = 15
J. Corporation *obreros* from Ataura and Matahuasi = 23
K. Corporation *empleados* from Ataura and Matahuasi = 12
L. The corporation *obreros* forming the three work-groups
and age-sets = 97

Work groups		*Age groups*	
Carpenters	= 27	Young	= 15
Process workers	= 34	Middle	= 48
Mechanics	= 32	Old	= 30

Total number of men interviewed in depth, C + D + F + G = 76
Total number of men interviewed with
relation to work and life-histories E + L = 200
Total number of men interviewed = 276

Glossary

Accion Popular	Centre political party
Ahijado	God-son
Ayllu	Inca community
Al partir	Dividing the costs and profits of work
Amigo	Friend
Amigo de confianza	Trusted friend
APRA	Centre Nationalist political party
APRA-Rebelde: MIR	Left splinter of APRA
AEY: Association de Empleados de Yauli	Yauli white-collar workers' association
Banda	The other side
Barrio	Quarter of a town or village
Bracero	Mexican labourer
Campamento	Corporation barrack
Chibaro	Sub-contract through debt
Cofradia	Religious brotherhood
Colono	Colonist
Compadrazgo	Ritual co-fatherhood
Comunero	Community member
Comunidad	Community
CGTP: Confederacion General de Trabajadores del Peru	General Confederation of Peruvian Workers
CTP: Confederacion de Trabajadores del Peru	Confederation of Peruvian Workers
Conquistadores	Spanish conquering soldiers
Contratista	Contractor
Corta-monte	Tree-cutting festival
Curaca	Inca lord
Empleado	White-collar worker
Encomendero	Spanish colonial administrator
Enganchador	Labour sub-contractor using debt

Enganche	Sub-contract through debt
Faena	*Corvée* labour service to Spanish administrator
Fiesta	Festival
Hacendado	Plantation or ranch owner
Hacienda	Plantation or ranch
Hatunruna	Indians working in mines earning money for tribute to Spanish administrators
Huaccha	Shepherding both personal and hacienda sheep
Ipoteca	To mortgage
Labor	*Labour:* Mariategui's pamphlet
Mercantil	Store
Minifundia	Smallholding
Minifundista	Smallholder
Minka	Payment for services in kind
Mita	*Corvée* labour service to Inca and Spanish Crown
Mitayos	Mita labourers
Mitimye	Inca resettlement system
Obrero	Blue-collar worker
Padrino	Godfather
Paisano	Compatriot
Partidario	One of the 'al partir' workers
Pension	Bed and breakfast
STMO: Sindicato de Trabajadores Metalurgicos de La Oroya	Oroya Metalworkers' Union
Sociedad Nacional de Mineria	National Mining Society
Sole	Peruvian currency
Tindaruna	Indian working in mine as *corvée* labour for Spanish administrator
Transportista	Transporter, carrier
Trueque	Payment for goods in kind
Uyay	Exchange of household members
Yanacona	Indian working as free labour in mine

Bibliography

Accidentes de Trabajo, 1970, *Ministerio de Trabajo*. Lima.

Adams, R. N., 1959, *A community in the Andes*. Seattle: Washington University Press.

Alavi, H., 1972, 'The State in post-colonial societies', *New Left Review*, 74: 59–82.

Alba, V., 1968, *Politics and the labour movement in Latin America*. Stanford: Stanford University Press.

Alberti, G., 1974, *Poder y conflicto social en el Valle del Mantaro*. Lima: Instituto de Estudios Peruanos.

Alexander, R. J., 1965, *Organised labour in Latin America*. New York: Free Press.

Anderson, M., 1971, *Family structure in nineteenth century Lancashire*. Cambridge: Cambridge University Press.

Amin, S., 1975, *Accumulation on a world scale*. New York.

—— 1976, *Unequal development*. New York: Monthly Review.

Arensberg, C. M., and Kimball, S. T., 1965, *Culture and community*. New York: Harcourt.

Arrighi, G., 1973, 'Labour supplies in historical perspective', in Arrighi, G., and Saul, J. (eds.), *op. cit.*

Arrighi, G., and Saul, J. (eds.), 1973, *Essays on the political economy of Africa*. New York: Monthly Review Press.

Baer, W., 1965, *Industrialisation and economic development in Brazil*. Illinois: Irwin.

Banco Central, 1961, 'Cuentas Nacionales del Peru', in Thorp, R., and Bertram, G., *op. cit.*

Banton, M. P., 1969, *West African city*. London: Oxford University Press.

Barnet, R. J. and Muller, R. E., 1974, *Global reach – the power of the multinational corporations*. New York: Simon and Schuster, Touchstone.

Bates, R. H., 1971, *Unions, parties and political development*. New Haven: Yale University Press.

Berger, J., and Mohr, J., 1975, *A seventh man*. London: Penguin.

Beynon, H., 1973, *Working for Ford*. London: Allen Lane.

Blanchard, P., 1974, 'The Peruvian working class: 1880–1920'. Ph.D.: London University.

Blauner, R., 1964, *Alienation and freedom*. Chicago: Chicago University Press

Boggio, M. S., 1972, *La Mineria Peruana*. Lima: La Confianza.

Bollinger, W. S., 1972, 'The rise of U.S. influence in the Peruvian economy, 1869–1921'. M.A., Los Angeles: California University.

Bonilla, H., 1974, *El minero de los Andes*. Lima: Instituto de Estudios Peruanos.

Bourricaud, F., 1970, *Power and society in contemporary Peru*. New York: Praeger.

Brody, H., 1973, *Inishkillane. Change and decline in the West of Ireland*. London: Allen Lane.

Brant, V. C., 1977, 'Do colono ao boia-fria', *Estudios Cebrap*, 19:37–93, Sao Paulo.

Brundenius, C., 1972, 'Anatomy of imperialism', *Journal of Peace Research*, 3:189–207.

Bullon, G., 1969, *Ataura*. Huancayo.

Bundy, C., 1972, 'The emergence and decline of a South African peasantry', *African Affairs*, 71:369–88.

Burawoy, M., 1976, 'The functions and reproduction of migrant labour', *American Journal of Sociology*, 81:1050–87.

Cancian, F., 1967, *Economics and prestige in a Maya community*. Stanford: Stanford University Press.

Cardoso, F. H., and Faletto, E., 1970, *Dependencia y Desarrollo en America Latina*. Mexico, Siglo XXI.

Castells, M., 1975, 'Immigrant workers and class struggles in advanced capitalism', *Politics and Society*, 5:33–66.

Castles, S., and Kosack, G., 1973, *Immigrant workers and class structure in Western Europe*. London: Oxford University Press

Castro Pozo, H., 1946, 'Social and economic-political evolution of the communities of central Peru', in Steward, J. H. (ed.), *Handbook of South American Indians*, II, 483–99. Washington: American Ethnology Bulletin.

Censo, 1961, *Censo Nacional, 1961*. Lima.

Cerro de Pasco Documents, 1902–70, Land titles.

—— 1902–70, Internal correspondence.

—— 1910–30, External correspondence.

—— 1910–25, Reports on *Comunidades* and *Haciendas*.

—— 1906–70, Complete production records.

—— 1916–70, Annual Reports of the Cerro de Pasco Corporation;

—— 1968, The Mines.

Chaplin, D., 1967, *The Peruvian industrial labour-force*. Princeton: Princeton University Press.

—— 1971, *Population policies and growth in Latin America*. Lexington: Lexington Books.

CIDA, 1966, Comite Interamericano de Desarrollo Agricola. *Tenencia de la tierra y desarrollo socio-economico del sector agricola: Peru*. Washington, D.C.

Colley, B. T., 1969, *Memoirs*. Oroya, CdeP. A high-ranking CdeP executive.

Cornelius, W. A., 1971, 'The political sociology of cityward migration in Latin America', in Rabinovitz, F. F., and Trueblood, F. M. (eds.), *Latin American Urban Research*, 1, Sage.

Craig, R. B., 1971, *The Bracero programme*. Texas: Texas University Press.

Dandler, J., 1969, *El sindicalismo campesino en Bolivia. Mexico*: Instituto Indigenista Interamericano.

Daniel, W. W., 1969, 'Industrial behaviour and orientation to work', *Journal of Management Studies*, 6.

Del Carpio, G., 1967, 'Plumbismo cronico occupacional en nuestro media', *Salud occupacional*. Lima: Instituto de Salud Occupacional.

De Negri, M., 1911, *La crisis del enganche*. Lima.

Dennis, N., *et al.*, 1956, *Coal is our life*. London.

De Wind, A., 1970, 'A history of the political economy of mining in Peru', M.A., Columbia University.

—— 1977, 'Peasants become miners', Ph.D., Columbia University.

Diaz Alejandro, 1970, *Essays on the economic history of the Argentine Republic*. New Haven: Yale University Press.

Di Tella, T., *et al.*, 1967, *Sindicato y comunidad*. Buenos Aires: Editorial del Instituto.

Dos Santos, T., 1969, 'The crisis of development theory and the problem of dependence in Latin America', in Bernstein, H. (ed.), 1973, *Underdevelopment and development*. Harmondsworth: Penguin.

Doughty, P. L., 1970, 'Behind the back of the city', in Mangin, W. (ed.), *op. cit.*

Epstein, A. L., 1968, *Politics in an urban African community*. Manchester: Manchester University Press.

—— 1967, 'Urbanisation and social change in Africa', *Current Anthropology*, 8 (4).

Etzioni, A., 1961, *A comparative analysis of complex organisations*. Glencoe: Free Press.

Fisher, J., 1975, 'Silver mining and silver miners in the Viceroyalty of Peru, 1776–1824', Miller, R., *et al.* (eds.), *op. cit.*

Fitzgerald, E., 1976, *The State and economic development. Peru since 1968*. Cambridge: Cambridge University Press.

Foster, J., 1974, *Class struggle in the industrial revolution*. London: Weidenfeld and Nicolson.

Frank, A. G., 1969, *Capitalism and underdevelopment in Latin America*. New York: Monthly Review.

Friedland, W. H., and Nelkin, D., 1971, *Migrant: agricultural workers in America's northeast*. New York: Holt Rinehart and Winston.

Fröbel, F., *et al.*, 1977, 'The tendency towards a new international division of labour', *Review*, 1 (1): 73–88.

Furtado, C., 1963, *The economic growth of Brazil*. Berkeley: California University Press.

—— 1970, *Economic development of Latin America*. Cambridge: Cambridge University Press.

Giddens, A., 1973, *The class structure of advanced societies*. London: Hutchinson.

Glade, W. P. and Anderson, C. W., 1963, *The political economy of Mexico*. Madison: Wisconsin University Press.

Gluckman, M., 1960, 'Tribalism in modern British Central Africa', *Cahiers d'Etudes Africaines*, 1: 55–70.

Goldthorpe, J., 1968, *The affluent worker*. Cambridge: Cambridge University Press.

Habakkuk, H. J., 1967, *American and British technology in the nineteenth century*. Cambridge: Cambridge University Press.

Harriss, D., 1978, 'Complementarity and conflict. An Andean view of women and men', in Lafontaine, J. (ed.), *Sex and age as principles of social differentiation*. London: seminar.

Hart, K., 1973, 'Informal income opportunities and urban employment in Ghana', *Journal of Modern African Studies*, 11 (1).

Herrick, B., 1965, *Urban migration and economic development in Chile*. Cambridge, Mass.: Massachusetts Institute of Technology.

Higgins, B., 1956, 'The dualistic theory of underdeveloped areas', *Economic Development and Cultural Change*, 4: 99–115.

Hobsbawm, E., 1968, *Industry and empire*. Letchworth: Garden City Press.

—— 1975, *The Age of Capital*. London: Weidenfeld and Nicolson.

—— 1974, 'Peasant land occupations', *Past and Present*, 62.

Hoggart, R., 1957, *The uses of literacy*. London: Chatto and Windus.

Holmberg, A., 1960, 'Changing community attitudes and values in Peru', in Adams, R., (ed.), *Social change in Latin America today*. New York: Vintage.

Huizer, G., 1972, *The revolutionary potential of peasants in Latin America*. Lexington.

Hyman, R., 1977, *Strikes*. London: Fontana.

Instituto Nacional de Planificacion, 1970, *Plan del Peru*, 1971–75. Lima.

Jachanowitz, A., 'La instalacion metalurgica de La Oroya', *Boletin Oficial de Minas y Petroleo*, 3. Lima.

Jensen, V. H., 1950, *Heritage of conflict*, Ithaca, N.Y.: Cornell University Press.

Kalecki, M., 1972, *Selected essays on the economic growth of socialist and mixed economy*. Cambridge: Cambridge University Press.

Kapferer, B., 1969, 'Norms and the manipulation of relationships in a work context', in Mitchell, J. C. (ed.), *op. cit.*

—— 1972, *Strategy and transaction in an African factory*. Manchester: Manchester University Press.

Kerr, C., 1954, 'The inter-industry propensity to strike', in Kornhauser, A. (ed.), *Industrial conflict*. New York: McGraw-Hill.

Kerr, C., *et al.*, 1962, *Industrialism and industrial man*. London: Heinemann.

Kilby, P. (ed.), 1971, *Entrepreneurship and economic development*. New York: Free Press.

Kruijt, D., and Vellinga, M., 1977, 'La politique économique des enclaves minières au Perou', *Tiers-Monde*, XVIII (72): 797–831.

Laclau, E., 1971, 'Feudalism and capitalism in Latin America', *New Left Review*, 67: 19–38.

Laite, A., 1974, 'Paisano', *Journal of Peasant Studies*, 1 (4): 509.

—— 1977, 'The migrant worker', Ph.D., Manchester University.

—— 1978, 'Processes of industrial and social change in highland Peru', in Long, N., and Roberts, B. R. (eds.), *op. cit.*

—— 1978, 'Industrialisation, migration and social stratification at the periphery', *Sociological Review*, 26 (4).

—— 1980, 'Miners and national politics in Peru: 1900–1974', in *Journal of Latin American Studies*, Vol. 12, part 2, November.

Lambert, R. D., 1963, *Workers, factories and social change in India*. Princeton: Princeton University Press.

Larson, M. S., and Bergman, A. E., 1969, *Social stratification in Peru*. Los Angeles: California University Press.

Ledesma, G., 1964, *Complot*. Lima.

Lewis, O., 1952, 'Urbanisation without breakdown', *Scientific Monthly*, 1 (75): 31–41.

Liverpool, 1954, *The dock-worker*. Liverpool University; Sociology Department.

Lomnitz, L., 1977, *Networks and marginality. Life in a Mexican shanty-town*. New York: Academic Press.

Long, N., 1972, 'Kinship and associational networks among transporters in rural Peru', London: Institute of Latin American Studies.

—— 1973, 'The role of regional associations in Peru', in Drake, M. (ed.), *The process of urbanisation*. Bletchley: Open University.

Long, N., and Roberts, B. R., 1978, *Peasant co-operation and development in Peru*. Austin: Texas University Press.

Lopez, E. P., *et al.*, 1967, *Mexico's recent economic growth*. Austin: Texas University Press.

Lora, G., 1977, *A history of the Bolivian labour movement*. Cambridge: Cambridge University Press.

Lukes, S., 1967, 'Anomie and alienation', in Laslett, P., and Runciman, W., (eds.), *Philosophy, politics and society*. Oxford: Blackwell.

Malpica, C., 1970, *Los duenos del Peru*. Lima: Ensayos Sociales.

Mangin, W., 1959, 'The role of regional associations in the adaptation of rural populations in Peru', *Sociologus*, 9 (1): 23–55.

—— 1970, *Peasants in cities*. Boston: Houghton Mifflin.

Mann, M., 1973, *Consciousness and action among the Western working-class*. London: Macmillan.

Martinez Alier, J., 1972, *Los Huacchilleros del Peru*. Lima: Instituto de Estudios Peruanos.

Marx, K., 1957, *Capital*. London: Allen and Unwin.

—— 1962, 'The eighteenth Brumaire of Louis Bonaparte', in *Marx–Engels: Selected Works*, 1. Moscow.

Mayer von Zulen, D., 1919, *The Cerro de Pasco Mining Company*. Lima.

Mayer, P., 1971, *Townsmen or tribesmen*. London: Oxford University Press.

Maynard, E., 1964, 'The pattern of community service development in selected communities of the Mantaro Valley, Peru', in *Socio-economic development of Andean communities*. Cornell University, Anthropology Department, 3.

McLaughlin, D. H., 1945, 'Origin and development of the Cerro de Pasco Corporation', *Mining and Metallurgy*, 26: 509–11.

Meillassoux, C., 1972, 'From reproduction to production', *Economy and Society*, 1 (1): 93–105.

Miller, R., 1975, 'Railways and economic development in central Peru, 1890–1930', in Miller, R., *et al.* (eds.), *op. cit.*

Miller, R., *et al.*, 1975, *Social and economic change in modern Peru*. Liverpool: Centre for Latin American Studies, 6.

Ministerio de Trabajo, 1971, *Accidentes de trabajo*, 1969–70. Lima.

Mitchell, J. C., 1956, 'Urbanisation, de-tribalism and stabilisation in southern Africa', in Forde, D. (ed.), *Social implications of industrialisation and urbanisation in Africa south of the Sahara*. Paris: UNESCO.

—— 1969, *Social networks in urban situations*. Manchester: Manchester University Press.

Moore, W., and Feldman, A. (eds.), 1960, *Labour commitment and social change in developing areas*. New York: SSRS.

Morawetz, D., 1974, 'Employment implications of industrialisation in developing countries', *Economic Journal*, 84: 491–542.

Morriss, M. D., 1965, *The emergence of an industrial labour force in India*. Los Angeles: California University Press.

Mostajo, F., 1913, *Algunos ideas sobre la cuestion obrera*. Peru: Arequipa University.

Nash, J., 1979, *We eat the mines and the mines eat us*. New York: Columbia University Press.

Noriega, A., 'El enganche en la mineria en el Peru', *Boletin de Minas*, 4–6. Lima.

Parsons, T., 1949, 'The kinship system of the contemporary U.S.', in Parsons, T., *Essays in sociological theory*. Glencoe: Free Press.

Payne, J. L., 1965, *Labour and politics in Peru*. New Haven: Yale University Press.

Peace, A., 1975, 'The Lagos proletariat: labour aristocrats or populist militants?', in Sandbrook, R., and Cohen, R. (eds.), *op. cit.*

Petras, J., and Morley, M., 1974, *How Allende fell.* Nottingham: Spokesman.

Petras, J., and Zeitlin, M., 1968, 'Miners and agrarian radicalism', in Petras, J., and Zeitlin, M. (eds.), *Latin America: reform or revolution?* New York: Fawcett.

Pike, F. B., 1967, *The modern history of Peru.* New York: Praeger.

Poppino, R. E., 1968, *Brazil.* New York: Oxford University Press.

Portes, A., 1977, 'Migration and underdevelopment', *Occasional Paper.* Duke University, Sociology Department.

Poulantzas, N., 1973, *Political power and social classes.* London: Sheed and Ward.

Price, R., 1972, *The French Second Republic.* London: Batsford.

Purser, W. F., 1971, *Metal mining in Peru, past and present.* New York: Praeger.

Quijano, A., 1968, 'Tendencies in Peruvian development and class structure', in Petras, J., and Zeitlin, M. (eds.), *op. cit.*

Roberts, B. R., 1973, *Organising strangers.* Austin: Texas University Press.

—— 1975, 'The social history of a provincial town: Huancayo 1890–1972', in Miller, R., *et al.* (eds.), *op. cit.*

Rock, D. (ed.), 1975, *Argentina in the twentieth century.* London: Duckworth.

Sanchez Albornoz, N., 1974, *The population of Latin America.* Berkeley: California University Press.

Sandbrook, R., and Cohen, R. (eds.), 1975, *The development of an African working class.* London: Longman.

Sandbrook, R., 1975, *Proletarians and African capitalism.* Cambridge: Cambridge University Press.

Schapera, I., 1947, *Migrant labour and tribal life.* London: Oxford University Press.

Schofer, L., 1975, *The formation of a modern labour-force.* Berkeley: California University Press.

Scobie, J. R., 1964, *Argentina.* New York: Oxford University Press.

Scott, W. H., *et al.*, 1956, *Technical change and industrial relations.* Liverpool: Liverpool University Press.

Shanin, T., 1974, 'The nature and logic of the peasant economy', *Journal of Peasant Studies*, 1 (1): 63–81.

—— 1972, *The awkward class.* London: Oxford University Press.

Sheth, N. R., 1968, *The social network of an Indian factory.* Manchester: Manchester University Press.

Skeldon, R., 1977, 'The evolution of migration patterns during urbanisation in Peru', *Geographical Review*, 67 (4).

Stavenhagen, R., 1975, *Social classes in agrarian societies.* New York: Anchor.

Stewart, N., 1946, *Henry Meiggs.* Durham, N.C.: Duke University Press.

Sulmont, D., 1974, *El desarrollo de la clase obrera en el Peru.* Lima: CISEPA.

—— 1975, *El movimiento obrero en el Peru: 1900–1956.* Lima: Universidad Catolica.

Thomas, W. I., and Znaniecki, F., 1958, *The Polish peasant in Europe and America.* New York: Dover.

Thompson, E. P., 1965, *The making of the English working class.* London: Gollancz.

—— 1967, 'Time, work-discipline and industrial capitalism', *Past and Present*, 38: 91–4.

Thorp, R., and Bertram, J., 1978, *Peru, 1890–1977.* London: Oxford University Press.

Trebous, M., 1976, *Migration and development: the case of Algeria.* Paris: OECD.

Tschopik, H., 1947, *Highland communities of central Peru*. Washington, D.C., Smithsonian Institute of Anthropology, No. 5.

United Nations, 1966, *The process of industrial development in Latin America*. New York.

—— 1975, *Demographic yearbook*. New York.

UNIDO, 1973, *Multinationals and developing countries*. New York.

Van Olsenen, C., 1976, *Chibaro*. London: Pluto.

Van Velsen, J., 1966, 'Labour migration as a positive factor in the continuity of Tonga tribal society', in Wallerstein, I. (ed.), *Social change: the colonial situation*. New York: Wiley.

Walker, C. R., and Guest, R. H., 1952, *The man on the assembly line*. Cambridge, Mass.: Massachusetts Institute of Technology.

—— 1956, *The foreman on the assembly line*. Cambridge, Mass.: Massachusetts Institute of Technology.

Wallerstein, I., 1974a, 'The rise and future demise of the world capitalist system', *Comparative Studies in Society and History*, XVI (4): 387–415.

—— 1974b, *The modern world system*. New York: Academic.

Weber, M., 1968, *Economy and society*. New York: Bedminster.

Willmott, P., and Young, M., 1957, *Family and kinship in east London*. London: Pelican.

Wolf, E., 1950, 'An analysis of ritual co-parenthood: compadrazgo', *Southwestern Journal of Anthropology*, 6: 1–18.

Wolpe, H., 1972, 'Capitalism and cheap labour-power in South Africa', *Economy and Society*, 1 (4): 425–56.

—— 1974, *Urban politics in Nigeria*. Berkeley: California University Press.

Woodward, J., 1958, *Management and technology*. London: HMSO.

World Bank, 1976, *World tables*. Baltimore: Johns Hopkins University Press.

Author index

This index gives the author's name, the page on which the author is noted and the note number.

Subject index

Subjects referred to by notes are indexed by page and note number.